-3072

Ten Percent of Nothing

Ten Percent of Nothing

The Case of the Literary Agent from Hell

Jim Fisher

Southern Illinois University Press
Carbondale

Printed in the United States of America
07 06 05 04   4 3 2 1

Library of Congress Cataloging-in-Publication Data
Fisher, Jim, date.
Ten percent of nothing : the case of the literary agent from hell / Jim Fisher
p. cm.
Includes bibliographical references and index.
1. Deering, Dorothy. 2. Literary agents—United States—Biography.
3. Swindlers and swindling—United States—Biography. I. Title.
PN149.9.D44 F57 2004
364.16'3—dc22   2003025211
ISBN 0-8093-2575-6 (cloth binding : alk. paper)

Printed on recycled paper. ♻

The paper used in this publication meets the minimum requirements of
American National Standard for Information Sciences—Permanence of
Paper for Printed Library Materials, ANSI Z39.48-1992. ⊗

I worked very hard trying to get my writers published. My problem is I'm too good-hearted. I'm too trusting and gullible. I can't change the past. I have lost everything, and will never trust anyone again.
—Dorothy L. Deering

As a nonfiction crime writer, I have come across more than my share of sociopathic personalities. As one who feels guilty about everything, I find these people fascinating. When sociopaths end up in jail, neurotics like me end up writing about them.
—Jim Fisher

Contents

CONTENTS

Illustrations

Preface

IN THE SUMMER OF 1997, I received a call from a friend I'll call Don who was in a state of agitation. A combative courtroom attorney and former Green Beret who had fought in Vietnam, Don was not easily shaken. I couldn't imagine what had caused him so much grief. As it turned out, Don's problem had to do with, of all things, a literary agent.

Don had paid this agent to read, then market, his mystery novel. He had tried to find someone who didn't charge fees, but none of those he queried was interested in his work. He had written the fee-charging agent after coming across her prominent advertisement in the back of a writer's magazine. Since money wasn't a problem, Don wasn't put off by the fees. He was excited when she said she loved his book and would take him on as a client. Several months passed without word from the agent. Finally, when he couldn't wait any longer, Don gave her a call. The news wasn't good; six publishers had rejected the manuscript. But Don was not to worry; she was still determined to find a publisher who wanted his mystery. Feeling better, Don resumed waiting and hoped for the best.

Several months went by, and nothing happened. Just when he was losing hope, the agent called. She had found a publisher who wanted his book. Don was going to be a published author; congratulations. The agent said she was quite pleased with the terms she had negotiated on his behalf. The publishing agreement was in the mail, and she urged him to sign. He was a lucky man, she said. It wasn't easy to get a first novel published.

Don spent the next few days in a state of bliss. He hoped he had written a good book, but there was always doubt. Now he felt like a real writer and even began thinking about his next book. He called relatives and friends to pass on the exciting news.

Don had built a lucrative, high-profile law practice, was respected in his profession, and was widely known as a tough courtroom warrior. While his successes in life had been satisfying, nothing matched what he was feeling now. He had never experienced such intense exhilaration. If cloud nine existed, he was on it.

The publishing contract arrived, and when Don read it, a hole opened up in his cloud and he plunged to earth. His agent had hooked him up with a vanity press. According to the contract, Don had to purchase, at the retail price, seventeen hundred copies of his own book. That came to seven thousand dollars. He had the money, but what would his friends and relatives think when they learned he had paid to publish his work? Don didn't know much about the business of writing, but he knew that authors were supposed to be paid for their work, not have to pay to see their work in print. And what really added injury to insult was that his literary agent owned the vanity press.

At first Don was furious, then depressed, then anxious and unsure of what to do. His confidence had been shattered. Maybe this was how some writers got their start. Perhaps it was an opportunity he shouldn't pass up. He wanted to call his agent for advice, then remembered that she owned the publishing company. After several days of brooding, Don called me.

I don't know what surprised me more: that Don had written a mystery novel or that he had found a literary agent. In my opinion, it would have been bad enough had she just steered a client to a subsidy publisher. Who needed an agent for that? That she also owned the vanity press was, in my mind, outrageous. I had to admit to Don that I had no idea this kind of thing went on. Because of what seemed to me a blatant conflict of interest, I wasn't even sure this kind of publishing contract was legal. I advised him to grab his wallet and run and, if possible, find an agent who worked from commissions.

Don turned down the vanity deal and dumped the agent but didn't look for new representation. The experience had destroyed his resolve to continue writing. The agent had done something to Don no one else had been able to do; she had broken his spirit.

It was my friend's encounter with the agent-publisher that led me into the subculture of the aspiring writer, fee-charging agents, and vanity publishers. I had assumed that people who called themselves literary agents earned commissions from the sale of manuscripts. My subsequent investigation into what one New York City editor referred to as the "genteel racket" introduced me to Dorothy L. Deering, the agent from hell. By successfully impersonating a literary agent for ten years, Dorothy operated one of the longest-running confidence games in American history. What follows is the story of how she managed to swindle so many writers for so much money over such an extended period. During her decade of infamy, she took more than her clients' money; she stole their dreams and broke their hearts.

This book could not have been written without the enthusiastic support of Special Agent Clay Mason and the FBI. The retribution made possible through Mason's efforts will probably be the only satisfaction that the victims of this long-running swindle ever receive.

Several employees of the Deering Literary Agency and Sovereign Publications cooperated with the author and the FBI. All of the Deering employees in Georgia and Kentucky were good-faith employees who had no knowledge of any criminal activity.

Author's Note

ON THE BASIS OF MY INVESTIGATION of the Deering Literary Agency and Sovereign Publications, I am certain that none of the firms' nonfamily employees in Acworth and Kennesaw, Georgia, as well as Nicholasville and Lexington, Kentucky, had any knowledge of unethical or criminal activity. These were good-faith employees who did their best to serve the best interests of Deering and Sovereign authors. Several employees, Jim Russo in particular, eagerly assisted the FBI and this author.

Ten Percent of Nothing

Oh my God! What is she doing in this business?
                                                    —Ted Nottingham, client

1 Queen of Fees

DOROTHY L. WATSON GREW UP IN KETTERING, OHIO, a quiet
bedroom community on the edge of Dayton in the southwest corner of
the state. The second oldest of four children, raised by William and Betty
Watson in a traditional, middle-class family, Dorothy graduated with
good grades from Fairmont High School in 1962. Instead of enrolling in
college, the quick-witted, soft-spoken girl with thick black hair and a
round, delicately featured face, married Robert Helm, her high school
boyfriend from the class of 1960. Robert worked with his father in the
family-owned food distribution business. Dorothy's older sister, Judy,
four years her senior, was married and lived nearby. Still at home were
Dorothy's younger siblings, William Paul and Vicki. Her brother, a bad-
tempered twelve-year-old who was perpetually in trouble, made his parents miserable, while his ten-year-old sister, Vicki, the family cutie, made
them proud.

In 1967, Dorothy and Bob, fearing that they were incapable of producing a child, adopted a two-week-old boy through an agency in Co-
lumbus. They named him Michael. Eight months after the adoption,
Dorothy gave birth to Christopher. Four years later, after being married
nine years, Dorothy and Bob divorced. Unable to afford the cost of raising the children, Dorothy relinquished custody of Michael and Chris to
Bob and his new wife.

Free of marriage and her children, Dorothy could pursue her dream
of becoming a professional entertainer. Having taught herself to play the
piano and the guitar, Dorothy moved to San Jose, California, where, with
the help of a booking agent, she went on tour as a folk singer performing

1

in Holiday Inns and other chain motels along the interstate and in small towns across America. She performed three years, her singing career coming to a close as the war in Vietnam ended.

Back in Dayton and again living with her parents, Dorothy ran into Ralph Weatherford, a boy she knew from the high school class ahead of hers. They soon married. A union organizer for the United Auto Workers, Ralph was on the road much of the time. They divorced four years later. Thirty-four, single again, with her two children being raised by her first husband, Dorothy was back under her parent's roof.

Two years passed, and while Dorothy was depressed about a life that seemed to be going nowhere, her mother died. Grief-stricken and desperate for something new, Dorothy traveled to San Diego to visit her sister Vicki, who was now married. While in California, Dorothy came unglued emotionally and checked herself into a mental ward.

While recuperating in the hospital, Dorothy met and fell in love with a thirty-three-year-old car salesman from Huntington, West Virginia, named Charles F. Deering. Chuck, as he insisted on being called, had put himself in the mental ward to dry out and to collect his wits after a nasty divorce from his California wife who had taken the house, the car, and their three kids. He was a big, back-slapping kind of guy who told her stories that made her laugh. Dorothy had grown tired of the ordinary working stiffs she had known back in Dayton. Chuck Deering was a flashy dresser with a big smile and a head full of schemes. He was exciting. Together they would go far, set the world on fire. This was the man Dorothy had been searching for. Feeling bored, depressed, and hopeless, Dorothy had found, in the mental ward of a San Diego hospital, her unlikely cure. When Charles Deering asked Dorothy to be his wife, she said yes.

Although there are probably few less promising beginnings than a mental ward romance, Dorothy and Chuck, upon their release from the hospital, climbed aboard his Harley and thundered into Mexico to tie the knot. Back in San Diego, the newlyweds set up housekeeping in an apartment not far from the lot where Chuck sold cars. The honeymoon didn't last. Chuck grew restless and started to drink again. In the meantime, his first wife became fed up with their three boys, aged ten to thirteen, and dumped them on Dorothy. Stuck with three unruly kids that weren't even hers and a husband who couldn't hold down a job, Dorothy realized she had made a big mistake. This life was not the kind she had dreamed for herself. Ambitious and bright, with talent she had not yet discovered or harnessed, Dorothy felt hopeless and trapped. Once again, she sank into depression.

In 1985, five years after marrying the engaging guy she had met in the California mental ward, Dorothy found herself living in Crossville, a small town nestled in the mountains of east central Tennessee. Because Chuck wasn't selling many cars, Dorothy got a bookkeeping job at a local carpet store. With her fifteen-year-old son Michael now living with the family, there were six people to support. There wasn't enough money. Something had to be done, and Dorothy did it—she began stealing cash from the man who owned the carpet store. Small amounts at first, but when she realized she could skim the money and cover her tracks, she started stealing larger sums. Over the period of a year, she stole thirteen thousand dollars, an amount too big to conceal. Her boss called the police, and she was charged with felony theft. Facing a term in prison, Dorothy, in return for a suspended sentence, pleaded guilty to felony embezzlement. Her ability to tell a convincing sob story kept Dorothy out of jail. She felt no shame for what she had done because, in her mind, she simply did what she had to do. When it came to money and the survival of her family, the end justified the means.

Having worn out their welcome in Tennessee, the Deerings moved north to Lexington, in the heart of Kentucky's horse country. Dorothy's brother Bill, now thirty-six, happened to be selling carpets in Lexington at the time. The bad-tempered kid, having been kicked out of college for cursing a professor, had turned into a boiler-room hustler who hawked carpets over the phone, then slipped out of town with down payments when too many customers began demanding the return of their money. As big and cheesy as Chuck but not nearly as friendly, Bill Watson personified the "fly-by-night operator." Chuck had found a pair of part-time jobs in Lexington selling cars and toolsheds. Dorothy had found a house to rent in Nicholasville, a small town just south of the city. If Chuck could control his drinking and do what he did best—sell things—the Deerings might make it in Kentucky. Now that she had a criminal record, Dorothy did not want to be forced to steal.

A few months after moving to Kentucky, Dorothy drove to Denver to visit her sister Vicki, who was living in Colorado with her second husband, a man with the impressive name of Blake Richardson. Vicki was putting Blake through chiropractic school and, in her spare time, writing short stories. Vicki was excited about her writing and believed she had talent. She was confident enough in her work to let Dorothy read some of her best stuff. As Dorothy read Vicki's writings, she experienced a defining moment in her life. She, as a former professional entertainer, was the creative one in the family. Vicki's stories were all right, but Dorothy could do much better. She loved books and had good taste in literature. She should be the writer; she could do it. Why hadn't she thought of this before? That's what her life had been lacking—she needed to be creative, to realize her potential. A new world suddenly opened up to her. Finally, a reason to live. Dorothy would become a successful author. She was excited, and when she made up her mind to do something, it got done. Dorothy would let nothing stand in her way.

Back in Nicholasville, inspired by her sister's literary aspirations, Dorothy quickly wrote a three-hundred-page science fiction novel called "The Sleepers." Convinced she had written an excellent, best-selling book, she picked up the 1987 edition of *Writer's Market* to look for an agent.[1] When none of the New York City agents in the non-fee-charging section of the directory showed interest in her book, Dorothy lowered her sights and paid a fee agent from Florida, or perhaps Wisconsin, to represent her work. That agent didn't have any success placing her book, so she hired another fee charger who couldn't find a publisher either. After wasting her money on a third fee agent, Dorothy probably realized that it would be a lot easier to become a fee-charging literary agent than a published writer. All it would take was a schedule of fees, some letterhead stationery, and a listing in *Writer's Market*. As she might have figured it, instead of unpublished writers dropping their manuscripts over publishing house transoms, they could pay her to do it. What was so difficult about mailing off manuscript packages to New York City? Who needed a good education and publishing experience for that? Maybe she'd blindly send something out that would catch the eye of an editor. Dorothy probably thought that's how literary agents got their start. Someone had to be willing to represent writers who couldn't get regular agents.

Dorothy probably had no idea how many potential clients—aspiring writers desperate enough to pay a hefty fee to an agent of last resort—were out there. She had no way of knowing whether there was room in the genteel racket for another fee-charging agent. (Of the 210 agents listed in the 1990 *Writer's Market,* twenty-five charged reading fees of seventy-five dollars or more. Only six of these entrepreneurs were aggressively advertising for clients in the back of *Writer's Digest,* a monthly magazine read widely among aspiring writers.) Whether Dorothy realized it or not, she had tapped into a pulsating vein of hopeful writers willing to pay for literary representation. She would also come to realize that this vein produced a steady source of fresh blood, that there were more than enough aspiring writers to keep fakes like her in business.

When the 1989 edition of *Literary Market Place* came out, it contained an advertisement for the Dorothy Deering Literary Agency of Nicholasville, Kentucky.[2] Her dream had become a reality. All she needed now were clients willing to pay fees up front.

The first response to Dorothy's ad in *Literary Market Place* came sooner than she had expected. Ted Nottingham, an Indianapolis minister, had written a spiritual book that he had already placed with a small press. He called Dorothy and asked her to work out the details with the publisher. There would be no advance—the company was too small—but Nottingham wanted a professional to look over the contract. He also asked Dorothy to find publishers for two other books he had written in the same genre. She accepted the assignment. Since he had already found a publisher for his first book, which would make finding a home for the other two much easier, Dorothy did not charge Nottingham a fee for reading his manuscripts or up-front money—a contract fee—to cover her costs of marketing the two books. Dorothy had one client, her first, and already she would be able to claim a manuscript sale to a publisher. It looked like becoming a literary agent was going to be easier than she had thought.

Dorothy's inclusion in the 1990 edition of *Writer's Market* further established her presence as a player on the literary scene. Listing her home address on Jason Drive, her twelve-line entry blended in nicely with the style, content, and format of the directory and had at its heart, "We are a new agency and are anxious to work with new, unpublished authors." Under the heading FEES was this contradictory statement: "Charges a reading fee; provides free critiques." Dorothy did not include that she also charged her clients an annual three-hundred-dollar contract fee that supposedly went toward marketing the manuscript. So, for four hundred dollars, the client hired an ex-felon with no literary experience who worked out of her garage in Nicholasville, Kentucky. Since no writer with a bit of sense would pay good money for that, Dorothy, under the RECENT SALES part of her *Writer's Market* entry, did a little "puffing." She listed three books without identifying their authors or publishers. She included her own unpublished science fiction novel, "The Sleepers," the book Ted Nottingham had placed with the small press, and a title she had made up.

For Dorothy, life suddenly had meaning and was full of promise. Chuck, on the other hand, seemed lost and unable to get anything going. He had quit his sales jobs in Lexington and wanted to move to Georgia to work with Dorothy's brother, Bill, who had set up another boiler-room carpet-selling operation in Acworth, a small town twenty miles north of Atlanta. This meant Dorothy would have to move her agency, which was not difficult at this point in her career. It required only changing addresses from one small town to another.

Dorothy rented a large, older home at 1507 Oakmont Drive in Acworth, where she would continue to expand a literary business based entirely on writer-paid fees. To help her with the paperwork—mailing form letter responses to writers inquiring about representation; producing boilerplate critiques for writers who had paid the reading fee; sending out acceptance letters contingent on the payment of the three-hundred-dollar contract fee; mailing bundles of manuscripts off to New York; and keeping track of the rejections—Dorothy asked her sister Vicki and her husband, now Dr. Blake Richardson, to come to Georgia and move in with her family. Vicki, the one whose literary aspirations had jump-started Dorothy's life, accepted the offer.

According to the 1991 edition of *Writer's Market,* the Deering Literary Agency, at its new address, was under the codirectorship of Dorothy Deering and Vicki Richardson. This time, under RECENT SALES, Dorothy simply said "Confidential." Why lie when she didn't have to?

In 1991, Ted Nottingham, Dorothy's first client, started to wonder whether his agent knew what she was doing. According to the status sheet she had sent him listing the twenty or so publishers who had rejected his two manuscripts, she was firing off books shotgun style without any regard to the different needs of each publisher. Had he been submitting his manuscripts himself, he would have known not to send them to any of the publishers on Dorothy's list. Having only spoken to Dorothy on the phone, Nottingham figured it might be a good idea to drive down to Georgia and see what this woman looked like. On the telephone, she *sounded* professional enough, but who knows how she would come off in person.

Instead of finding a well-groomed literary agent in business attire working in a modern, well-lit place, Nottingham encountered a woman in a farm dress working in a cluttered house full of relatives. The moment the Indianapolis writer laid eyes on Vicki, he thought, "Oh my God, what is she doing in this business?" He also met Chuck, who seemed to be working for the women.

Nottingham drove back to Indiana with mixed emotions. Any fool could see that these folks were not literary people. But he had no reason to believe they were dishonest, and he didn't doubt for a minute that Dorothy Deering, despite her obvious limitations, was ambitious, hardworking, and shrewd. She was a quick study who wanted to get ahead. Against his better judgment, Nottingham decided to stay with the Deering Agency. As a man of the cloth, he was not one to look down on anyone. Someday, Dorothy Deering might be a big-time agent. This was America, where anything was possible.

Early in her career, Dorothy acquired a stable of clients who would remain, above everything else, loyal. Craig Andrews, an automotive engineer from the Detroit area, was one of them. An unpublished writer who had just finished his sixth fantasy novel, Andrews was selecting, out of the 1991 *Writer's Market,* agents to query. He had put the Deering Agency on his list because, according to their directory entry, they were interested in working with unpublished writers. Of the agents to whom Andrews wrote, Dorothy was the first to respond and the only one who expressed an interest in his book. She sent him a three-page flyer that contained a brief history of the agency and a lot of puffing.

> The Deering Literary Agency began in 1989 in Nicholasville, Kentucky. During that first year, Mr. Deering was transferred to Atlanta with the corporation he was with and at that time, Mrs. Deering consolidated her Houston Office with our Georgia Office.

Having introduced Chuck as some kind of business executive and herself as a literary agent who had offices in two states, Dorothy didn't want prospective clients to be put off by her agency's address.

> From Acworth, we can reach the publishing centers quickly by telephone, fax, air express or priority mail. Since works of literature and genre works sell on their merit alone, we can cover the markets as well as a New York agent, but we are just far enough away to provide a fresher outlook.

A careful reader of Dorothy's flyer may have wondered whether perhaps there wasn't more to author representation than having a fax machine. And if manuscripts sold on their merits alone, why would any writer with a good book need an agent in the first place? Finally, what kind of literary agency found it necessary to sell itself to potential clients? Wasn't it supposed to be the other way around? Didn't writers, particularly unpublished ones, have to sell themselves to the agent? In other words, why would a successful literary agent need a flyer?

Instead of smelling a rat, Craig Andrews was intrigued and impressed with the Deering story. Dorothy, having stated that good manuscripts virtually sold themselves, continued to lay it on.

> We are a young, aggressive, sales oriented agency. We are not locked into the "old system" of representation. We have incorporated the best of the old ways, the unerring accuracy of computers, and the determination of an experienced sales and marketing director. We know that this blue ribbon combination will result in the proper placement of your work with interested professionals in your particular field of writing. We have spared no expense in obtaining the latest in computer equipment, scanners, laser printers, copiers, etc., to better serve our clients.

Dorothy made her company seem more like a Kinko's franchise than a literary agency. In referring to her sales and marketing director, she must have been thinking of Chuck. If manuscripts could be sold like toolsheds, carpets, and cars, Dorothy would have been onto something.

For those writers still reading her flyer, Dorothy saved the most important part for last: the justification for up-front money. First, the $125 reading, or manuscript evaluation, fee:

> This fee pays for the services of the staff members that are involved in making a representation decision. These staff members spend a great deal of time on these manuscripts. We do specialize in new authors and it is unreasonable for these services to be performed and not paid for.

In 1992, only a handful of fee agents charged so-called contract or representation fees. Since they were really after the fee, the quality of the client's manuscript was not an issue. As a result, virtually no writer willing to pay the up-front money was ever rejected, which made the reading fee, as a manuscript screening technique, superfluous. Dorothy charged a contract fee and justified it as follows:

In most cases we charge a fee of five hundred dollars per manuscript. In our
experience, that is approximately what the cost of marketing a manuscript is
over the period of representation.

The period of representation was one year, and no client since Ted
Nottingham would escape what was then one of the stiffest contract fees
in the business. If Dorothy brought in three hundred reading fees a year
and "represented" an average of one hundred manuscripts, she could
make, by working out of her house, $87,500 a year. Since Dorothy's
method of "marketing" a manuscript involved packing it into a box with
four or five others and mailing it to a publisher she had found in *Writer's
Market* along with a form cover letter, 90 percent of the contract money
was profit.

Dorothy Deering, like others before her, had found a way to become
a successful literary agent without having to sell manuscripts. All she had
to do was sell herself and the writer's dream of being published. She had
become a player in the genteel racket.

Selling dreams is a tricky business. Once the fantasy merchant makes
the sale, the buyer has to be gently brought back to reality. If not, the buyer
becomes a pain in the seller's ass when high expectations aren't met. Even
before she had the dreamer's money, Dorothy laid the groundwork for
the inevitable kiss-off. In a tone of condescension common to fee hustlers, she ended her flyer this way:

> Now comes the hard part, especially for new authors who do not know the
> ropes. A publisher will not usually respond for a period of from two months
> to even as long as six months. In reality, the longer a publisher keeps it [the
> manuscript], the better the chances are that they may be interested in that
> manuscript. We will be the first ones on the phone to you if and when there is
> an offer. Please feel free to call our office about every five or six weeks to check
> on the progress of things. . . . We are not miracle workers. We cannot sell the
> unsalable manuscript. We can only try to do the best of our ability, using our
> best efforts. The book marketplace is tough and very demanding. We make no
> promises that a particular work will sell.

Craig Andrews wasn't rich, but as an automotive engineer, he had a
good job and certainly could afford to send Dorothy Deering her $125
reading fee. The way he figured it, if that was what it took to get on the
road to being published, it was a small price to pay. A few weeks after he

sent Dorothy the reading fee and his novel, "The Godmanchester Stone," Andrews received a three-page manuscript evaluation form that had been filled out by someone named Cheri A. Anderson.[3]

Craig was thrilled to see that Dorothy's reader had given his work an overall rating of "excellent." Finally, an opinion from someone he didn't know who thought he had written a good book. With his evaluation came even better news: an encouraging letter from Dorothy Deering offering to take him on as a client. She had also enclosed a contract that called for the one-year, five-hundred-dollar contract fee.

Craig Andrews had been up against the inexperienced author's worst fears about publishing: If you weren't published, you couldn't get an agent, and without an agent, you couldn't get published. He had invested an enormous amount of time and energy in his writing and so far had nothing to show for his efforts. He believed he had no choice but to help Dorothy Deering market his "excellent" manuscript. Just having an agent made him feel like a real writer. He liked that feeling. Now when people asked him about his new book, he could say that his *agent* was shopping it around to publishers. This part of being a writer was the most exciting.

About a month after Craig Andrews signed on as a Deering client, Diana Kemp-Jones, a science fiction writer from San Pedro, California, paid Dorothy fifteen hundred dollars to represent three of her fifteen unpublished novels. Over the next three years, these two clients, Craig Andrews and Diana Kemp-Jones, would pay Dorothy tens of thousands of dollars for the representation of twenty-one manuscripts.

When it came time to bill a writer for another year's worth of representation, Dorothy would send the client a letter that read,

> My plans are to send it [the manuscript] to many, many more small presses and foreign presses. One I sold recently, I sent it to forty-seven American publishers, then to the Dirves Livres in Paris. They bought it and I then immediately sold it in this country. There is no rhyme nor reason to selling a book. I just have to keep at it.

Dorothy's contract extension letter reflects clever and effective deception. It's clever in that while sounding detailed and informative, there are no material facts, including the title of the book in question, the author's name, or the identity of the American publisher. It's effective because in a fairly subtle way it keeps the dream alive. There may be no rhyme or reason to manuscript selling, but there was to selling dreams, a skill Dorothy had mastered.

Dorothy Deering had transformed herself from a neophyte into one of the most aggressive and successful fee agents in the genteel racket. She was well on her way to becoming the agent from hell.

2 Atlantic Disk Publishers

BY 1993, AS A RISING STAR IN THE literary fee business, Dorothy's days of being dependent on a husband who couldn't hold down a job were behind her. Chuck depended on her; she was now head of the family, the one calling the shots. She was close to living the life she had always dreamed of. She had money, respect, and a future that promised excitement and, yes, even glamour.

When she spoke to a client, she could tell that the writer felt privileged to be talking to a literary agent. She could never go back to the old ways, not now, not after tasting the good life. With her agency now prominently listed in several writer's magazines, publishing directories, and trade journals, Dorothy had built a giant net designed to gather up aspiring writers who had lost hope of ever acquiring literary representation from agents who didn't charge fees. And there were so many of them! It seemed that everyone in America had written a book. No wonder nobody read anymore; they were too busy writing. Every month, hundreds of query letters and manuscripts poured into the agency, and every month, almost as many manuscript evaluation sheets and agency contracts flowed out. In the meantime, boxes and boxes containing the works of her clients were trucked to publishers in New York City, where most of the material simply vanished. Instead of pitching her clients' manuscripts to editors, Dorothy spent most of her time talking potential clients into signing up with the agency or keeping old clients on board for another year. She was working herself silly, but not for her clients.

While Dorothy worked the phones, Chuck kept the paper moving. They had become an effective team. Dorothy did the selling, and Chuck ran the fee mill. In fact, he was so organized and efficient, Dorothy awarded him the title of business manager. Now it was Dorothy out in the world selling and Chuck behind the scenes doing the grunt work. Dorothy's success as a literary entrepreneur had saved her marriage. Chuck's emergence as a key figure in the agency that bore his name had the effect of pushing Vicki, Dorothy's sister and codirector, aside. So what to do with Vicki? Dr. Blake Richardson, the husband she had put through chiropractic school, was no longer around, and she had two children to support. Dorothy had an idea—why not start a literary agency for Vicki? She could work out of the house and pick up writers who had been missed by the Deering net. Who knows, Vicki might even attract some of Dorothy's disgruntled, former clients.

To accommodate her own growing business and the second agency, Dorothy rented adjoining offices in a tiny strip mall on West Alabama Road in Acworth. Calling this new firm A Rising Sun Literary Group, Dorothy began running display ads for the agency in the back of *Writer's Digest* magazine that read,

> **It's a Tough Market**
> for new and unpublished authors, but A Rising Sun Literary Group can help scale the mountains.[1]

The two agencies shared the same street address and fax number but had different suites (104 and 106) and telephone numbers. Dorothy was careful not to run the Deering and Rising Sun ads in the same edition of the magazine. Dorothy also advertised the new agency in *Literary Market Place* and arranged for an entry in *Writer's Market.* That's all it took. Query letters were soon pouring into A Rising Sun. Quite often, a writer would query both agencies. When that happened, the business went to Vicki. Because she was new and just starting out, she charged only ninety-five dollars to read a manuscript and three hundred dollars to represent it for a year.

The great thing about starting a new agency was the absence of a blank record of manuscript sales. How could a brand new literary agency be expected to have any publishing deals to brag about? The Deering Agency, on the other hand, had been around for almost five years. What recent, or even old, manuscript sales did Dorothy have to show for all that fee money? Except for Ted Nottingham, her first client, who had placed the book himself with a small press, Dorothy had nothing to report. This poor record was becoming a problem, particularly in the area of talking old clients into re-upping for another year. Dorothy was saying, "Show me the money," and they were responding with, "Show us the results." That was a tall order for someone who really wasn't a literary agent. Since she couldn't actually sell her clients' manuscripts, Dorothy decided on a way of maintaining the *illusion* of legitimacy.

Her back against the wall, Dorothy came up with a way to get her clients published; she would do it herself. She would form another company. Dorothy would solve the problem threatening her literary agency and at the same time generate a new source of revenue. She would make her clients pay to have their manuscripts published on computer disks, and it would cost them only five hundred dollars a pop. The money would be paid in advance, of course. She had found the perfect Deering style solution. She would call her new company Atlantic Disk Publishers, Incorporated—ADP for short.

Dorothy announced the formation of her new publishing enterprise in what she pretentiously called a press release, sent to every client and potential client she had ever dealt with. Chuck had put together the mailing list, which included more than two thousand writers. It was a good start. Referring to ADP as "a new publisher rising," Dorothy established her credentials as a *publisher* with a lie as preposterous as it was ingenious and effective. She wrote, "Mrs. Deering is the daughter of Betty Morrow of the original Morrow publishing family."[2] The fabrication was clever because she knew no one would even think of checking it out and ingenious because she realized that writers would consider this affiliation important. Dorothy, in telling this whopper, had crossed the line between blatant puffing and false advertising.

In the sentence following the announcement that she was one of *the* Morrows, Dorothy returned to her regular brand of hard-core puffing: "She travels to speak and conduct workshops at writer's conferences all over the United States." Had this statement been true, it would have been a lot worse than the lie. Having established herself as a literary figure of considerable influence, Dorothy, in her own press release, felt obliged to quote herself.

> Says Mrs. Deering, "We are part of the new computer age and will publish authors' manuscripts on disks. We have unlimited marketing in this area and

expect to publish over one hundred titles in the first year. This is an exciting age we live in and ATLANTIC DISK PUBLISHERS, INC. is a part of the new technology for our time.

We take mass market fiction, literary fiction, adventure, thrillers, romance, mystery, suspense, young adult, humor, ethnic, fantasy, science fiction, futuristic, mainstreams, political, religious, short story collections as well as nonfiction and will pay thirty-five percent royalty to our authors. . . . Be sure your manuscript is in the best possible form, edited in spelling, grammatical errors, tense and sentence structure problems, as we will only accept the cream of the crop."

Indeed, Dorothy would have to possess "unlimited marketing ability" to distribute and sell computer books of virtually every genre known to man. So much for specializing. Since every writer receiving this press release had already been praised by Dorothy, the agent, for their fine manuscript, they all had reason to believe they were the "cream of the crop." Moreover, if Dorothy, as ADP, turned down one writer, she would, as a vanity publisher, be making history.

Had Dorothy intended to keep any of the promises outlined in her press release, she would have been forced to hire someone who knew something about publishing. Instead, she installed Chuck as "publisher and editor-in-chief," introducing him to potential authors as follows:

Mr. Deering, who has functioned as the co-director and business manager of the Deering Literary Agency, was a national corporate contract negotiator before joining his wife in their prospering office.

What a "national corporate contract negotiator" was or did, Dorothy left to the imagination of her readers. They would also have to figure out what that had to do with publishing. But it sounded good, a lot better than former used car salesman who had also sold toolsheds and hustled carpets for her brother, "Boiler-room Bill."

To be his ADP editorial assistant, Chuck would hire Teresa Nelson, a part-time clerical employee of the Deering Agency. Dorothy also put her son Michael Helm on the ADP payroll. It was hard to envision what Michael, a twenty-six-year-old antisocial drug addict, would be doing for Dorothy's Atlantic Disk authors. His job, basically, would be to keep out of sight, stay off the telephone, and do as little harm as possible. This assignment was not tough but would prove to be more than he could handle. Dorothy, in selecting her ADP personnel, had managed to assemble a staff who knew less about publishing than she did.

Diana Kemp-Jones, the science fiction writer from San Pedro, California, who had nine of her novels under representation by Dorothy, became one of the first of her clients to sign on with ADP. In the fall of 1993, she paid Dorothy twenty-five hundred dollars to have five of her manuscripts published on disk. With four of her nine manuscripts still unpublished, Diana had to decide, after seventy-two publisher rejections, whether to pay Dorothy the two thousand dollars to have her manuscripts represented for another year. Having already paid Dorothy more than ten thousand dollars in reading and contract fees, with nothing to show for it but a five-book vanity deal costing her another twenty-five hundred dollars, Diana perhaps should have cut her losses and run. But having invested so much in Dorothy, Diana believed she had no choice but to remain hopeful. To help Diana make the right—or wrong—decision, Chuck Deering, in his capacity as Dorothy's business manager, sent this long-time client the following letter:

> I was reviewing your file today and noticed that your contracts on four of your works have expired. We have contacted many publishers and producers concerning your work and unfortunately they decided to pass on it *right now*. This does not mean they never want to see it again, rather it means they may view it more favorably in the near future. The number of new publishers and producers is increasing with every passing month. I plan to contact these in the coming weeks and months. We should not give up just because some publishers passed on your work. Your writing is just as good now as it was when we first took it to represent. . . .
>
> I have included the contract extension agreement with this letter. I hope it meets with your approval. We have lowered the fees to the MINIMUM possible because I believe your work has the potential to sell. Please return the copy of the extension agreement to me as soon as possible. If you have any questions, CALL ME.

If Diana called anyone, it should have been the attorney general of Georgia. Instead she sent Chuck Deering a check for two thousand dollars. Who would have believed it was easier getting money out of people this way than by selling cars? You sent them a letter, and they sent you money. Thank God for writers.

This is too good to be true.
—Dorothy Deering, referring to Northwest Publishing

3 Northwest Publishing

A FEW MONTHS BEFORE DOROTHY ANNOUNCED the formation of Atlantic Disk Publishers, she and a hundred or so fee agents around the country began receiving promotional literature from a new publishing house in Salt Lake City called Northwest Publishing, Inc., or as it came to be known, NPI. Formed in October 1992 by James B. Van Treese, NPI claimed it specialized in the publication of mass-market paperbacks by first-time authors, all of whom had been rejected by other publishers. Supposedly, Van Treese was giving them another chance. In return, authors would contribute up front one-half of what Van Treese claimed to be the cost of producing their books. Insisting that these were not vanity deals, Van Treese coined the term *joint venture publishing.*

Whatever he called it, joint venture had the stink of subsidy publishing all over it. And no writer, however desperate, wanted to be thought of as a vanity author. If Van Treese had any chance of selling his new publishing scheme to a large number of writers, he would need a sales force of supposedly independent operators, like Dorothy Deering, who could convince their clients that joint venture publishing was not only legitimate but the wave of the future. Since vanity publishing does not produce royalties, there was nothing in it for the agent. That's why, as an incentive, Van Treese offered 10 percent of the writer's contribution as a so-called finder's fee. The client, led to believe there would be royalties, was not to be told that 10 percent of his joint venture payment was going to the agent in the form of a kickback. If writers ever discovered the true role of the agent in Van Treese's operation, the scheme would collapse. Jim Van Treese and the fee-based literary agent was a marriage made in hell.

The typical NPI deal involved a writer's contribution of between four and eight thousand dollars, depending on the agent's assessment of how much the client was willing to pay. The joint venture author would receive, as a return on investment, a 40-percent royalty on the sale of the first twenty-five hundred paperbacks. On copies sold after that, the author's percentage would drop to the more standard 15 percent. An author, for example, who contributed $4,825 to the publication of a $5.95 paperback, got back $5,950 on the sale of twenty-five hundred copies. Assuming that ten thousand copies of the book had been printed, the author's cut on the sale of the remaining seventy-five hundred paperbacks would come to $6,693.75. So, on a $4,825 investment, the author would make a profit of $7,818.75.

Granted, this amount was not a lot of money for a book that had taken six months to a year to write. But it was a start in the right direction. If the book took off, and it could happen, the writer might end up rich and famous. NPI gave the aspiring writer a chance to invest in his own success. Either the writer believed in his book or he didn't. Jim Van Treese gave writers the opportunity to put their money where their mouths were, and if only ten thousand copies of the book sold, there were the intangible benefits of being a published author. Family members, colleagues, and friends who had scoffed at the idea of starting a new career as a writer would suddenly become respectful, perhaps even envious. For a mere $4,825, the writer, at the very least, would get respect and a chance. That was the deal, the lure, and the pitch.

On paper, Van Treese's joint venture idea looked good, but in reality, it was hopelessly flawed. The typical print run of an author-subsidized book is in the neighborhood of two thousand to ten thousand copies. Legitimate subsidy publishers sell the product, not the dream of becoming a commercially successful author. Under Van Treese's system, before the author can make any money at all, ten thousand books have to be sold. Assuming that Van Treese actually matched the writer's contribution, which he didn't, there was no way he could afford to manufacture and market that many books. Assuming, for a moment, that he could afford to produce that many books, how could he sell ten thousand copies of a cheaply made, poorly edited book that no one, outside the writer's family and friends, knew existed? Finding one of these books on the shelf of a Barnes and Noble store would be as likely as coming across a cold can of beer. If Van Treese actually believed for one second that joint venture was a viable concept for publishers and writers, he hadn't done the math or was as naïve as his victims. That he was recruiting agents to sell his idea suggested otherwise.

In the spring of 1994, Van Treese sent Dorothy Deering a copy of NPI's first catalogue. Containing 187 titles, some available for purchase, but most listed as "soon to be published," it was quite impressive. The lead book, its dust jacket featured in a full-page ad, was a novel of "love, space and war" by former astronaut Mike Mullane. Entitled *Red Sky,* with cover blurbs from Stephen Counts and Chuck Yeager, this hardcover book was obviously not a joint venture publication and grossly misrepresented the typical NPI product. Targeting prospective joint venture authors rather than book buyers, the catalogue proclaimed that *Red Sky* was backed by

- seventy thousand copies, first printing
- $125,000 marketing budget
- twenty-eight-city author tour
- national advertising
- eighteen-copy floor display
- advance reading copies
- full-color posters, 16" x 24"

Van Treese's catalogue, featuring *Red Sky* as show money, would help agents like Dorothy sell NPI to clients whose manuscripts they had been unable to sell to regular publishers.

Dorothy was impressed with Jim Van Treese and his new publishing company and sent him a novel about Hurricane Andrew by a client from Florida named Howard Markowitz. A few weeks later, Markowitz was sent, directly from NPI, a publishing contract calling for a $4,825 author's contribution. Appalled at being offered a vanity deal, Markowitz called Dorothy to find out why she had sent his manuscript to a subsidy publisher. Caught off guard and angry that Van Treese had gone directly to her client before she had the chance to make the pitch, Dorothy called Northwest and spoke to Van Treese's son, Jason. After Jason's apology for the goof, the two of them had a long talk. By the end of the conversation, Jason realized there was a live wire down in Georgia who had a barrelful of clients. He said he would speak to his father about the Deering Literary Agency.

The next morning, Jason called and invited Dorothy and Chuck Deering to Salt Lake City, where Jim Van Treese would give them a personal tour of Northwest Publishing. A few days later, Jason picked them up at the airport and drove the pair to their hotel before taking his guests to NPI headquarters in Midvale, a small town off I-15 on the southern edge of the city. There they met Jim Van Treese, a medium-sized, dark-haired man in his late forties, wearing blue jeans and an open-collared shirt. For Dorothy, it was love at first sight. Here was a tightly wound, rough-around-the-edges kind of guy who made no secret of the fact he intended to make a lot of money and to share the wealth with people who helped him get it.

Van Treese was impressed with Dorothy as well. Here was a woman, from Georgia or wherever, with a buffoon of a husband, who had built something out of nothing. Like him, she wasn't in the literary business because she liked books. She was in it because she liked money.

After taking the NPI tour, Dorothy was even more impressed with Jim Van Treese. He proudly showed off his expensively furnished office, the machine he used to print and bind cheaply made paperbacks, his typesetting software, and the small warehouse where he stored cartons of NPI books. (At that time, Van Treese was actually publishing three hundred of the ten thousand copies he was under contract to produce.) There was no doubt in Dorothy's mind that Jim Van Treese was a rising star in the publishing world.

That evening, over wine and lobster at a five-star restaurant, Van Treese explained how agents like Dorothy were key to his success. By agents like her, he meant agents who charged fees because they really weren't in the business of selling manuscripts. While she didn't have sales, Dorothy did have clients and access to hundreds of manuscripts, a mountain of slush he—they—could turn into gold. To Dorothy, five hundred manuscripts were nothing more than a tower of used paper; to Van Treese, these works represented $3 million in joint venture money. If Dorothy could talk half her clients into NPI deals, they could both make a lot of money. An agent could rock along on reading and contract fees, but after a while, that well would run dry. But if Dorothy hooked up with Van Treese, she'd get a piece of the joint venture pie and, because her clients would be getting published, maintain the credibility she needed to keep the fees rolling in.

Van Treese didn't have to ask whether Dorothy wanted in; the look on her face told it all. She was staring, glassy-eyed, at the man who was going to take her to a place in life she had only dreamed of. She had hit the jackpot and was on her way. Tell us what to do, she said. We'll do whatever it takes.

The deal was this: Jim Van Treese would become a silent partner in the Deering Literary Agency.[1] NPI would be pitched to every Deering client—past, present, and future. As a clandestine representative of Northwest Publishing, Dorothy would receive from Van Treese an annual salary of ninety thousand, her office rent paid, new computers, and money to hire more personnel to handle the additional paperwork. Dorothy nearly fell out of her chair at that offer, but there was more: Van Treese would pay Dorothy a 10-percent finder's fee on every joint venture deal that came through her agency. And for every ten deals she brokered, he would allow her to give one of her clients a standard, nonvanity contract. This would allow her to claim that not all of her published clients had signed joint venture deals. From his experience with his other agent partners, Van Treese expected Dorothy to take this offer for books she and her friends had written, which is exactly what she would do.

Back at the hotel that night, a triumphant Dorothy talked excitedly about her good luck and what lay ahead. She kept saying, "This is too good to be true." She was referring, of course, to herself and not her clients.

Before flying back to Georgia the following morning, Dorothy signed the contract Van Treese had drawn up containing the terms they had discussed in the restaurant. It was now official; Dorothy Deering and Jim Van Treese were partners.

Two weeks later, Jim and his son flew to Georgia to see what they had purchased. After dinner at the Deering house, Jim shocked Dorothy by announcing he was taking every manuscript she had, including copies, back to NPI. The next day, there wasn't a single manuscript in the agency. Van Treese left behind a batch of signed NPI publishing contracts with a blank space for Dorothy to fill in the author's contribution, a collection of NPI form letters, and written instructions on how to talk clients into joint venture deals.

Having sold her clients' manuscripts to Jim Van Treese, Dorothy had become a sales representative for NPI. But to do that job effectively, she had to continue impersonating a literary agent, and for that she needed her principal prop, an office full of manuscripts. Moreover, if she couldn't get her hands on a client's manuscript, say, when a writer called or a letter had to be written, she could lose a contract extension or a joint venture kickback. She was lost without those manuscripts—Van Treese should have left her at least one copy of each. She couldn't function without them.

Dorothy, Chuck, her son Michael, and one of Chuck's boys, Daniel Craig, spent the week after the Van Treese looting calling clients, asking them to send additional copies of their manuscripts. Each client was told that Dorothy, because she liked to send as many manuscripts as she could to publishers, had simply exhausted her supply. This was, of course, just what the client wanted to hear. With visions of editors the length and width of Manhattan reading their works, clients were running to copy shops all over the country to replenish Dorothy's supply. Within a few days, manuscripts began pouring in, filling up Dorothy's shelves and file cabinets. For now, everybody was happy. Dorothy had set her sights on a rising star, and her clients thought their manuscripts were making the rounds in Manhattan.

Still eager for new NPI authors, Jim Van Treese next turned his attention to A Rising Sun, the agency Dorothy had started for her sister Vicki. A month or so after acquiring Dorothy's manuscripts, Van Treese invited both Dorothy and Vicki to Salt Lake City. This time Dorothy left Chuck at home. Van Treese wanted to meet Vicki and make the same deal with her.

Dorothy got the ball rolling by sending clients the NPI contract—signed by Van Treese with the author's contribution, usually $6,375, typed in— accompanied by a letter that read,

> I am so excited that I had to send these [the NPI contracts] to you immediately. We have an offer on [title of the client's book] that I truly believe is beneficial and profitable to you. We have dealt with Northwest before and they have proven themselves to be people of their word and conduct their business in a very professional manner. It is exceptional that a first time author gets an offer to publish with this type of return.
>
> I have gone over this [the contract] with my attorney and believe me when I tell you that it is the best in the industry. Although it is a joint publishing

agreement, you will make the highest royalty percentage, higher than any of the big publishers are paying.

I went to Salt Lake City and went through Northwest Publishing, and it is a fine operation. I have seen their printing presses and they have the finest art department I have ever seen. I had the opportunity to see every cover they have ever done and they were all beautiful.

As your agent, I highly recommend these publishing agreements. Mr. Van Treese is in the process of buying a chain of 31 bookstores on the West Coast and is going to make them into super stores. He has unlimited distribution and marketing capabilities. He uses some 5,000 reviewers.

Congratulations, and I shall look forward to hearing from you soon. Please give me a call when you receive these contracts.

In terms of their immediate reaction to being asked to kick in six thousand dollars to have their books published in paperback, Dorothy's clients fell into three broad categories. About half rejected the proposal outright as being either ridiculous or perhaps even bogus. Maybe they didn't buy the five thousand reviewers—whatever that meant—or the thirty-one bookstores. Maybe it was the tone of Dorothy's letter—the "truly believe" and the "believe me when I tell you"—language that suggested dishonesty and put them off. Maybe they just didn't have the money. A much smaller group jumped with joy over the offer, while the rest needed more prodding than just a pitch letter. It was the writers in this last group that Dorothy and Van Treese had to work on. Dorothy would spend hours on the telephone with these clients, assuring them that joint venture publishing was an excellent way for them to realize their dreams of becoming commercial writers. Van Treese would also call the reluctant writer to praise the book and to characterize it as a potential best seller that would receive his personal attention when it came time to promote the work. This one-two punch was usually enough to close the deal.

Clients who wanted to be published by NPI but couldn't get their hands on that kind of money were encouraged by Dorothy to borrow it against their mortgage, pension fund, or some other asset. If that wasn't possible, they could always try to borrow it from a relative or a well-heeled friend. If no one would lend them the money, Dorothy would arrange a payment plan of monthly installments. These clients, because they paid their contributions in increments, were charged the most, even though they could afford it the least.

After the NPI contract had been signed and the client's check had cleared, Dorothy would send the joint venture author the following letter.

> First of all, congratulations on the sale of your manuscript. Book contracts are hard to come by in this day and age. One in 2,000 sells, so you have something to be proud of.
>
> I just wanted to let you know what happens after the sale of a manuscript. After the contracts are signed and returned to the publisher, there is a wait. I know you are used to that. The publisher puts your book in the library room in the date sequential order of publication. When the time comes for them to work on your book, it is taken down and assigned an editor. That editor will call you and work directly with you. Prior to that time, you will not hear from that publisher.
>
> Please be patient and "write another book" while you're waiting.

Since no legitimate literary agent would push a client toward a vanity book deal, Dorothy risked exposure and the loss of her business. She told the handful of clients who were insulted by the NPI pitch that it was her job to pass along *all* publishing offers. That didn't explain why she had *recommended* the NPI deal—"As your agent, I highly recommend these publishing agreements"—but it was usually enough to calm them down. If that didn't work, she could always apologize and promise to make it up to them by trying even harder to find a royalty-paying publisher for their manuscripts.

Six months after hooking up with Dorothy Deering, Jim Van Treese knew he had picked a winner. That gal down in Georgia could *sell.* Holding up her end of the bargain, she pitched the hell out of NPI, almost making it sound better than a standard publishing agreement. By the end of 1994, roughly 250 Deering clients had signed Northwest contracts, providing Van Treese with a million and a half dollars, minus Dorothy's $150,000 finder's fee. She had even talked Howard Markowitz, the Florida client who had been insulted when he was contacted directly by Van Treese, into a $6,375 author's investment.

Now that she knew how to turn manuscript piles into towers of gold, Dorothy, with this new, aggressive ad in *Writer's Digest* magazine, pulled out all the stops.

Manuscripts Wanted
Accepting new clients—specializing in new authors. Serving all English speaking countries, with agents in book-starved Russia.[2]

Agents in book-starved Russia? Dorothy had become the master of the beautifully constructed lie, an absolute genius. As fee artist, vanity publisher of books on disk, and chief manuscript supplier for Jim Van Treese, Dorothy had found her niche in the literary world. She had never worked so hard or been more pleased with herself. But with success came problems, especially in the business of selling dreams that can't come true.

In this business, things do not happen overnight.
—Dorothy Deering to anxious ADP clients

4 Lies, Lies, and More Lies

DOROTHY HAD PROMISED HER ADP AUTHORS that the sales catalogue would be out in January 1994. That didn't happen. Three months later, Dorothy sent the sixteen-page booklet, which contained only fifty-five titles, to her clients—past, present, and potential. This catalogue contained an order form for the seven disks actually available for purchase (at six dollars apiece). Such was the extent of her "unlimited marketing" capacity. Two hundred clients had paid Dorothy five hundred dollars to have ADP publish their books. In return for the money—one hundred thousand dollars—all they got was this catalogue and seven disks. Most didn't even get into the catalogue. The writers who did get their works on disk were longtime clients, like Ted Nottingham and Diana Kemp-Jones, or friends of the family.

Once Dorothy had the up-front money, she lost interest in ADP, "the new voice of the publishing world." She now focused on supplying manuscripts for Jim Van Treese and NPI. ADP had become small potatoes and a pain in her neck.

By midsummer 1994, with nearly two hundred ADP disks behind schedule, new clients to be signed up, old clients to be renewed, and joint venture deals to be hawked, Dorothy was working sixteen-hour days. ADP authors were driving her crazy with their incessant calling about the status of their books. ADP had been a terrible mistake. Had she met Jim Van Treese a few months earlier, she would not have become involved in such a ridiculous scheme. Now she had to find a way to get these people off her back.

To buy a little time, Dorothy would have to lie. She realized that running out of lies was like running out of money, that if she wasn't careful, she'd squander her quota. But she had to hold these writers off until she figured something out. With stalling in mind, Dorothy sent ADP authors the following letter.

> I ask that you be patient, and want you to know that things are happening as far as advertising and distributions are going. We have signed with Baker and Taylor, the largest distributor in the United States, and we are currently in negotiations with Ingram, another large distributor. We are still in negotiations with the four major companies that own all of the airport bookstores. We will go onto the Internet as soon as all the "bugs" are worked out of the disks. We have 20,000 catalogues out and are receiving orders each day. If the disks are ready, they are shipped out immediately. Each and every day I am improving our reading program.
>
> In this business, things do not happen overnight and we need all available man hours of all our people to make this happen. I ask that you please be patient and please do not call to ask these questions. I shall try to keep you better informed by mailings such as this.

It was all a lie, of course. Nothing was happening, overnight or otherwise, at ADP. But the letter achieved its purpose. Writers, accustomed to their lowly position in the literary hierarchy, do not want to be thought of as pests or, worse, dilettantes. They also do not want to anger the person who makes decisions regarding their books.

Dorothy's letter bought her breathing space, but it also raised the expectations of her authors. They pictured their disks on sale at airports around the country, travelers picking up a disk before they boarded the plane, twenty thousand catalogues, Baker and Taylor, and all the rest. Weeks passed before it became apparent to many that Dorothy's promises were not being kept. By the end of the summer, Dorothy was again being harassed by ADP callers. She had to get this monkey off her back. Unlike practitioners of pigeon-dropping or the bank examiner's scam, she couldn't pick up and leave when things got hot.[1] If she was going to make it in the literary dream business, she would have to develop a method of cleansing herself of the people she had screwed. Otherwise they would eat her alive, put her out of business. Bankruptcy wouldn't work; her business was flourishing.

The solution finally came to Dorothy—she would simply claim to have sold ADP. But who could she say had purchased it? Whoever it was, when the mob of angry writers appeared at their door, they would deny it. That's why she decided to tell her ADP authors and clients that the new owner was none other than Jim Van Treese. Since more than half of her ADP authors had signed NPI deals, the last thing they would do was annoy Jim Van Treese. In that sense, he was bulletproof, the perfect phantom buyer of her phantom company. In her letter announcing that she no longer owned ADP, Dorothy, after referring to Van Treese as "highly reputable," wrote,

> He [Van Treese] deals with over 5,000 independent book sellers and large book distributors. He also has bought a chain of 31 book stores on the West Coast and will be putting his books and CD-ROMs in them and turning them into super stores.

To keep some of the more obnoxious ADP authors at bay, Dorothy declared,

> Due to the corporate change, there will be a delay of several months in publishing your disk, but I can personally assure you that Mr. Van Treese is a man of high integrity and will fulfill the contractual agreements with you and much more.

This "highly reputable" man of such "high integrity" had started NPI after serving a prison term in Oklahoma for penny-stock fraud. He also had a criminal record in Texas and had been investigated by the U.S. Securities and Exchange Commission concerning stock fraud in Utah. Endorsement of Van Treese by Dorothy, herself a convicted thief, was a little like John Dean listing Richard Nixon as a reference in applying to be an election judge.

Among Dorothy's clients at this time was Tom Mahon, a high school teacher and football coach from Pompano Beach, Florida. He had become a Deering client in November 1993 and had paid Dorothy (in addition to the reading fees) fifteen hundred dollars in contract fees to represent his three thrillers, "Axis II," "Sebastian Yard," and "Apparition." Just days later, Tom also paid Dorothy a thousand dollars to have the first two titles published by ADP. Two months later, at a time when Dorothy knew she wouldn't be producing more than a handful of books on disk, she tried to talk Mahon into paying her another five hundred dollars to have his third novel published by ADP. She hit him up with the following letter.

> Things here at Atlantic Disk are progressing rapidly. We will soon be closing the September 1994 list and will need a decision from you within the next few weeks on "APPARITION."
>
> It has become bigger than even I anticipated at the onset. We have entered into a contract whereas our catalogue will be mailed to over 14,000 bookstores and to most all the library systems, along with the computer network advertising, the individual catalogue mailings, airport bookstores, etc. There will be free-standing displays available for the bookstores. We expect sales to be substantial.
>
> Let us hear from you soon.

Although tempted by her letter, Tom decided to wait and see how ADP handled his first two books before sending Dorothy another five hundred dollars. He was pleased, however, that things were looking so good for ADP and his two thrillers.

In April 1995, more than a year after these two books were due to come out, the ADP catalogue finally was issued. "Axis II" was listed, but "Sebastian Yard" was not. When Mahon tried to order a few disks to hand out to family and friends, someone at ADP's sales department told him that title was not yet available for purchase. "Sebastian Yard," he learned, was being featured in the fall catalogue.

Leafing through the catalogue, Mahon noticed that what looked like blurbs from book reviewers were mostly quotes from Dorothy, Chuck, and Vicki Richardson, an "A Rising Sun Representative." He wondered if Vicki was related to Dr. Blake Richardson, who was identified in the catalogue as a "Critic." Tom Mahon was disappointed that only one and not both of his books were in the spring catalogue, but he had no reason to believe that ADP was a sham or that Dorothy Deering was not what she claimed to be. That's why, shortly after the publication of the catalogue, he allowed himself to be talked into paying Jim Van Treese $6,375 to have NPI publish his thriller, "Axis II."

When September came and went without the fall edition of the ADP catalogue, Mahon wondered whether he was a victim of some kind of publishing scam. He was also worried about the deal he had made, through Dorothy, with Northwest Publishing. Other than the copy Dorothy had sent him, Mahon had never seen an NPI book. He had looked in bookstores, public libraries, and publishing directories for references to NPI. He found nothing. It was as though NPI didn't exist. In one bookstore, Mahon asked the manager if he had ever heard of Northwest Publishing. The manager said he had not, prompting Mahon to reveal that he had paid the company a lot of money to publish his book. Well, that explains it, the manager said; our stores don't stock vanity published books. No one did.

Frustrated with the Deering Literary Agency, disappointed with ADP, and more and more suspicious of NPI, Mahon wrote Dorothy a letter voicing his concerns. At her urging, he had invested nearly ten thousand dollars into his books. That gave him a right, he thought, to some straight answers. Instead, he received this angry and insulting letter from some Deering underling named Cynthia Gray:

> In response to your letter of October 5, 1994, I have enclosed a status report for *Apparition.* I assure you the Dorothy Deering Literary Agency is still and will continue to be a very prominent force in the literary community. Atlantic Disk Publishing is a separate entity altogether. As to the periodic reports given to our authors, we are glad to send status reports to you. If you will read clause IV, part C of the agent/author contract, it specifically states that status reports are given on a "request basis only." Please understand that we must prioritize our time to maximize representation for our authors. In order to do so, we must ask that your requests for updates are no less than six weeks apart. You will be notified of any significant replies from a publisher immediately!
>
> The Dorothy Deering Literary Agency is listed in the 1994 and 1995 edition of the LITERARY MARKET PLACE. This is the market book that we have chosen to do our advertising. Northwest Publishing, Inc. is also listed in the LITERARY MARKET PLACE on page 159. I understand from your letter that you are "leery" of Northwest Publishing. I truly do not understand why, since they are right on schedule for publications. A publisher will not contact you with a status report during the time they are preparing your book for publications. They are very busy getting the manuscript prepared for print and do not have time to contact their authors unless a problem arises. Although we are aware that the waiting can be torturous, please be patient and let the publisher do his job.

Tom Mahon suspected that whoever Cynthia Gray was, she didn't write this letter. It was vintage Dorothy Deering. Moreover, Mahon was not impressed with the status report. It was nothing more than a list of publishers with names like Lodestar, Willowisp, and Woodsong, inappropriate-sounding places for a thriller.[2]

With Dorothy's Cynthia Gray letter, Mahon received another enclosure, this one designed to ease his mind about NPI. It was a copy of a letter that had supposedly been sent to Dorothy by an NPI author, one Dr. Terri W. Jenkins, who endorsed Northwest Publishing. The date of the letter, October 6, 1994, and its Dorothy Deering tone and syntax led Mahon to suspect it was as phony as the Cynthia Gray letter. To Mahon, it suggested that he was not the only Deering client worried about Jim Van Treese and NPI. The entire package—the Gray letter, the status report, and the NPI endorsement—smelled phony. Mahon's mind had not been eased. He had become even more suspicious that he had been swindled by a bogus literary agent. The Jenkins letter:

> This letter is to serve as moral support to any of you other clients who are currently dealing with Northwest Publishing, Inc. As you are aware, my book was sold to Northwest early in 1994, and like any other first time author, it was very difficult to send "my child" off to daycare and hear nothing for a long time. . . .
>
> I heard very little from them after signing my contract until September. I was able to learn where my work was in processing via a liaison in the company. When the work is about to begin typesetting, a letter will be sent identifying the person and telling how to reach them. In September, I was assigned an editor who reviewed my work very thoroughly, and we have spoken several times. . . .
>
> Please reassure any of your other authors that Northwest Publishing is a company of integrity and have [sic] given me no reason to believe that they will not fulfill every aspect of our contract.[3]

Tom Mahon was one of the first of Dorothy's NPI clients to smell a rat. He was asking her questions she could not afford to answer honestly. Clients like Mahon, people she had bled dry and who now were complaining, could be dangerous, particularly if they had big mouths. This high school teacher and football coach from Florida didn't seem like the kind of writer who could be easily intimidated or shamed into silence. This guy could be trouble.

A major publisher in the United States has shown considerable interest in reviewing your manuscript.

—Donald Phelan to potential clients

5 *Commonwealth Publications*

IN MARCH OF 1994, shortly after Dorothy had sold her clients' manuscripts to Jim Van Treese, she received a call from a fee agent and book doctor in Edmonton, Canada, named Donald T. Phelan. Prior to forming Canadian Literary Associates two years earlier, the ambitious, red-haired Irishman had, for a fee, counseled aspiring musicians on how to break into the entertainment business. Currently, he was seeking aspiring writers with the following ad in the *New York Times Book Review* and *Writer's Digest* magazine.

> **Manuscripts Required**
> Book length fiction in all genres required for presentation to North American, British and Australian publishers.

Phelan had called Dorothy to inquire about Northwest Publishing. He had heard that Van Treese offered kickbacks to agents whose clients signed joint venture deals with NPI. If that were true, Phelan was sitting on a gold mine because he had line-edited manuscripts nobody wanted stacked to his ceiling. Dorothy said it was true; agents received 10 percent of the amount each client had to contribute toward the publication of the book. This usually came to six hundred dollars per manuscript. You make a hundred NPI sales a year, and you're doing okay for very little work and virtually no overhead. Phelan agreed it was a sweet deal, that is if Van Treese was a man of his word. Dorothy assured Phelan that Jim Van Treese was a businessman of the highest integrity. He was a rising star who was going to make himself and his agent associates a lot of money.

Phelan, a thirty-six-year-old with a bachelor's degree in English and a minor in French from the University of Alberta, envisioned *himself* as a rising star in the publishing world. Unlike Jim Van Treese, who by trade was a boiler-room stock salesman, Phelan, a freelance editor and the president of his own literary agency, had literary pretenses. He also fancied himself as a writer, having written, like Dorothy Deering, an unpublished science fiction novel. Also like Dorothy, Donald Phelan was dwarfed by his own ego.

Phelan had to admit that Jim Van Treese had come up with a nifty way to milk money out of aspiring writers. He, too, saw joint venture publishing as a gold mine but not from the fee agent's point of view. Why settle for six hundred dollars per manuscript when you could get the whole six thousand dollars? After placing a handful of his clients' manuscripts with NPI for the standard 10-percent kickback, Phelan decided to start his own joint venture publishing company. He would go head-to-head with Jim Van Treese.

In the spring of 1994, Donald Phelan formed Commonwealth Publishing, Inc. (CPI), in Edmonton. Since he planned to use his literary agency, Canadian Literary Associates, as a major source of manuscripts, he named his wife, Lorraine, president of the joint venture press. To hide the fact he owned both firms, Phelan had his wife use her maiden name, L. Faye Hillman. By signing up his own clients to joint venture deals, Phelan saved the 10-percent kickback, putting him one up on Van Treese. He still planned to utilize people like Dorothy Deering to supply CPI with authors but would kick back only 5 percent. The way he figured it, NPI was already running out of steam, and when CPI became the only game in town, all the fee agents would come to him, 5 percent or not. Van Treese was giving the store away to a pack of greedy agents, a mistake Phelan would not make. As Phelan's star rose, Van Treese's would burn out, or so he hoped.

Donald Phelan, as owner of Canadian Literary Associates, was never an honest-to-God literary agent. He made his money on reading fees and expensive line-editing jobs he farmed out to minimum-wage freelancers. The reason he advertised himself as a literary agent instead of a book doctor was simple—aspiring writers, upon completing their manuscripts, didn't want an editing job; they needed an agent. Donald Phelan claimed to be that agent, but before he could represent and sell their potential best sellers, they needed to be fixed, and he was the man for that job as well. This is the literary version of the old bait-and-switch technique. Phelan had not invented this racket; it had been around for decades, and in North America the woods were full of operators like him.

Aspiring writers, mostly from the United States, would query Phelan after seeing one of his ads in the *New York Times Book Review* or *Writer's Digest* magazine. Feigning great interest in their book, he would ask to see the manuscript, along with the reading fee. Following the passage of enough time to make it appear that the manuscript had actually been read and evaluated, Phelan would send the potential editing job candidate the following letter.

> After carefully reviewing your manuscript, it is our considered opinion that [the title] has the potential to be an extremely marketable, commercial property. We are, therefore, eager to offer you our standard literary agreement for a single work. However, we hasten to add that there are certain technical difficulties with your manuscript which prevent us from offering it to publishers in its present form. Although they are not generally serious, those editorial concerns must be addressed before we can pursue the submission process any further. With your approval, we will initiate a complete line edit of [title] to eliminate these problems and ensure the saleability of your manuscript. . . . Remember, submissions are usually rejected due to a general lack of professionalism in their presentation and/or content. We are determined, as I am certain you are, to protect your book from suffering a similar fate.

By ensuring the "saleability" of the manuscript instead of its *sale,* Phelan had carefully worded his way out of potential claims of false advertising. Clever fox that he was, Phelan knew that few writers would note this distinction.

Craig Etchison, an English professor from the eastern panhandle of West Virginia, had written Phelan a letter asking whether Canadian Literary Associates would be interested in his fantasy novel, "The World Weaver." Phelan responded quickly to Etchison's query, saying that he was very interested in "The World Weaver" and wanted to see the manuscript as soon as possible. Thankful that he had found a literary agent willing, even for a fee, to seriously consider his work, Etchison wasted no time in mailing Phelan a copy of his manuscript. Two weeks later, in mid-April 1994, about the time Phelan was getting CPI off the ground, he sent

Etchison his your-manuscript-needs-work letter accompanied by the following editing proposal.

As for the process of line by line editing, only moderate changes are required in your case. We are, therefore, able to base our fee on an average of $2.00 (Cdn) per page. Given that *The World Weaver* is 280 pages in length, the following is the proposed schedule and attendant fees for completion of the necessary work:

a) Edit first half of MS
    Upon receipt of deposit for $280.00   1st month
b) Edit second half of MS
    Upon deposit of postdated cheque for $280.00   2nd month
Hand posted line by line edit
    for 280 page manuscript $560.00 (Cdn) TOTAL

Etchison had written to a literary agent and gotten a response from a book doctor. The writer didn't recall seeing anything about line editing in Phelan's magazine ad. Disappointed, he wrote Phelan a note declining his offer. That should have been the end of it and would have been, had Phelan not started his own joint venture publishing house. What he couldn't edit for a fee, he would publish. But first, he needed Etchison as a client, and he fulfilled that need by writing him another letter.

With reference to your novel, *The World Weaver,* a major publisher in the United States has shown considerable interest in reviewing your manuscript. While our editorial department has already informed me that you do not wish to undertake any further revisions, under the circumstances, I would be willing to represent your book on an "as is" basis.

Given the apparent enthusiasm of the publishing house concerned, I am confident that we will be able to secure an offer and hopefully negotiate an equitable contract.

Please telephone or fax me at your earliest convenience in order that we may forward the manuscript to the publisher without further delay.

While Dorothy Deering was the master of the bold, well-placed lie, Phelan showed himself to be the sly wordsmith. A major publisher with "apparent enthusiasm" over the prospect of "reviewing" Etchison's fantasy novel was a far cry from a major publisher who had read the manuscript and was enthusiastic about publishing it. Although Phelan was no less deceptive than Dorothy, he was far more subtle.

Phelan didn't charge a contract fee, so Etchison believed he had nothing to lose by signing with Canadian Literary Associates. He was impressed that Phelan had already spoken to a major publisher about his book. A literary agent liked his manuscript and had an editor enthusiastic about reading it—how could he not be at least a little hopeful? Etchison signed the agency contracts and began the agonizing wait. This is an intense period in the life of any aspiring writer, a time of hopes and doubts. It makes more than a few people a little crazy.

While it didn't seem short to him, Etchison's wait wasn't very long. In June, a mere three weeks after signing on with Phelan, the agent called with incredible news. A mass-market paperback house had offered to publish "The World Weaver." The contracts were in the mail to him. Etchison, excited and overwhelmed with joy, had a million questions, but Phelan, with another client on the line, didn't have time to talk. All he could say was that it was a Canadian publisher, a young, aggressive company in the market for hot-selling books like "The World Weaver." They could discuss the details later, after Etchison had a chance to look over the contracts. Getting your first novel published was a big deal. Congratulations!

For the next few days, Etchison was in heaven. The college professor was going to be a published novelist. He had the urge to stop strangers in the street and tell them the great news. His dream had come true. When the Canadian Literary Associates envelope arrived from Edmonton, Etchison tore it open and read Phelan's letter. Interestingly enough, the publisher, Commonwealth Publications, Inc., was also in Edmonton. Etchison had never heard of Commonwealth, but Phelan had said it was new and just beginning to open up big markets in the United States. Etchison read on:

> With reference to our recent telephone conversation, you will find enclosed the contract offer we recently received from Commonwealth Publications. Once you have reviewed it thoroughly, please feel free to call me with any questions or concerns you may have.
>
> I am rather pleased with the terms of the contract, particularly with regards to the extensive marketing plan Commonwealth is prepared to initiate once your book has gone to press.
>
> The royalty schedule they have proposed is also quite impressive and is obviously designed to virtually guarantee a high return for the AUTHOR—par-

ticularly from initial sales. As the contract indicates, your remuneration from royalties on 10,000 copies at $5.95 per book will be as follows:

40% royalty on the first 2,500 copies	$5,950.00
15% royalty on the remaining 7,500 copies	$6,693.75
TOTAL ROYALTIES	$12,643.75

While we are confident that this contract is most advantageous to you, the final decision as to whether or not to accept the proposal is, of course, yours.

At this point, not being familiar with the terms of regular publishing agreements, Etchison had no reason to suspect that CPI was different from, say, Random House. He did, however, think that ten thousand copies was a rather modest sales projection. And he hadn't seen any mention of an advance. Reading the contract itself, Etchison was okay until he came to a clause entitled "Author's Contribution," which read,

In consideration of the expenditures, services, and efforts to be incurred and undertaken by the PUBLISHER in accordance with the terms of this AGREEMENT causing the WORK to be published and marketed, the AUTHOR agrees to pay the PUBLISHER $3,850 (U.S.) to offset a portion of the PUBLISHER's cost. This fee shall be non-refundable and is due in cash or certified funds with the signed AGREEMENT.

This sounded like a vanity deal. Surely Phelan wasn't recommending that. No longer elated, Etchison picked up the phone. This had to be a mistake.

Phelan, anticipating initial resistance to joint venture publishing, had prepared himself for Etchison's call. If he were going to put Jim Van Treese out of business, he'd have to distinguish joint venture from subsidy publishing. And that's what he did. Phelan presented joint venture as a new concept that was sweeping the country. *The World Weaver* would sell like hot cakes in the United States and Canada, which meant that its author, having invested in his own success, would make a lot of money. Vanity publishing was for losers; joint venture was for people like Etchison who had written hot books that would sell like crazy in paperback. If Etchison didn't think he had written a commercial book, fine, this deal wasn't for him.

Etchison was impressed with Phelan's pitch. He said he would think it over. Phelan said fine, but he shouldn't take too long because these offers didn't remain open forever. There were thousands of writers out there who would jump at this deal.

Etchison thought it over, talked to his wife, and played with the numbers. The way he figured it, CPI would have to sell only sixteen hundred copies of his book for him to get his investment back. That didn't seem like a lot of books. He had the money, he had told everyone his book was being published, and his own literary agent assured him it was a good deal. He signed the contracts and withdrew $3,850 from his savings account.

What Craig Etchison didn't know was going to hurt him. He didn't know that Donald Phelan was not a legitimate literary agent, that he owned Commonwealth Publications, and that joint venture was inherently bogus.

It wouldn't be long before Craig Etchison and the other clients Phelan had signed to joint venture deals came to realize that he also owned CPI. Reacting to angry cries of conflict of interest, false advertising, and fraud, Phelan shut down Canadian Literary Associates and promised his former clients special treatment as CPI authors. That quieted things down for a while.

Now that Phelan couldn't play literary agent and publisher, he would have to do business with joint venture specialists like Dorothy Deering. At that time, she was down in Georgia hustling manuscripts for Jim Van Treese, but the moment NPI began taking on water, she and the other literary rats would abandon ship. He didn't like dealing with those people but knew that he had to. Writers trusted their agents. Without the agent, joint venture was a tough sell.

While Phelan reached out to the agents, Van Treese, tired of paying kickbacks and monthly stipends, was trying to replace them with in-house telemarketers. Given the vital role the agent played in the joint venture racket, this move was a risky one that Van Treese would live to regret.

We have recently endured many family illnesses and some tragic deaths.
—Dorothy Deering to ADP authors waiting for their disks

6 News and Notes

LOOKING AHEAD, DOROTHY MUST HAVE WONDERED whether 1995 was going to be as good a year for the Deering Literary Agency as 1994 had been. The arrangement with Jim Van Treese and her success at talking clients into NPI deals had saved the business. Through reading and contract fees, ADP contracts, and NPI sign-ups, she had grossed in the neighborhood of three hundred thousand dollars. Not bad for a woman who five years earlier had been working out of her garage in Nicholasville, Kentucky.

Dorothy faced the new year exhausted and justifiably worried. Her ploy to get her ADP authors off her back and onto Van Treese's hadn't worked. She had not received an NPI salary payment since September, and because Van Treese was now hustling her clients directly, she no longer pushed NPI, thus forgoing the kickback money. To make matters worse, *Writer's Digest* had received so many complaints from Dorothy's former clients, the magazine was forced to cancel the display ad that had brought in so much business. Dorothy still had ads, however, in other magazines, and was beginning to use the Internet to attract clients.

To survive without ADP or NPI, Dorothy had to rely entirely on reading and contract fees. Unlike commission-based agents, who can handle only so many writers, the fee agent can't prosper without hundreds of clients. Dorothy needed more of them, and one way to get them was to convert a higher percentage of potential clients into the contract-paying kind. After a potential client's manuscript had been evaluated, Dorothy would offer agency representation. To close the deal more often, Dorothy had created a new, higher-octane form letter. Beginning in 1995, this was what she hit them with:

> It is with great pride that I invite you to join the group of prestigious authors that is represented by the Dorothy Deering Literary Agency. I have enclosed contracts of representation for [title] and have already spoken to a few publishers who are willing to review your work with an eye toward publication.
>
> The Dorothy Deering literary agency now has agents in all book-starved Russian territories, Poland, China, Japan, all of the United Kingdom, Canada, Thailand, all of Europe and Africa. Your manuscript will be sent to all of these representatives. In the United States, your manuscript will have maximum representation. Upon receiving your signed contracts, you will be included in our catalogue that will be sent to over three hundred (300) publishers and every editor in those publishing houses. This is a new technique that we have created to give our authors the best exposure possible. We have had offers on over fifty percent of our contractual authors' works and have placed in excess of fifty manuscripts in the last six months.

Dorothy didn't represent any prestigious authors, hadn't spoken to any editors, didn't have literary affiliates around the world, hadn't printed a catalogue of her clients' works, and had sold only one book to a legitimate publisher. Whatever "maximum representation" meant, Dorothy didn't offer it. These claims were to false advertising what death was to sleep. Any writer who became a Deering client on the strength of this letter had been swindled.

In February 1995, their businesses in decline, Dorothy and Vicki moved their agencies from the strip mall on West Alabama Road to a house Dorothy had rented for the clan on Shiloh Road in the neighboring town of Kennesaw. (Without the NPI money, she couldn't afford the office rent.) Dorothy believed that Jim Van Treese had treated her unfairly. Her clients accounted for $1.5 million in joint venture money, and what did he do? He got greedy and cut her off. She had heard that Van Treese had replaced her with a crew of boiler-room types working by commission. The writers to whom they pitched thought they were NPI editors.

Dorothy was down but not for long. Shortly after the move to Kennesaw, she received a call from Donald Phelan, who wanted to know whether it was true that she no longer steered clients to NPI. Phelan asked because he hoped Dorothy would start pitching CPI to her clients. His standard contract called for an author's contribution of $3,850, a couple of thousand less than NPI required, but he planned to issue contracts in the thousands. Phelan could pay Dorothy only a 5-percent finder's fee, half of what Van Treese paid, but again, they were talking volume.

Eager to get back in the joint venture business, Dorothy said yes to Phelan's offer. Now calling herself chief executive officer of the Deering Literary Agency, Dorothy would pitch CPI to her NPI authors first. She wanted to sign up these writers before Van Treese's roof caved in, souring them on joint venture. It was all a matter of timing.

Shortly after the arrangement with Phelan was agreed upon, Dorothy talked Diana Kemp-Jones, the science fiction writer from California, into a $3,850 CPI deal. Diana had already paid for five ADP disks and had paid more than six thousand to have a book published by NPI. Dorothy also convinced Howard Markowitz, the Florida writer who had gone for two ADP deals and one NPI contract, to sign a contract with CPI. She would sign, early on, more than two dozen Deering clients who had invested in ADP or NPI, or both.

Writers rolled into the Deering fee mill as potential clients, were converted into clients, were subjected to a period when their manuscripts were supposedly rejected by legitimate publishers, then were carried out the back door as joint venture authors. Clients who could not be converted into vanity authors were transferred onto another conveyor belt that carried them through as many annual contract extensions as it took for them to realize where they had been and where they were going. Dorothy did the converting, while Chuck kept the belt moving at just the right speed.

When it came time to turn a client into a vanity author, usually six months into the agency contract, Dorothy would send the writer a CPI contract along with the following letter.

> We here at Deering Literary Agency are happy to present the following book contracts for you to review. Please look over the enclosed carefully. Sleep on it and discuss it with important individuals in your lives [*sic*].
>
> Please remember, as your agent, I am to present any offer to you that comes your way. I have reviewed the contracts myself and found them very viable and highly recommend them. You will also find enclosed their new fall list and a copy of their colorful book covers. It is your decision whether or not you choose to go with the offer. I will be here for support and answer questions that you may have regarding the contracts and even the publishing house.

It usually took more than this letter to get the client's money. A follow-up pep talk from Dorothy helped—"Your high-impact book will blast the market!"—and if that wasn't enough, this letter from Donald T. Phelan often closed the deal:

> As your agent may have already told you, we propose entering into a joint venture with you to publish your book. Both the title and the concept were well thought out, therefore, we are confident the book will be favorably received. This type of book continues to enjoy considerable popularity. Given proper production and marketing, your work should do very well.

Phelan wanted potential joint venture authors to believe that Commonwealth offered contracts only to writers who had written "well thought out" books that would "enjoy considerable popularity." In truth, no one could write a book bad enough to be rejected by Phelan. To suggest otherwise was a lie, and a big, important one at that. Van Treese, Phelan, and Dorothy Deering were professional liars. That was their business. They got away with it because the writers they lied to had grown weary of the truth.

With the fresh kickback money from Phelan pouring in, Dorothy was back on top and loaded with new ideas. She could now afford to publish an in-house newsletter to keep her clients informed of her literary exploits and to attract new clients into the fold. The quarterly publication, called *News & Notes,* would also give her a platform to launch new moneymaking schemes, to lecture anxious clients on the virtues of patience, and to maintain her illusion of legitimacy. It would also become a detailed record of her deceit.

To help her with her newsletter, Dorothy hired three young people and gave them fancy titles—managing editor, senior editor, and submissions editor—positions more appropriate for a publishing company than a literary agency. The fact that real literary agents didn't use newsletters, brochures, pamphlets, and the like to publicize their successes and to attract clients would not, in Dorothy's case, give her away. Dorothy was misappropriating her clients' money, funds acquired under false pretenses, to attract, through more false advertising, new money to misappropriate.

The first issue of *News & Notes* rolled off the press in the summer of 1995. In her front-page column, "Off the Wall Remarks," Dorothy tried to disarm the ADP authors she had left holding the bag with this transparent and ridiculous plea for sympathy:

> I want to take this opportunity to first of all thank each and every one of you for your kind words, cards and flowers during the past year. Charles is home from the hospital and slowly recovering from major reconstructive surgery from donating a kidney to his brother some time past. Sadly, John Deering passed away just eight weeks ago.

Why would a Deering client need to know this? Just how bad were they supposed to feel about the two-month-old death of the brother-in-law of a woman they had never met? What would possess Dorothy Deering to think that a client would care one way or the other about her husband's long-gone kidney? Her hapless clients had, in addition to the status of their manuscripts, ADP disks, and NPI and CPI books, their own kidneys to worry about.

Dorothy, in her column, also laid the groundwork for a scheme she had devised to milk more money out of clients who didn't go for the joint venture deals. If the client paid her an extra five hundred dollars, she would, on her next trip to New York City, personally pitch that client's work to several big-time editors. Dorothy, having never been to New York City on her own money, had collected, for sort of a pilot program, donations from a handful of clients to finance a four-day trip she and Chuck had taken to the Big Apple that previous March (presumably before Chuck gave up the kidney). Because they hadn't made any publishing appointments, the closest they got to editors were the lobbies of their buildings where they left boxes of manuscripts. But this was not how Dorothy described the junket in her column.

> We had great success wining and dining the publishers and had a good time in the process. We took editors to lunches and dinners at such places as Tavern on the Green, The Russian Tea Room, and Broadway Joe's. Our time in New York was spent beating on doors, talking to publishers and soaking our feet. And, oh those taxi cabs! One actually ran onto the curb to get around another cab. I have decided that the hack drivers in New York have a horn language we do not know and that they communicate with each other in some alien code. I enjoyed the airport limo that took us to and from the hotel much more.

Dorothy wasn't telling her readers—her clients—anything they really wanted to know. Instead of naming editors, publishers, book titles, authors, and deals in the works, she gave them the names of restaurants and her impression of cab drivers. She gave them what she had, and that would be enough.

Dorothy wanted her clients to know that doing business out of Kennesaw, Georgia, didn't mean that she wasn't a player on the world stage. To this end, she had this to report:

> We have managed to sell three books in Russia in this last week. When your copies come into the office, the first is sent to Moscow, the second to my agent in London. From London, the coverage is Europe, Japan, China, Australia, and several more countries. My Russian agent who covers all Russian territories and Poland, does the translating himself for my authors free of charge upon the sale of their book.

Using *News & Notes* as a pulpit from which to lecture, in her most condescending and high-horsed way, writers on how to be well-mannered clients, Dorothy told the following story.

> Recently, the wife of one of my author's [*sic*] phoned the office. This person had only been under contract for two weeks and we had already sent his manuscript to several publishers. She made unreasonable demands and spoke abusively to my staff. I absolutely will not stand for that!! This is a business and my staff works harder than any I know of in order to sell your books. Most of you are caring and nice to speak with and I have a good relationship with almost everyone I represent. I simply ask that you observe the "Rules of Common Courtesy." We work in a stressful business and need to focus on the positive. Unfortunately, patience is not usually present in artistic people. I ask that you write me another book while you are waiting.
>
>   Thanks, Dottie

Poor Dottie; what would people with jobs, families, health problems, and all the rest, folks who struggled to write books on the side, know about stress? Didn't they realize that the most difficult part of the publishing process was Dorothy's? How thoughtless of them.

On this theme—that clients didn't appreciate what she did for them—Dorothy, in an outlandish attempt to justify her punishing schedule of fees, published the following.

How Agents Get Rich!!!
How much money does an agent actually make on book sales? Why do we charge fees?

> Let's say that I sell a book for the normal standard royalty contract. The average print run is 3,000 selling for $7.95, average percentage is 8% for first-time authors. Providing all 3,000 books sell, the equation goes like this: 3,000 X $7.95 = $23,850.00 X 8% = $1,908.00 X 12% = $228.96 which is the agent's commission on sales. It costs approximately $700.00 to represent just one manuscript. I can't tell you how many authors resent the fact that agents charge fees. Now that you see how much I make on one sale, I hope your understanding is greater and maybe your appreciation for our hard work will increase.

From the fee agent's point of view, this made perfect sense. But what did it say to the writer? It said, based on Dorothy's figures, that writing was not good business (a message that contradicted her joint venture pitch). That from the two-thousand-dollar royalty check, Dorothy would receive—counting her reading and contract fees plus the 12 percent commission—$978. This figure meant that the client, for writing the book, barely made more money than the agent who sold it. Selling the book had more value than its creation. Writers would do better, financially, if they got into farming.

Dorothy's fee justification formula would have gone over big in a newsletter for, say, the Society to Create Agency Money (SCAM) but should have bombed in a publication read by writers. That it didn't cause a run on her agency for refunds is more amazing than the fact that she wrote it.

Dorothy's new managing editor, a young man named Richard Oliver, responding to clients skeptical of Dorothy's cozy relationship with a pair of joint venture publishers, explained it this way:

> There's been some confusion about the Deering Literary Agency's relationship between and with authors and publishers. When we represent authors to publishers, we walk a fine line between them both, trying to strike a deal that pleases all parties. We do our best, but at times, one part of the equation will be upset.

Mr. Oliver apparently didn't understand that the agent's first and only responsibility is to the client. The way he explained it, Dorothy was running a dating service rather than a literary agency. Real agents wanted unbalanced deals in favor of their clients. That Dorothy ran Oliver's article and the fee justification piece in a newsletter aimed at clients reveals how out of touch she was with the legitimate publishing world. It also shows how out of touch the writers who bought this propaganda were.

That summer, the Deering and A Rising Sun agencies split when Dorothy's sister, Vicki, married Chris Scott, the son of Randolph Scott, the movie cowboy of the 1940s and 1950s, and moved her agency to Savannah, Georgia. She had met Chris when he became a client of A Rising Sun. As one of a handful of writers whose ADP disks were actually produced, Scott's book, *Whatever Happened to Randolph Scott,* was available from NPI. Chris was now helping Vicki run the literary agency.

Dorothy's breakup with NPI had fractured her plan to use Jim Van Treese to get the ADP authors out of her hair. Her plea for sympathy in *News & Notes,* while working on some, hadn't made the problem go away. So, in late summer 1995, Dorothy announced that she had sold ADP to a man in London, Canada, named Wayne Ray. In a letter to her victims, she broke the news as follows.

> As many of you may know, we have recently endured many family illnesses and some tragic deaths. In addition, I have been in and out of the hospital due to my health. Things are improving, but with the terrific growth recently of the Deering Literary Agency, Inc., we have been hard-pressed to devote the time to ADP that it truly deserves. Mr. Ray can do this, and he is enthusiastic about his new titles and new authors.

Not nearly as enthusiastic, however, as Dorothy was about getting rid of this dog. Ray, of course, paid nothing for ADP. He put out a catalogue in November 1995 that included only a few new titles, then let Dorothy's brainchild slip into oblivion. Except for those clients she had also signed to NPI and CPI deals, Dorothy had found a way to separate herself from the ADP authors whose money she had spent on other things. With these people finally out of her way, Dorothy could be healthy again, and Chuck could get his kidney back.

From this point on it will be necessary for us to go to Hollywood every six months and to New York City every three months. It's all part of this game called publishing.

—Dorothy Deering

7 Paid Vacations

IN THE HISTORY OF JOINT VENTURE PUBLISHING, 1995 was, from the writer's point of view, a bad year because it was such a good year for the publishers. Van Treese, his agent associates, and his in-house sales force had talked more than seven hundred writers out of $4,377,000 in joint venture money. The previous year, NPI had grossed $1.2 million and the year before that, about eight hundred thousand dollars.

Like NPI, which was top-heavy with members of Van Treese's family, Commonwealth, now officially headed by Donald Phelan, also employed Phelan's seventeen-year-old son Ryan, Phelan's brother Michael, his two sisters, and his wife, Lorraine. Thirty-two-year-old Ken Molloy, Phelan's top assistant, ran the office on Thirty-third Avenue in Edmonton and oversaw the marketing, acquisitions, and publicity departments. Commonwealth employed, besides family members, an office manager, file clerks, a phone receptionist, some graphics people, a couple of typographers, a boiler-room sales force, and five author liaison officers whose job it was to hold the hands of anxious authors. Notably absent from this roster is even one editor, the heart and soul of publishing. In 1995 each author liaison officer was assigned 130 or so writers waiting for their books to come out and become best sellers. The time was rapidly approaching when this would not be a fun job to have.

To attract writers in all the genres, Phelan had created, under the Commonwealth umbrella, several imprints, such as Ravenmore (horror), Erin (Irish and Celtic fiction), Scarlet (romance), Loral (self-help), and Tree House (children). In Commonwealth brochures directly mailed to hundreds of aspiring writers in Canada and the United States, Phelan created the illusion of exclusivity to cover the odious whiff of vanity that came off joint venture.

> While Commonwealth Publications obviously cannot publish every manuscript we review, our acquisitions staff gives each and every submission careful consideration in terms of its overall marketability.
>
> Should we determine your book is commercially viable, a Publication Marketing and Royalty Contract will be offered for your consideration. If you do have a manuscript you would like us to review, please query with a synopsis or outline to: . . .

Phelan's "acquisitions staff," a crew of phone hustlers, were sending out joint venture contracts in response to one-page query letters. People who wrote CPI saying that they had an idea for a book they'd like to write someday when they had time got contracts. At Commonwealth, everything was commercially viable.

Back in Salt Lake City, Jim Van Treese's troubles were mounting, whether he realized it or not. By the summer of 1995, he had hundreds of authors clamoring for overdue books they had paid to have published. Despite this backlog, his eight boiler-plate pitchmen, keeping track of their joint-venture sales in what they called "dirt books," were still bringing in $350,000 a month. Not one penny of this money was being used to publish books, making the company a complete and increasingly unwise fraud. In addition, this multimillion-dollar operation had no bookkeeper and no accounting system whatsoever, not even, as incredible as it may seem, a corporate bank account of any sort. When a joint-venture check arrived, it was cashed, for a fee, at a check-cashing service. That year, the outfit received 1,777 checks totaling $4,377,739. From this amount, Van Treese paid the unbelievable sum of $124,128 in check-cashing fees, an unnecessary business expense if ever there was one. The cash was subsequently deposited in one of Van Treese's five personal bank accounts.

If he wasn't publishing books, what was Van Treese doing with the joint venture money? He was going to Las Vegas with his wife and son and gambling it away. While the Van Treese family played keno and fed the slot machines, hundreds of authors were calling NPI every week about their books. Many of these writers couldn't afford Las Vegas themselves because they had paid to have their books published.

In the meantime, Van Treese's boiler-room crew, sensing the end was near and finding new business increasingly difficult to drum up, were calling NPI authors with special deals for their next book. Since 250 of these writers were, or had been, Deering clients, word got back to Dorothy that her old partner had sneaked into the henhouse and was stealing her chickens. If anyone was going to sell her NPI authors another joint venture contract, it would be Dorothy, for the CPI kickback. Van Treese had a lot of nerve. To bar the henhouse door, Dorothy sent her NPI clients the following letter.

> It has come to my attention that certain joint venture publishers are contacting agent-represented authors in an attempt to solicit their next work. This is in direct violation of the Fair Business Practice Act and not ethical in this business. The proper way to do this is of course to contact the agent. If this has occurred please contact my agency and discuss it with Charles or myself.

If, within the genteel racket, there was a code of conduct, the stealing of a phony agent's kickback would indeed be wrong. Dorothy had a point. The nerve of that guy.

As the summer of 1995 wore on, more and more of the clients who had rejected Dorothy's joint venture pitch and therefore had no chance whatsoever to see their manuscripts in print, were starting to wonder what in the hell she was doing with the money they had sent her to find publishers for their books. As a result, much of Dorothy's time, and Chuck's, was being spent lying to these writers about the status of their manuscripts. When Dorothy and Chuck refused to take these clients' calls, the office staff incurred their wrath.

In the August-September issue of *News & Notes,* Dorothy and Chuck did their best to shame these callers into silence. Apparently unaware of how arrogant, condescending, and disrespectful they sounded, Dorothy and Chuck scolded the very writers who had paid for the newsletter they were using to give them hell. Chuck, a guy who would still be bouncing from one sales job to another had his wife not forged a successful career as a phony agent, lectured away:

> As much as Dorothy and I would love to talk to each of you when you call, IT IS IMPOSSIBLE with our workload. We have to spend our time calling and writing publishers and producers and doing follow up paperwork, for each and every author. Please be understanding and help us be more effective by utilizing our

staff. They are wonderful!!! I must also ask that you keep your calls brief, keep in mind that the author/agent team both work more efficiently when communication is on a positive note. Our staff works with each and every file and is here to assist you.

Old Chinese Proverb:

A spoonful of sugar sweetens better than a bagful of salt!!!

Chuck didn't elaborate on exactly what it was that made the Deering staff so wonderful, or how their wonderfulness benefited clients. What pleasure they were to derive from this was a mystery. However, if the clients wanted to be wonderful, too, they could quit calling the goddamned office.

Dorothy, with her enormous ego and equal tactlessness, made the same point. But the real message she conveyed was this: Dorothy thought her clients were idiots. To wit:

Many of you have been in the habit of calling our office about every month or so to request an update and as you know, we have been months behind due to Chuck's illness. Chuck is back working full-time now and has recuperated nicely, but we have grown so much that it is impossible for him to go back and "catch up" on these requests. I want you to know that your files are being worked constantly and that if we have ANY positive response, I shall call you immediately. Most New York agents *do not* send updates to their clients because there is no time for such reports. . . . Most of you realize that we work very hard for you; however, there are still a few inexperienced, uninformed first time writers that are not familiar with the extreme workload of a high profile agent. Some of you do not realize this fact as yet. This is the toughest market in the world and it takes an enormous amount of work to represent each and every manuscript to publishers and producers. Our staff is, as always, working overtime to assure quality representation, so, therefore, please bear with us. Allow us to do our job without the constant demands from authors for updates and various other requests. . . .

I have tried to make everyone aware of the demands of being a literary agent. Please remember your phone courtesy and business posture when speaking with members of my staff.

One wonders how many clients were truly relieved over Chuck's improving health. As to what New York agents did or didn't do, they certainly didn't have time to publish newsletters. It was a fact that clients' files were "being worked constantly." Chuck made sure no writer slipped into a new contract year without being sent an extension agreement, and no client, after six months of Deering representation, missed getting the joint venture pitch. That, they were good at. Constantly reminded of how overworked the Deerings were, readers of the newsletter may have wondered why, given their high-profile success as literary agents, they had so many clients. If they liked having a lot of clients, why didn't they hire more agents and more wonderful people to answer the telephone when clients called about their manuscripts?

Dorothy was not in the business of selling manuscripts; she was in the business of selling clients on the *idea* she was selling manuscripts. She had a problem because she was so good at the latter and so bad at the former. Eventually, clients had to catch on, and when they did, they became liabilities. Dorothy had to find some way to kiss off clients she could no longer milk. And if doing so also involved hitting them up with a parting fee, all the better. She didn't want them to go away mad, just go away and pay for the privilege. If she could do it, Dorothy would become the Thomas Edison of the genteel racket. Out of this necessity, Dorothy created the "Agent Option," a scheme she floated in the August-September issue of *News & Notes*.

The Agent Option worked like this: clients who were tired of making pests of themselves by calling the agency every month could become their own agents. By paying Dorothy a one-time fee of six hundred dollars, they would get a "Presentation and Submission Package" consisting of a list of publishers and editors along with advice on how to submit a manuscript, a Deering publication called *Author's Showcase* (which didn't exist), and letters from Dorothy Deering recommending the author-agent's books. The fee included a "dynamite synopsis" of the writer's book, along with an author biography, in two issues of the biannual *Author's Showcase*, a catalogue that would be circulated widely among publishers and movie producers. Subsequent entries in the catalogue would cost fifty dollars an issue.

The Agent Option seemingly was a good deal because once the manuscript was sold, the writer did not have to pay the agent's commission. Whether or not the Agent Option was really a wise investment depended on how you looked at it. The first year of Deering representation, with the reading and contract fees, cost the client $750. For this, the writer got nothing. Writers who paid Dorothy six hundred dollars *not* to represent them saved $150. It was a sweet deal for Dorothy as well. When a writer had a complaint, he could call and harangue himself. And if the manuscript didn't sell, the writer would have only himself to blame, never knowing whether he was a bad writer or simply a lousy agent.

Unfortunately for Dorothy, her you-be-your-own-agent scheme didn't get off the ground. The last thing a writer wanted to do was to fill Dorothy's role as an unhelpful agent. That would be like a singer trying to impersonate a third-rate Elvis impersonator. The impersonation of a bad impersonator was not the way to go.

Unfortunately for writers, another one of Dorothy's harebrained, money-grubbing schemes, the so-called Manuscript Express—client-financed excursions to New York and Hollywood—was a success. Clients were kicking in an extra five hundred dollars to have Dorothy and Chuck *personally* pitch their manuscripts to editors and movie producers. Dorothy had her clients competing with each other for preferential treatment.

In the August-September issue of *News & Notes,* in her appropriately titled "Off the Wall" column, Dorothy breathlessly reported on a recent manuscript-selling excursion to the West Coast.

> Charles and I went to Hollywood July 11 through 16th and had great success. We called on top executives at Paramount, Fox, Universal, Emperor Films, Imagine Films (Ron Howard), Warner Brothers, The Zanuck Company, Spelling, Orion, Columbia, Castle Rock (Rob Reiner) and many more....
>
> Chuck and I did have the opportunity to meet Michael Dorn who plays Worf in the Stark Trek series. This was, of course, a thrill for Chuck as he is a major "Trekker" [sic]. We saw Steven Spielberg and several other personalities. After all business was conducted, we had some time to play, so we went to Palm Springs to see friends. It was 102 degrees in the shade but enjoyable as the climate is dry. We all went out to Catalina Island and enjoyed some shopping. I am sure all of you girls will appreciate that. The best shopping trip was on Rodeo Drive and I enjoyed that thoroughly. At Universal Studios, I posed for a computer-generated photo. The picture was of me with Clark Gable looking into my eyes very romantically. Chuck and I posed for a picture that put us amid Captain Kirk, Spock and Bones. This now occupies a permanent place on our wall of personalities in the office.

Were clients supposed to believe that Dorothy and Chuck, in four days (minus travel) in Los Angeles, had visited with the executives of twelve film companies and still had time to visit friends in Palm Springs, shop on Catalina Island and Rodeo Drive, and take the Universal tour? When Dorothy said she had "called on" people like Ron Howard, Rob Reiner, and Steven Spielberg, what did she mean? If she hadn't actually spent time with these people, why was she dropping their names? Instead of having a fake photograph of herself and Clark Gable, Dorothy would have been better served having a computer shot of Steven Spielberg gazing romantically into her eyes. That photograph could have graced the front page of *News & Notes.* By painting a picture of herself and Chuck as a pair of rubes on vacation, spending clients' money on Rodeo Drive, Dorothy revealed just how fine she was with the people financing her fantasy life.

Given the good time had by all, it's not surprising that Dorothy announced that "From this point on, it will be necessary for us to go to Hollywood every six months and to New York every three months. It's all part of this game called publishing." To entice clients into being represented on their upcoming trip to the Big Apple, Dorothy wrote,

> The last New York trip was at the end of March of this year and produced some great results. We sold four books as a direct result of personally presenting and pitching the manuscripts we took with us.
>
> We have booked reservations for September 19th and will be taking several manuscripts with us. As per your contract, if your desire is to have us personally pitch your book to the senior editors, managing editors and editors-in-chief, please have at least six copies and a $500 expense money order, cashier's check or VISA information to us before September 5th. This will allow us enough time to prepare our materials and presentation.
>
> It is exciting to wine and dine these editors for you and lots of work.... Don't forget to get your request in early as we can only take a limited number each time we go.

Here was an agent who crowed about having her picture taken with a dead movie star but wouldn't provide clients with the specifics about the recent sale of four manuscripts to New York City publishers. This telling vagueness characterized Dorothy's report, in the October-November issue of *News & Notes,* of the September excursion to New York City.

> This trip was quite productive. Of course, it is too early to announce any sales from the meetings I had with seven different publishers. I always end up selling at least three or four manuscripts from these business trips.

The true story of Dorothy's interactions with the Who's Who of New York City publishing, told from the point of view of an editor, goes like this: One morning an editor with a large publishing house in Manhattan was informed by the receptionist that a literary agent named Dorothy Deering was in the lobby waiting to see her. The editor had never heard of Dorothy Deering and didn't have any appointments scheduled for that morning. Not wanting to be rude, and a little curious, the editor went to the lobby to see what the agent had to say. She was taken aback by the sight of a tall, rawboned man and his plump, sawed-off companion. Dressed like tourists, they stood next to a stack of manuscripts almost as tall as the agent. Pointing to the tower of paper they had lugged into the lobby, the woman said, "Well, here they are." With that, she and the big guy turned on their heels and strode out of the building. (The boxes were sent back to Dorothy with a note asking her not to phone, visit, or mail any more manuscripts to the publisher.)

Had the clients who couldn't afford to have Dorothy take their works to New York City witnessed this, they may not have felt so bad, unless they thought about how she marketed the manuscripts she didn't handle personally. Either way, the picture wasn't pretty.

Between trips to Hollywood and New York City, Dorothy and Chuck found time to be wined and dined in western Canada by Donald Phelan. The publisher of CPI, impressed with Dorothy's ability to sign up so many of her clients to joint venture contracts, was showing his gratitude and cementing his relationship with this go-getter. Dorothy not only was unashamed of her cozy association with a vanity publisher but was so proud of it she treated her clients to another one of her breathless reports. This one was published in the October-November issue of *News & Notes.*

> The trip to Edmonton, Alberta, Canada was also highly productive. Commonwealth Publications, who are [*sic*] publishing my Callie books, showed us a wonderful time at the West Edmonton Mall, the largest mall in the world. We stayed at the Fantasyland Hotel in the mall and had a theme room that had an igloo and a dog sled for a bed. Don Phelan, the publisher at Commonwealth, said that he could not have us there in Canada and not sleep in an igloo.

It's astounding that Dorothy, so good at manipulating writers, couldn't resist the urge to strut in front of the people she had deceived to make it all possible. So full of herself, she must have actually believed that her clients would enjoy reading about how she had slept in a fake dogsled inside a phony igloo in a placed called Fantasyland. Her clients must have believed that Phelan was paying for all of this to get to their potential best sellers, not just their money. Otherwise, Dorothy wouldn't have had any clients.

After regaling clients with her adventure in Alberta, Dorothy got down to the business of promoting the successor to Jim Van Treese.

> Commonwealth Publications is a relatively new publisher who offers standard royalty contracts, advance contracts, as well as joint venture contracts. We had an opportunity to discuss the various contracts and what they mean to an author with Mr. Phelan in depth.
>
> The definition of a joint venture contract is a contract in which the author is expected to pay a small portion of the publishing costs. As getting published is so very hard for new authors, this is a good choice if the company meets certain standards. The first one is that they publish the books in a timely manner and not run a year or two late. The second and perhaps most important is that they market the books efficiently. Other important factors are artwork, editing, of course royalties, and that if your book sells that they will pay for all subsequent printings. These are questions we asked Mr. Phelan at Commonwealth and they came up roses. He is a red-haired Irishman and we like him very much.

In these in-depth discussions about CPI, Phelan probably didn't tell Dorothy that he was being sued by one of his authors, a former client of his literary agency named Steve Esrati. A retiree from Shaker Heights, Ohio, Esrati had written a novel about Nazi atrocities against American and Canadian prisoners of war called "Comrades, Avenge Us." When he paid CPI his author's contribution of $5,175, Esrati didn't know that his literary agent owned the joint venture publishing company. The book didn't come out when promised, and in July 1995, months after its publication date, Esrati hired a Canadian attorney and brought suit against Commonwealth Publications. Esrati was asking the court to either declare his CPI contract null and void or order Phelan to publish all ten thousand copies of his book. Not content to leave it at that, Esrati had written letters to the Royal Canadian Mounted Police, the Better Business Bureau in Edmonton, the Canadian Authors Association, the Writers' Union of Canada, and the Writers Guild of Alberta accusing Phelan of misrepresentation and fraud. When Phelan responded that Esrati's book had been, in fact, published and was selling well in Canada (a lie), the battle was joined. To silence Esrati, who was advising writers online to avoid CPI, Phelan threatened to bring a $10-million defamation suit against his former client.

If Dorothy wasn't aware of *Esrati v. Commonwealth* and the plaintiff's crusade to tell the world that Phelan was a crook, she should have been. One thing is certain, if Dorothy did know, her clients would be the last people she would tell. Rumors about Van Treese's gambling binges had been floating around the genteel racket for months, information Dorothy wanted to keep from her clients as well. The mere whiff of scandal would panic her joint venture authors and send her business into a nosedive.

Seemingly oblivious to the concept of conflict of interest, or perhaps so caught up in her fantasy she couldn't appreciate the inappropriateness of what she was revealing, Dorothy saved the best for last.

> Now for the clincher: Chuck and I have accepted the positions of National Directors of Marketing and Distribution for not only Commonwealth Publications, but for their mother company, Anthem Marketing and Distribution, for the entire United States. We will, of course, still be literary agents, but will also be effective in our new positions. They are moving us to Nicholasville, Kentucky, where this literary agency began. The move will take place October 15th of this year, so please be a little patient with us over the next three or four weeks until we are in place and functional. This position will give my authors a great advantage. Moving is simple for a literary agency as being an agent could be done from a desert island with all the media functions of today.

Jim Van Treese had paid the Deerings to move from Kentucky to Georgia; now Donald Phelan was paying to move them back. Dorothy would reward the publisher who paid for the move by signing more than 150 writers to CPI contracts. Dorothy now had seven hundred clients, proving that one could at least impersonate a literary agent from anywhere in the country. How long one could get away with it was another question.

We were victims the same as you.

—Dorothy Deering to NPI authors

8 The Dead Publishers Society

WHILE THE DEERINGS WERE STUFFING their clients' manuscripts into storage bins until they got settled in their new home, the Van Treeses were in Nevada gambling away their authors' joint venture money. By January of 1996, the publishing end of NPI had been at a standstill for months. Employees were abandoning the company and spreading stories about the Van Treeses. That January alone, Van Treese, his wife, and his son had dropped $441,000 in casinos around Nevada with names like Peppermill, State Line, Silver Smith, and Stardust. Joint venture checks generated by Van Treese's still active sales force were converted into hundred-dollar bills and delivered to Van Treese's house in zippered leather satchels. NPI authors whose books were long overdue knew that something had gone wrong in Salt Lake City. Writers whose books were approaching their publication dates were finding out. No one was at home at NPI, unless the caller was a joint venture prospect.

In February, things got worse. NPI was now under investigation by the Utah attorney general's office and inspectors from the U.S. Postal Service. The state authorities were looking into allegations of consumer protection violations, while the Feds were checking into the possibility of mail fraud. That month joint venture sales dipped to two hundred thousand dollars, a three-year low.

Sales continued to plummet, and by March, Van Treese, having for years treated his authors' joint venture money as an asset rather than a corporate obligation and debt, was so deep in the hole the company couldn't be saved. Instead of putting this money toward the publication and sale of books that created income and profit, he used it to pay for salaries, wages, commissions, and office costs. Eventually, he didn't even use it for these things. On the chance he would hit it big in Las Vegas and get himself out of this mess, he was using it to gamble. With joint venture money down to a trickle and very little left to gamble with, Van Treese made a last-ditch effort to raise $1.5 million from a group of venture capitalists. When that failed for NPI and hundreds of its coinvesting authors, it was over.

On the first of April, a Monday, shortly after what was left of Van Treese's office staff settled into their work, the place was raided by a half-dozen state and federal investigators bearing search warrants. One of the NPI employees was on the telephone with an author when the cops hit the door. "Oh, my God!" she screamed into the phone, "we're being raided!" The phone went dead, and the writer went nuts.

No one from the Van Treese family was in the building that morning, and no one was taken into custody. The investigators sent everybody home. As the officers loaded a truck with a hundred boxes of documents and several computers, the NPI phones continued to ring.

The next day, those NPI employees who returned to the job found they no longer had computers on their desks. The cops hadn't taken any manuscripts, galleys, or books but had taken pretty much everything else. There was nothing left to do but answer the phones and tell sweet lies to the callers.

The state and federal raid on Northwest Publishing, Inc., produced the following headline in Salt Lake City: "AT NORTHWEST PRESS, ALL IS VANITY."[1] The article, while favorable to neither Van Treese nor NPI, presented joint venture authors in a realistic but unflattering light.

> Unpublished authors of The Great American Novel held dear their dreams of becoming a Michael Crichton or Sue Grafton, of endorsing checks with lots of zeros after the dollar sign. Then reality sets in as rejection letters mount.
>
> Enter their prince in shining armor—the publisher who says, "I'll publish anything!" And for $5,000, the fairy tale comes true.

News of the police raid and NPI's impending crash spread quickly among the twenty-one hundred or so writers directly affected. The news was bad even for NPI authors whose books Van Treese had actually published. Given that these paperbacks were cheaply made, badly edited, if edited at all, and produced in small quantities, their authors were victims as well.

Of the twenty-one hundred victims, 250 had been, or were, Deering clients. Dorothy's NPI authors were so shocked and confused, they were calling for advice rather than to chew her out. Except for a handful of her clients like Tom Mahon, an ADP and NPI victim, Dorothy's writers hadn't figured out the role she had played in the loss of their money, their books, and their pride. The Florida high school teacher and coach who became suspicious of NPI after signing the publishing contract, but was assured by Dorothy that Van Treese was a man of integrity, now understood full well that he and the others had been sold down the river by a bogus agent. Mahon was one of the first to figure out kickbacks were involved, but he didn't know the details or the extent to which Dorothy had enriched herself at her clients' expense. He would try to find out and, like Donald Phelan's nemesis, Steve Esrati, do everything he could to expose what he considered a criminal enterprise.[2]

Dorothy understood the business and public relations implications of the NPI scandal on the agents who had served up their clients to Van Treese. Clients who had acted on Dorothy's advice might come to blame her for their financial losses and emotional misery. And if word ever got out about the kickbacks, there would be hell to pay. In a move to dissociate her agency from Northwest and to portray herself as a victim of Van Treese's bad management, Dorothy issued the following memo to her NPI authors:

A few years ago, when we first began having any dealings with Northwest, they were a good publisher with marketing set up through Ingram, the largest distributor in the U.S. and were a large functioning company. Since then, possibly through being overwhelmed with business and deadlines, bad management or whatever other reasons, they have not answered many phone calls, not dealt with authors in a professional manner and not published their books on time if at all. As of this date, no royalties whatsoever have been paid to this agency.

. . . On a personal note, I know how heart breaking this is and want all of you to recoup what is yours, but I personally have no control over the situation. We have done everything we could from this end. When your contracts were signed, Northwest was flourishing and we had no indication things would change.

. . . Many agents were almost put out of business by this publishing house and we were very close. A few of those lost businesses and one even lost his family. I know it is easy to blame someone when something like this happens and agents always seem to be fair prey, but Northwest left me hanging, owing me tens of thousands of dollars and I shall get no royalties from all of your books either. We never owned any part of Northwest or were involved in any decision-making processes. We were victims the same as you. Compassion seems to be at a premium here. Please try to understand that there are other points of view and other sides to everything and we were hurt very badly too.

The people who read Dorothy's letter were in this fix because of her. Now she was a victim because she wouldn't be getting her hands on royalties she never expected to earn. The only ones to profit from the mess were the casinos in Las Vegas, the check-cashing company, Van Treese's boiler-room crew, and kickback agents like Dorothy who got theirs up front without taking risks. Instead of blaming Dorothy, most of her NPI victims felt her pain along with their own. Except for Tom Mahon and a few others, Dorothy's NPI clients still didn't see joint venture publishing for what it was—a racket—and Dorothy for what she was—an accomplice.

To Dorothy's relief, the NPI authors she had victimized did not rise up against her. They had their angry and teary eyes focused on Jim Van Treese. Everybody hated Jim Van Treese, even some of his former employees who had formed a coalition to lobby for the payment of back wages they claimed were owed to them. None of these employees, of course, had known that their boss was running a sham publishing company. The head of the coalition was asking for money to help finance the cause. This caught Dorothy's attention and got her thinking.

As a publisher, Northwest was dead. But as a vehicle to squeeze a few more bucks out of its victims, it was an opportunity Dorothy couldn't pass up. Dorothy decided that on the ruse of raising money to sue Jim Van Treese, she would ask each NPI author to send her $125. If only half of her NPI writers took the bait, she could make a quick fifteen thousand dollars.

Over a weekend in May, Dorothy, Chuck, and Chuck's son, Daniel Craig, called 250 NPI clients to make the pitch. For a mere $125, they could recover the rights to their books and maybe get some of their money back.

Craig Andrews, the auto engineer from Michigan who had been a Deering client since 1991, responded positively to Dorothy's pitch. In addition to having paid her three thousand dollars in agency fees and $6,125 to have a novel published, Andrews, thanks to Dorothy, had recently signed a three-book deal with Commonwealth that cost him $8,250. Andrews had taken seventeen thousand dollars out of his 401(k) retirement fund to finance his dream of being a published author. In a letter accompanying his $125 check, Andrews wrote, "I am on your team and will discuss with you any communication (from NPI) that comes my way."" Having invested so much money on the advice of his agent, Andrews simply couldn't afford the realization she was a liar and a fake. It would take a lot more than the collapse of NPI to convince him.

Being writers, many of Van Treese's victims were telling their stories and beating up on themselves. One NPI author posted the following online:

> **Dead Publishers Society:**
> Northwest Publishing, Inc. unofficial motto: "Your royalty statement will be a few weeks, months or years late, depending upon your gullibility."

A month after the raid on NPI headquarters, Van Treese began Chapter 11 bankruptcy proceedings and, sixty days after that, sought complete protection against his creditors by filing Chapter 7. Interviewed by phone by a reporter for the *Salt Lake Tribune,* Van Treese said, "The market I've built over the last four years is enviable. I have as much integrity as anybody—every month was getting better—we were absolutely on top of where we should be."[3]

By then investigators had discovered that some twenty-one hundred writers had paid Van Treese $10.5 million to have their books published. Less than one-third of these manuscripts were ever published, and of the books that did come out, only fifty to a hundred copies of each were printed. There was no marketing.

To hear Van Treese tell it, he had been sabotaged by unreasonable writers, incompetent employees, and greedy literary agents. He was a businessman who had tried to help writers realize their dreams. There were no bad guys here, just victims. Everybody was a victim.

We are going to publicize each and every author we publish as if they were a Norman Mailer or Daniel [sic] Steele.

—Dorothy Deering

9 Sovereign Publications

IN APRIL OF 1996, the month federal and state investigators raided NPI, the Deerings and their newly hired staff were getting ready for business in a pair of offices on the second floor of a turn-of-the-century building in downtown Nicholasville. As the owner of one of the largest agencies of its kind in America, Dorothy could afford the two suites on North Main across the street from the Jessamine County Court House. This move made Nicholasville the only town in Kentucky where one could retain a lawyer and a literary agent without moving one's car.

Once settled in her new offices, Dorothy, as her first order of business, published the spring-summer edition of *News & Notes.* Printed on hot pink paper, it would be her most flamboyant, widely read, and bogus newsletter yet. The so-called pink edition would lure hundreds of new writers into Dorothy's lair. It was as deadly as it was pink.

In her "Off the Wall with Dorothy" column, one of the country's most aggressive fee agents strode into the lion's cage carrying a whip, a chair, and a lot of baloney to feed the beasts.

> As usual, Chuck is somewhat behind on his updates, but be assured that we are doing everything possible to market your work and if he is late, please be patient. That is the least important thing we do for you (the updates) and sometimes the more important things take precedence, i.e., negotiating book deals and movie deals, talking to publishers, talking to you on the phones and the substantial paperwork in this business. If you should visit us, we will take you on the grand tour. I believe you will be surprised at the processes involved. We also have on display many of the 450 books we have sold over the last eight years.

The process—the compilation of long lists of publishers who had supposedly rejected manuscripts submitted to them by the Deerings— would have indeed surprised her clients. They also would have been dismayed. Had Dorothy actually realized that a client would make the trip to Nicholasville, she wouldn't have offered the tour. Clients wouldn't have been too impressed with Chuck, his boys, and Dorothy's adopted son Michael Helm. They'd also notice that all the books on display that Dorothy had "sold" had been published by one of two joint venture presses, one of which had gone belly-up.

While a personal tour of the Deering offices in Nicholasville wouldn't impress many clients, the pink edition listings of 106 manuscripts recently "sold" by Dorothy was extremely effective. It was impressive because readers of the newsletter had no way of knowing that every book on the list was a CPI title.

Shortly after moving back to Kentucky, Dorothy made a big decision. After having sold 150 joint venture deals for Donald Phelan, Dorothy, figuring that the Canadian publisher would eventually follow Van Treese into bankruptcy, decided to enter the joint venture sweepstakes herself. Since 1994 she had sold, for Van Treese and Phelan, four hundred joint venture deals from which she had made a mere two hundred thousand dollars. The publishers had made millions. It was now her turn to get a shot at the really big money.

Phelan's leap into publishing had cost him his literary agency, but that had been a nickel-and-dime operation. Dorothy couldn't afford to lose the Deering Agency, a gold mine in itself. Unlike Phelan, she wouldn't even try to hide the fact she was also in the joint venture business. Once the agent convinced the joint venture client that they would both make a lot of money off the deal, the conflict of interest issue became irrelevant. That writers were smart enough to write books didn't mean they couldn't be led down the vanity path by a dream-selling agent-publisher.

Dorothy felt certain she could make tons of money as a joint venture publisher. Van Treese had gambled his company away in Las Vegas, and Phelan, doing business not far from the North Pole, had shot his wad. It had also been fortunate for Dorothy that the NPI debacle had been ignored by the mass media and by journalists covering the publishing industry. With seven hundred clients, hundreds of ex-clients, thousands of potential clients, and a mailing list of everybody ever represented by

A Rising Sun, Dorothy had access to a mother lode of manuscripts, each representing a potential of four to six thousand dollars. Because these manuscripts were hers, Dorothy wouldn't have to share a penny of this money with anyone. Dorothy was a master salesperson. When she got on the phone with a client, she was all charm. By comparison, Van Treese and Phelan were a pair of boiler-room galoots.

The main reason Dorothy was so eager to get the pink edition of *News & Notes* off the press was to announce the formation of her new joint venture company, Sovereign Publications. The announcement, in typical Deering style, was so over the top it pushed the envelope of credibility. But because so many of the aspiring writers who would read Dorothy's pitch were as naïve about publishing as she was, the unintentional kitsch of the announcement touched the right nerve and was a perfect shot.

> What makes Sovereign different from the others is that after numerous years of hard-earned experience in the publishing field, we are going back to the way publishers were in the past, with personal attention to each and every book, not just a number on a spreadsheet. We are going to publicize each and every author we publish as if they were a Norman Mailer or Daniel [*sic*] Steele. Publishers allow the book stores and chains to strip covers off the books and return unsold books for full credit. We are paying the freight to have them shipped back to us for redistribution or for sale in our bookstore that will be open by next spring.

Atlantic Disk Publishers had been the wave of the future; now Sovereign was the wave of the past. Not content to just publish her clients' books, Dorothy was also going to sell them in her own bookstore. That would have been a first: a store that sold only joint venture paperbacks published by the company owned by the agent-bookseller.

Dorothy announced the hiring of her new Sovereign staff as though they were high-profile acquisitions—first-round draft picks—from the world of publishing. Apparently unaware that potential Sovereign authors had no interest in, or need to know, who these people were, Dorothy named her senior editor, submissions editor, and director of marketing. She then described the dream, hers as much as her clients', that she would be selling over the next few months.

> We will not put a lid on the amount of copies we print. The first printing will be 5,000 and then we will print in increments of 1,500, thereafter, as the mar-

ket demands. . . We have contracted artists for the covers and children's books from California and New York, the very best. The quality of our books will be second to none.

We will distribute through Baker & Taylor, the largest book distributor in the U.S., our own distribution company, national news agencies such as Smith and Anderson, as well as many other distributors. We are going to go to Frankfort [*sic*], Germany to the book fair each year to sell foreign rights and we will aggressively cultivate the film market as far as many of our published works as possible as the film industry is crying out for new fresh works. We will take our titles to the ABA each year to market to the chains and news agencies. Our premier list for the 1997 catalogue will boast some 80 titles. We had to keep the numbers small to insure the marketability of the entire line. Sovereign is the publisher to watch in the future!

By conjuring up images of quality book covers, movie deals, and bookstore chains, Dorothy painted the picture her clients wanted to see. She knew what they dreamed of because she shared their fantasy. This was the woman who had posed in a photograph with Clark Gable. If there was one line in her dream sequence that made any sense, it was the one Dorothy saved for the last: "Sovereign is the publisher to watch in the future." Finally, and prophetically, the truth.

Dorothy, as chief executive officer, now spent all of her time behind the window at 106 N. Main Street that read SOVEREIGN PUBLICATIONS while Chuck continued to act as the literary agency's master file clerk. The only clients of interest to Dorothy were those thinking about joint venture deals. It was Chuck's job to keep the rest of her clientele happy and to make sure they paid their contract fees on time. In his role as the literary agency's head cheerleader, Chuck, in his most recent *News & Notes* column, "Chuck's Desk," asked Deering clients to be patient, then proclaimed, "We have more book sales than ever before and are making a lot of headway. In addition to our contracts multiplying, movie deals are also on the rise—this is defiantly [*sic*] the 'Golden Year' for us."

It was nice to know that the Deerings were having their golden year, but what's good for the bank robber is bad for the bank. In the genteel racket, what's good for the agent is bad for the client. To impress readers of the pink edition with how hard he was working, albeit against their interests, he signed his column "Sincerely, Chuck (overworked and under-appreciated) Deering." It was lucky for him that Deering clients did not understand what he was up to. From this point on, with Dorothy preoccupied with her joint venture publishing company, Chuck, with the help of his son, Daniel Craig Deering, would run the literary agency. Chuck, compared with his son, a ninth-grade dropout, was highly literate.

On the Sovereign side, Dorothy hired, as her executive assistant, Mary Layne, a Nicholasville friend from before Dorothy moved the agency to Georgia. Dorothy brought in Stephanie Baker, an English instructor at nearby Sullivan College, as her senior editor. Amy Franklin, the daughter of one of Dorothy's CPI authors, would serve as Sovereign's submissions editor. Shane Centers, a recent graduate of the University of Kentucky, was her new director of marketing. None of these people apparently realized that joint venture publishing was bogus, nor did they know that Dorothy was a phony. They were simply good-faith employees who knew zilch about the real world of publishing. However, it must have become hard, even for them, to ignore the fact that Daniel Craig Deering and Michael Helm were not the type of people one would expect to find working in a literary agency, but they were family.

Dorothy didn't know any more about publishing than her new employees. What she knew she had learned from Jim Van Treese, the father of joint venture. As a result, Sovereign was modeled after NPI, right down to the standard author's contribution of $6,125. Like Van Treese and his heir, Donald Phelan, Dorothy, while she knew how to make money the joint venture way, had no more idea of how to survive as a legitimate publisher than her predecessors. That is, she knew nothing about actually producing books and nothing about how to sell them once they were printed. And even if she had, no one wanted to buy books from a company that published everything submitted.

The key to joint venture success involved making it look like the real thing, and although Dorothy couldn't *be* the real thing, she knew just enough to create a rough imitation. To do this, like Phelan, she created, under the Sovereign publishing umbrella, eleven genre imprints. For example, Sherlock Press was for mysteries, Candy Apple Press for children's books, Midnight Tales for horror books, and Sunset Trails Press for westerns.[1]

Jim Van Treese had published, as a nonvanity book, former astronaut Mike Mullane's novel *Red Sky* as joint venture bait. Dorothy didn't know any astronauts, so she turned to her first client, Ted Nottingham, the Indianapolis minister who had asked Dorothy to look over a contract from a publisher who had already agreed to publish his manuscript. Nottingham, five years later, was still her only legitimately published client. He had written a novel called "The Final Profit," which he intended to publish himself. He had already created the cover art and seen to all of the technical details of having it printed. Dorothy made him an offer: if Nottingham put the Sovereign imprint on his paperback, she would pay to have it published. It sounded like a good deal for both parties, and Nottingham agreed. Dorothy would pay the printer. He would be a step above self-published, and she would get, without any effort or know-how, a nice-looking book bearing the company's name. Dorothy would have her *Red Sky,* her own joint venture bait. Jim Van Treese had shown her the way.

The summer of 1996 would be one to remember for a lot of people. The pink edition had done its job better than Dorothy had any right to imagine. Nearly one hundred clients bought the Sovereign pitch. By fall, Dorothy and Chuck had seven hundred thousand dollars in the bank, making them the nouveau riche of the publishing world. They had no idea what to do with all the money except, like Jim Van Treese, to spend it on themselves.

It generally takes time for a company to succeed, but in joint venture publishing, it takes time for the business to fail. For Northwest and Commonwealth, things started seriously coming apart two years out, a time when one-third to a half of the publishing dates of the coinvestors' books were past due and the money that had been paid to publish them squandered. At this stage, the new money could no longer cover the old, and the pyramid began to crumble. In the fall of 1996, Dorothy and Chuck were sitting on top of their brand new pyramid, and from there, things looked mighty good.

We consider the content of the article in WRITER'S DIGEST *not only an insult to our firm, but a threat to our authors.*

—Ken Molloy for CPI

10 Storm Warning

IN 1996, AS SUMMER TURNED INTO FALL and Dorothy and Chuck luxuriated in the honeymoon phase of joint venture publishing, Donald Phelan, estranged from his first hundred authors, scrounged for new money. He needed to bring in at least $250,000 a month just to keep CPI afloat. He had predicted NPI's collapse but hadn't seen Sovereign coming. That ungrateful lout down in Kentucky was doing to him what he had done to Van Treese.

Left to his own resources, Phelan amassed rosters of potential joint venture authors by raiding writer's magazine subscription lists and acquiring the names and addresses of writers who had registered their manuscripts with the government for copyright protection. Phelan would mail these people a large, glossy brochure proclaiming Commonwealth as "North America's fastest growing mass market publisher." At a time when the future for CPI was bleak and predictable, Phelan conveyed the following message to the objects of his desire.

> The future is bright for Commonwealth Publications, Inc. and its authors, assured by our steadfast dedication to inspiring and nurturing the artistic qualities in our existing and prospective writers throughout North American and around the world.

Festooned with dozens of colorful book covers and laced with author testimonials—"Commonwealth Publications did a wonderful job on my book from beginning to end"—the CPI brochure was impressive. Nowhere did it mention, however, that CPI authors were also coinvestors. While the brochure and CPI ads in writers' magazines generated numerous query letters, without the assistance of the agents, joint venture sales dropped off.

In addition to having lost his sales force of literary agents, Phelan was threatened by bad publicity arising from an expanding base of angry and vocal authors. Several CPI authors had sent letters of complaint to the Writers' Union of Canada, a nonprofit organization in Toronto, and to the Better Business Bureau of Central and Northern Alberta. As bad as that was, it got worse. *Writer's Digest* magazine had received so many complaints, it published in the October 1996 issue the following "storm warning":

> We've received complaints from writers about Commonwealth Publications, Inc. (7964-45 Ave., Edmonton, Alberta TGE 5C5). The Writers' Union of Canada is advising its members not to deal with the company, and the Better Business Bureau of Central and Northern Alberta says the company has an "unsatisfactory record" based on its "failure to eliminate the basic cause of customer complaints" brought to the attention of BBB.

The *Writer's Digest* alert sent shock waves through the joint venture community. Writers were flooding CPI with phone calls, faxes, letters, and e-mail. For Dorothy Deering, the trouble at CPI was both good news—Commonwealth was a competitor—and bad, because she had signed 150 of her clients to CPI contracts. Moreover, this kind of joint venture publicity could poison Sovereign's well. Even the whiff of scandal could cut down the flow of joint venture money. Dorothy had no choice but to enthusiastically endorse Donald Phelan and CPI, assuring her Commonwealth clients that, for them, the future was still bright. Having been banned from *Writer's Digest* in 1994, Dorothy joined in accusing the magazine of libel. Phelan couldn't have agreed more. Phelan and Deering, joint venture adversaries in a battle for survival, had become partners in adversity.

The *Writer's Digest* alert, while scaring a lot of CPI authors, brought many to Phelan's defense. It was not, after all, in their best interest to see their publisher fail. William B. Kerr, a retired navy captain from Ponte Vedra Beach, Florida, was one of these writers. Ten months earlier, Kerr had received, out of the blue, a letter from Donald Phelan expressing interest in his two unpublished novels. He had no idea how Phelan had gotten his name or learned of the manuscripts. Kerr, intrigued by CPI and impressed with the colorful brochure, sent Phelan summaries of his books, "Path of the Golden Dragon," and "The Red Hand." Just three weeks after responding to the CPI letter, Kerr received a telephone call from the publisher himself. Phelan said he was so impressed with the summaries and Captain Kerr's impressive background, he offered to publish the two novels, sight unseen. The CPI contracts, straight royalty deals, and the two manuscripts, crossed in the mail. Kerr signed the agreements and became one of a handful of Phelan's nonvanity authors. Unaware that Commonwealth was a joint venture outfit and unaware that Phelan was using him as a dupe, Kerr was understandably shocked by the warning in *Writer's Digest* magazine. In defense of his publisher and perhaps worried about the upcoming publishing dates for his books, Kerr wrote *Writer's Digest* the following letter:

> I am struck by the incendiary connotation of this article. Unfortunately, you provide nothing to substantiate either the Writers' Union of Canada actions or the Better Business Bureau quoted comments. While I am unable to defend Commonwealth (from allegations which you failed to discuss), I must state that my relatively brief association with members of the Commonwealth staff have been pleasant, efficient and business-like, which is more than I can say for certain U.S. publishers.
>
> In short, I feel it only fair to your reading public, not to mention good journalistic ethics, to publish, in detail, the reason/s for both the Writers' Union of Canada and the Better Business Bureau of Central and Northern Alberta, in effect, "black list" of Commonwealth Publications, Inc.[1]

Captain Kerr sent a copy of his *Writer's Digest* letter to Donald Phelan, who sent copies to all of his writers. He also phoned Kerr to thank him for his support and to advise him that he was putting Kerr's two novels on the publishing front burner.[2] Phelan, by distributing an all-author memo from his executive vice president, Ken Malloy, went on the attack.

> As some of you are already aware, a highly inflammatory article regarding Commonwealth Publications, Inc. appeared in the October 1996 issue of WRITER'S DIGEST magazine. Primarily, this is due largely to one individual disgruntled author's industrious defamation of our firm. The Writers' Union of Canada has joined in this clamor because as a matter of policy they are opposed to cooperative publishing agreements—not because of any direct knowledge of impropriety on our part.

After lashing out against the Alberta Better Business Bureau, Malloy wound up his memo with a warning.

We consider the content of the article in WRITER'S DIGEST not only an insult to our firm, but a threat to our authors insofar as this public defamation of our reputation could well jeopardize our relationships with buyers in the North American book trade. Obviously, this situation will not go unchallenged and the entities responsible will be taken to the fullest extent possible.

Phelan, besieged with problems from several quarters, had become obsessed with one writer, Steve Esrati, the retiree from Shaker Heights, Ohio, who had brought suit against him eighteen months earlier. At great expense to himself, Esrati refused to drop the case; he wanted his joint venture money back or the publication of ten thousand copies of his book, "Comrades, Avenge Us." In Ken Malloy's "storm warning" memo, Steve was the unnamed, disgruntled and industrious writer who was defaming CPI. Tireless in his crusade against Phelan, Esrati was doing everything he could to publicize his story. He was driving the publisher crazy; Phelan would have to find some way to shut him up. Writers like Esrati who didn't respond to threats were dangerous and bad for business.

A Rising Sun, the literary agency Dorothy had started for her sister Vicki, folded at the close of 1996, a little more than a year after moving from Acworth, Georgia, to Savannah. The agency had been operated by Vicki, her husband Chris, and Lynn Watson, the wife of Dorothy's carpet-hustling brother. Without the kickback money from Van Treese and, later, Phelan, the agency floundered, then crashed, leaving forty or so clients without representation. When these writers phoned A Rising Sun, their calls were automatically routed to Nicholasville, Kentucky, from where they were told that A Rising Sun has been "absorbed" into the Deering Literary Agency. Dorothy Deering would honor their Rising Sun contracts until they expired. Dorothy was not about to let these fee-paying clients slip into the night, particularly now that she owned a joint venture publishing company. A Rising Sun's liabilities would be turned into Deering assets.

Glenda Ivey, one of Vicki and Chris Scott's clients, had paid six hundred dollars to have two of her manuscripts represented. Ivey had heard that it was not a good practice to pay contract fees, but being from Atlanta, she liked the idea of having an agent from Georgia. She also had been impressed with the eye-catching advertisement for A Rising Sun in *The Literary Market Place*. In fact, according to that advertisement, the

Savannah agency was a member of the Association of Authors' Representatives and had literary affiliates in the "Russian Territories."[3]

Ivey paid the contract fees and waited. Months went by, and she was still waiting. No one from the agency had called, so she started calling them. Chris Scott kept saying that her manuscripts were out and they were hopeful. Don't call us, we'll call you. Finally, three months before her contracts ran out, Chris, for the first time, called Ivey. He didn't have any news about her manuscripts; he just wanted to offer her a deal, a hundred-dollar discount if she paid next year's contract fees early. She declined his generous offer, and he never called again. So much for the benefits of a Georgia agent.

In January 1997, before her contract with A Rising Sun expired, Ivey called Chris Scott to ask for copies of her rejection letters and the return of her manuscripts. Chuck Deering picked up the phone and informed Ivey that she was now represented by the Deering Literary Agency of Nicholasville, Kentucky. The owner and CEO, Dorothy L. Deering, the daughter of William Morrow of the publishing Morrows, would honor Chris Scott's commitment. Ivey told Chuck that all she wanted were her manuscripts and rejection letters. Chuck promised to have those items in the mail the following day. Although she had considered herself finished with A Rising Sun, Ivey was curious to know what happened to Chris Scott and the Savannah agency. Chuck explained that Chris and his wife Vicki didn't know what they were doing. They had simply run the agency into the ground. He didn't tell Ivey that Vicki was Dorothy Deering's sister. That would have made Vicki one of William Morrow's daughters, too.

Shortly after their phone conversation, Ivey received a package from Chuck Deering. Instead of keeping his promise to send the manuscripts and rejection letters, Chuck had mailed her the infamous pink edition of *News & Notes.* Ivey was not impressed with the overall appearance of the newsletter; it looked like a flyer announcing the opening of a supermarket. She was even less impressed when she realized that Dorothy Deering, a literary agent, wanted her clients to pay her company to publish their manuscripts. That a literary agency would recommend vanity publishing was bad enough; that the agent owned the subsidy press was outrageous. Who were these people and how were they connected to those incompetents in Savannah? Ivey tossed the pink vanity publishing flyer into the trash and gave up on her manuscript copies and the rejection letters. Maybe she should try to get an agent who worked in New York City.

Ivey had forgotten Chuck Deering and the daughter of William Morrow, but they had not forgotten her. A few days before the expiration of her Rising Sun contract, Chuck, the master file clerk, called Ivey to offer her a special deal: a full year of Deering representation, for both books, for just six hundred dollars, a whopping four hundred dollars off the regular price. Color him soft, but Chuck felt terrible about her bad experience with those louts in Savannah; this was his way of making things right. As someone who was obviously serious about writing, she owed it to herself.

Ivey accepted Chuck's deal, but under one condition—he was not, under any circumstances, to submit her manuscripts to a vanity publishing company, and that included the outfit owned by Dorothy Deering. Chuck gave Ivey his solemn promise: *no vanity contracts.* This was from the man who had pledged to send her the rejection letters, a promise he couldn't keep because they didn't exist.

Six months after signing the agency contracts and two months after it had dawned on her that she had probably hooked up with the Kentucky version of A Rising Sun, Ivey received the following letter from Chuck Deering:

> I have tried to reach you by phone with little success. The reason I am trying to contact you is we have received an offer of publication for *Sarah's Revenge* from Sovereign Publications. It is a co-publishing offer (not a vanity press offer!). I have reviewed the copy of the contract they sent me and it seems a really good deal for a co-publishing contract. You may have been contacted by Sovereign. The parts I like are the payback arrangements and the escalation clause. I told them to contact you and see what you think. Please give me a call and we will discuss the offer or we will reject it and keep on searching. The choice is yours!
>
> I do want to emphasize that any offer of publication from a legitimate publishing house, such as Sovereign, should not be dismissed lightly. The market is tough and sometimes an author must take charge of their literary destiny to overcome the bias and unfeeling, shortsightedness of the well-meaning editors at the MAJOR publishing houses. . . . *Sarah's Revenge* deserves to be published!

Ivey, taking Chuck's advice, took charge of her "literary destiny" by dismissing Chuck's offer, not lightly but emphatically and with feeling:

This is also a good time for me to admit that I am somewhat troubled by your company's affiliation with Sovereign. I see it as a conflict of interest. My opinion is based on the lack of information I have received from your office regarding the marketing of my manuscript. I can only assume that the possibility of placing my work with a company that offers standard royalty contracts was not fully exhausted before it was presented to a company that would require a sizable investment on my part. . . .

Mr. Deering, I am concerned that, after six months, the only publisher I'm aware of that has received my manuscript from your agency is that of a co-publishing firm that happens to be closely affiliated with DEERING. . . . I would like nothing better than to learn that my thinking is way "off base."

Ivey's thinking, of course, was not off base. Neither of her manuscripts had gotten out of Nicholasville, Kentucky. She hadn't fully learned her lesson from A Rising Sun, but she caught on a lot sooner than many others, and it saved her a lot of money and heartache.[4]

As slick as he was, Chuck Deering didn't win every time out, and the same was true of Donald Phelan at CPI. In May 1997, to avoid a legal face-off with Steve Esrati, Phelan backed down and settled the suit. Phelan had no choice, the author of "Comrades, Avenge Us" had a winning case, and he refused to be intimidated. In return for the writer's pledge not to divulge the terms of the settlement, and to quit bad-mouthing CPI, Phelan agreed to publish ten thousand paperback copies of Esrati's novel and to reimburse him for his legal expenses.

The paperbacks were published and shipped to Shaker Heights, Ohio, where they took up considerable space in Esrati's garage. All he had to do was find some way to sell them. Once the books were printed, Phelan stopped making payments toward Esrati's legal bills. With one of the settlement terms breached by Phelan, Esrati was free to start bad-mouthing CPI again. Suddenly, the writer was posting messages online, writing letters, talking to people about his experiences with Phelan and doing all he could to bring down CPI. Other Commonwealth authors, convinced they would never see their books or their money, joined in. Many of these writers were Deering clients, and they were starting to see the light. For Dorothy, this couldn't and wouldn't be good.

the Dorothy Deering Literary Agency

1153 Alabama Rd. Suite 104
Acworth, GA 30101-2606
404-591-2051 FAX: 404-591-0369

October 6, 1994

Craig L. Andrews
11644 Brandywine
Brighton, MI 48116

Dear Craig,

First of all, congratulations on the sale of your manuscript. Book contracts are hard to come by in this day and age. One in 2000 sells, so you have something to be very proud of.

I just wanted to let you know what happens after the sale of a manuscript. After the contracts are signed and returned to the publisher, there is a wait. I know you are used to that. The publisher puts your book in the library room in the date sequential order of publication. When the time comes for them to work on your book, it is taken down and assigned an Editor. That Editor will call you and work directly with you. Prior to that time, you will not hear from that publisher.

I have enclosed some material that I thought would be informative for you.

Please be patient and "write another book" while you're waiting.

Take care,

Dorothy Deering, Agent

Follow-up letter to client who signed joint venture contracts with Northwest Publishing, October 6, 1994

News & Notes

The Deering Literary Agency

Issue: Spring/Summer

In This Issue: Introducing Sovereign Publications, Announcing Upcoming Hollywood/New York Trip, Off the Wall with Dorothy Deering, Chuck's Desk by Charles Deering, Author Showcases and more. . .

We Proudly Announce: Sovereign Publications

By: Dorothy Deering

After years of planning and countless requests from our authors, we have finally taken the big step and are proud to announce the opening of Sovereign Publications, our new publishing house. We are publishing outstanding works of fiction and nonfiction.

There are many things that go on in this business that authors do not know about. One is that most large publishers publish only a few new authors each year and usually take a loss on them to offset the profits on their big name authors. To publicize them, they only put them in their catalogues.

What makes Sovereign different from the others is that after numerous years of hard-earned experience in the publishing field we are going back to the way publishers were in the past, with personal attention to each and every book, not just a number on a spread sheet. We are going to publicize each and every author we publish as if they were a Norman Mailer or Daniel Steele. Publishers allow the book stores and chains to strip the covers off the books and return unsold books for full credit. We are paying the freight to have them shipped back to us for redistribution or for sale in our book store that will be open by next spring. I see nothing wrong with the way the publishing industry used to operate, how the large publishers got to be large publishers.

We have already sent out nine standard royalty contracts to a few of our well-published authors and twelve joint venture contracts so far to a few of our first-time authors. We are reviewing all of our files and offering the opportunity to our very best authors only. We have spent the last year setting up this company, getting our distributors in place, hiring the right people and we are ready to rock and roll!

Our Senior Editor is Stephanie Baker who we literally stole from Sullivan College by making her an offer she couldn't refuse. (Right, Vito and Chuck Carleone!) She is a full professor of English and a published author. Her experience is impeccable. We hired Shane Centers from Cumberland College who has a degree in English and Communications and was their Communications Director. He is our Marketing Director. We are Bringing in Amy Franklin from Vidor, Texas as our Submissions Editor. She attended BYU and has edited all of Larry Franklin's manuscripts. Larry is one of our clients who writes wonderful westerns and action adventure fiction. She will arrive the third week in August. We are hiring a full-time in-house publicist who will give all books equal attention. Then we have our current staff who will continue to run Deering Literary Agency and sell manuscripts to other publishers, as well as Sovereign.

We will not put a lid on the amount of copies we print. The first printing will be 5,000 and then we will print in increments of 1,500, thereafter, as the market demands. We will print mass market paperbacks, some hardback books, and a few trade paperbacks. The publishing format is contingent upon the genre and type of book. We have contracted artists for the covers and children's books from California and New York, the very best. The quality of our books will be second to **none**.

We will distribute through Baker & Taylor, the largest book distributor in the U.S., our own distribution company, national news agencies such as Smith and Anderson, as well as many other distributors. We are going to go to Frankfort, Germany to the book fair each year to sell foreign rights and we will aggressively cultivate the film market for as many of our published works as possible as the film industry is crying for new fresh works. We will take our titles to the ABA (American Book Association) each year to market to the chains and new agencies. Our premier list for 1997 catalogue will boast of some 80 titles. We have had to keep the numbers small to insure the marketability of the entire line. **Sovereign** is the publisher to watch in the future!

Dorothy Deering's newsletter announcing the formation of her vanity press

O ff the Wall with Dorothy

By: Dorothy Deering

It has been a while since the last newsletter and I want to personally apologize for the delay. We have just been so very busy that there has been no time to put it all together.

Our new offices are spacious and directly across from the courthouse in downtown Nicholasville. I invite each and every one of you to come visit us at the new facility if you get to Kentucky. I am so very proud of the authors we are representing currently. I feel that we have some of the very finest writing talents and we are selling your books right and left. I also want to praise you for the professional way you correspond with us and talk to us. It is much appreciated. This business is tough and a little common courtesy goes a long way after dealing with New York publishers and Hollywood producers all day.

As usual, Charles is somewhat behind on his updates, but rest assured that we are doing everything possible to market your work and if he is late, please be patient. That is the least important thing we do for you and sometimes the more important things take precedence, i.e., negotiating books deals and movie deals, talking to publishers, talking to you on the phones and the substantial paperwork involved in this business. If you should visit us, we will take you on the grand tour. I believe you will be surprised at the processes involved. We also have on display many of the over 450 books we have sold over the last eight years.

"Blood Moon" by producer Keith Strandberg is finally done. Production would up the last week in June and the novelization by Dan Neidermeyer will soon go to press. This is a hot one and I recommend you see it when it comes to a theater near you. Dan has five plays being produced in September along; "Zapped," "To Race Again," an adaptation of The Prince and the Pauper," "Words by Fanny," "Light in the Fields," and "Martyred: The Cheat Bitterman Story." Two meetings took place this week with investors and a major television station concerning making "Martyred" into a movie. Congratulations, Dan!

The Manuscript Express

Periodically we take manuscripts to New York or Hollywood to *personally* present them to the publishers and/or producers. This is an extra personal push that numerous authors have requested. Of course, this is a completely optional action. If you would like for us to personally present your material to the Senior Editors, Editors-in-Chiefs or Producers, please have at least 6 copies and a $500.00 expense check or Visa information to us before the following dates:

New York........................**Deadline:** August 10, 1996.........................**Trip date:** Aug. 15th
Hollywood......................**Deadline:** August 25, 1996.........................**Trip date:** Sept. 5th

We can only take ten properties to be effective in our presentations, so I encourage you to make the arrangements as soon as possible. Call the office to reserve your place today as the list is already filling up. This is not required, but it is a dynamite way to sell manuscripts and screenplays. The last trip to New York yielded four sales and the last trip to Hollywood yielded three options and two sales. We initiated these trips at the insistence of many authors. If this sounds interesting to you call Chuck at 1-606-887-5862 to discuss your options.

You may think that it is very glamorous to make these trips but I can assure you that it is all work, even when we are wining and dining these publishers, it is work. From 7:00 a.m. until 11:30 p.m. we run around New York or Hollywood for you. On the last trip, we walked our legs off, especially when a cabby let us out three blocks from the publisher in the rain and we were carrying many manuscripts and brief cases. It is work that is gratifying and successful.

Sovereign Publications

World Headquarters

JOINT VENTURE ROYALTIES

April 29, 1997

Dear James:

Here are some figures that I have worked up for *"Glimpses"*. I know that you will want to see these numbers before you sign your first publication contract with Sovereign Publications.

Author's Share of Investment (Based upon a print run of 5000 books and up per contract)	**$5,875.00**
Author's 40% Royalty (First 2500 books sold per contract)	**$6,990.00**
Author's 10% Royalty (Second 2500 books sold)	**$ 961.13**
Author's Total Return	*$7,951.13*

NOTE: The author gets 40% of RETAIL on the first 2500 copies and 10% of gross receipts thereafter. (See your contract for future escalations of royalties.) The author also has no other out-of-pocket expenses; you pay nothing after the initial contract. These figures are in addition to royalties on subsequent printings.

If you have any questions, please feel free to contact me. All of us here at Sovereign look forward to seeing *"Glimpses"* in major bookstores all over the United States and possibly the world.

106 North Main Street, Suite B, Nicholasville, KY 40356-1234 (606) 887-5935
Fax (606) 885-5455 E Mail: deeringlit@aol.com SAN: 299-0598

Letter from Sovereign Publications stating fee and royalty schedules to clients offered contracts, April 29, 1997

Dorothy Deering's

SOVEREIGN DIGEST

A Quarterly Newsletter

Winter 1998 Edition

Dorothy Deering's glamour shot in *Sovereign Digest*'s quarterly newsletter, winter 1998

Sovereign Publications

WORLD HEADQUARTERS

Dear Author,

Opportunities to publish are far and very few. Your choice is clear, <u>publish or perish.</u> 90 days from now, there will be 1000 more authors submitting more manuscripts to our publishing house. At that time, the past will be the past. The window of opportunity comes and goes with all authors. If you miss this window of opportunity, you may be left with self-publishing or vanity as your only remaining option. <u>We want you now!</u>

Notice: This publishing contract offer will be voided and revoked thirty days from post-mark of this letter.

If the reason you are declining is a financial one, why don't you give our finance department a call to inquire about a payment plan?

<u>Please call me</u> to secure your future as a published author.

Sincerely,

Bill

<u>Bill Richardson</u>
<u>Vice-President of operations</u>

106 N. MAIN STREET / NICHOLASVILLE, KY 40356 / 606-887-5935
E. Mail address: sovpublish@aol.com Web site: http://www.appapub.com

Sovereign pitch letter written by Bill Richardson

Advertisement that ran in *Writers' Journal* when Dorothy Deering knew the company would be closing its doors

Sovereign Publications

Friday, June 26, 1998

Dear Diane,

Great news! *Sovereign Publications* is fulfilling the dreams of our authors with incredible success. Publisher, Dorothy Deering has created a few additional openings for publication in her next publishing season. Dorothy wants to bring your dream to *Sovereign Publications* to be published under her prestigious imprint of *Appaloosa Press*. Please apply this gift certificate of $1000.00 toward your publishing contract. Join *Sovereign Publications'* other authors who are becoming successfully published with Dorothy Deering's help. Please call me immediately to apply this gift and secure your publishing contract and publication date with America's fastest growing publishing house, *Sovereign Publications*.

Sincerely,

Bill Richardson,
Vice-President of Operations

"Please accept my offer and let me help you with your publishing. I've built my publishing company by helping unknown authors & first-time authors fulfill their dreams. I will help you!"

Dorothy Deering, Publisher and CEO
Sovereign Publications

Infamous "Death Heads Units" Sovereign Publications gift certificate, June 26, 1998

Clay Mason, special agent of the FBI, February 2002. Photo by the author; used with permission of Clay Mason.

11 *Little Brother*

BY FEBRUARY 1997, working from Sovereign's "world headquarters" across the street from the old Jessamine County court house, Dorothy had signed 150 clients to joint venture deals. She had raised, within a year, more than a million dollars. Representing the Deering Literary Agency, Chuck, with the help of Daniel Craig, had raised about four hundred thousand dollars in reading and contract fees. The Deerings were again busy and flush.

The Deering Literary Agency and Sovereign Publications, a pair of companies that produced nothing in the way of services or products, firms supported entirely by Dorothy's client base, provided good-paying jobs for Dorothy, Chuck, Chuck's three sons, and Dorothy's son Michael to the tune of about $250,000 per year. She paid the nonfamily employees, a staff of five, hourly wages. About half the client money that came in went out as payroll and office expenses. The Deerings, in pursuit of the good life, were spending the rest of the money on furniture— Dorothy had rented, at seventeen hundred dollars a month, a sprawling suburban house in Lexington—cars, jewelry (a seven-carat diamond ring for Chuck), and a pair of Caribbean cruises. Dorothy also employed the services of a housekeeper. None of this income came from the placement of a single client's manuscript, or from the publication and sale of a Sovereign book. In fact, the only book that had been produced was Ted Nottingham's. Dorothy was not spending profit; she was, in effect, practicing deficit spending. The Deerings were incurring an enormous debt without creating a way to repay it. At Sovereign, there was not enough money left over to produce books.

Dorothy would have to make a big decision, and make it soon. The honeymoon was over; the publication dates of at least fifty Sovereign books were fast approaching, and there was no way any of these titles were getting into print. Dorothy could follow one of two plans. She could end the false pretense, give back what she could, and plead for mercy. That would mean, of course, that she would have to give up the office, the house, the cars, and the perks of ostensible success. Because of that, this option of limiting the damage and taking responsibility for her actions had no appeal. Dorothy decided on plan B. She would keep up the sham as long as she could, accumulate as much money as possible, and then when she couldn't maintain the illusion any longer, file for bankruptcy to escape her creditors and victims. To carry Sovereign through this post-honeymoon phase of its operation, Dorothy needed a ruthless hustler who could keep angry authors off her back, and when the whole enterprise burst into flames, take the heat. Chuck fit the bill to a tee, but Dorothy needed him at the agency. She needed someone she could count on, a family member who shared her lack of ethics. The choice was obvious; she'd hire her younger brother, Bill. On the upside, Bill was currently unemployed, had extensive boiler-room experience, and was desperate for money. On the downside, he knew nothing about publishing and there were warrants out for his arrest in Georgia, where he had been accused of ripping off a group of carpet buyers. Whereas his status as a fugitive might have troubled another prospective employer, Dorothy had no qualms. She probably figured Nicholasville was as good a place to hide as any. Taking the last name of Vicki's second husband and giving him the title of vice president of operations, William Paul Watson would run Sovereign Publications as Bill Richardson.

In February 1997, Richardson (as he will now be called) and his wife Lynn moved into a small house they had rented on Buckhorn Street on the south side of Lexington. Dorothy had agreed to pay her brother a salary of two thousand dollars a week, plus a 10-percent cut of every joint venture contract he sold. The kickback incentive would turn out to be a bad idea because it put him in fierce competition with Chuck's son, Daniel Craig Deering, a kid Richardson didn't like anyway. The two men would fight whenever Richardson sold, or would try to sell, a joint venture deal to a Deering client behind the agent's back.

While Richardson possessed the essential qualifications for his assignment, he wasn't a perfect fit for the job. For one thing, he didn't look like a top publishing executive. Beneath a thin layer of charm lived a foul-mouthed bully who had no respect for writers. He was big and intimidating, and he wasn't about to take any crap from a bunch of authors who thought they were special just because they had written a book. Richardson probably thought selling joint venture contracts wasn't going to be different from selling carpets.

One of the first moves Richardson made upon taking up his new job, after being briefed by Dorothy on the ins and outs of joint venture publishing, was to craft a twelve-page notebook he and others would use when selling Sovereign contracts. The so-called pitch book, a standard boiler-room tool, contained the basic spiel, plus canned responses to every question, objection, expression of doubt, or form of sales resistance. Armed with this notebook, the seller had an answer for everything. In fashioning this script, Richardson had the advantage of using whatever lies he needed to make the case and paint the dream.

David Brannon, the son of the woman who owned the janitorial company that serviced Dorothy's offices, needed a job, so Dorothy hired him to work in Sovereign's graphics department. Richardson, unhappy with the hiring because he didn't need a graphics person and didn't like the fact he hadn't been consulted, handed Brannon the pitch book and told him to start selling joint venture to writers who responded to Sovereign's newspaper and magazine ads. Brannon cemented his position on Richardson's bad side by dating Dorothy's assistant, Mary Layne, with whom Richardson was fighting for control of the company.

In May 1997, a couple of months after Brannon came on board, the Richardson-Layne feud came to a head during a staff meeting in Dorothy's office. In response to Richardson's complaint that Layne wasn't following his orders, Layne screamed, "I don't have to do anything for you!" Richardson yelled back that she did because she now worked for *him.* Layne broke into tears and appealed to Dorothy for support. Richardson, in a grab for total control, gave his big sister an ultimatum: it was either Layne or him; one of them would have to go. Dorothy felt she had no choice but to fire Layne on the spot. She didn't want to do this; Layne was a friend, but without her brother Bill, there could be no plan B. A week later, David Brannon followed his girlfriend out the door. Richardson had killed two birds with one stone. When he hit the exit, Brannon took with him a copy of Richardson's pitch book, blank joint venture contracts, and samples of the various form letters Dorothy used to hook her clients.[1]

That spring, Richardson continued to clean house. He fired two young staffers, daughters of one of Dorothy's CPI authors, to make room for a personal secretary, a thirty-three-year-old Lexington woman named Carolyn Thue. Single, with twin babies her mother helped care for, Thue got the six-dollars-per-hour job by responding to Richardson's help-wanted ad in the *Lexington Herald-Leader*. Thue would answer the phone, do light filing, and run errands to the bank and post office. She had a high school education and had no idea how publishing worked. Since her boss didn't either, this lack of knowledge would not be a problem.

Richardson, working with a long, updated mailing list, launched a direct-mail campaign that featured a flyer of his own creation.

> Opportunities to publish are far and very few. Your choice is clear, *publish or perish*. 90 days from now, there will be 1000 more authors submitting more manuscripts to our publishing house. At that time, the past will be the past. The window of opportunity comes and goes with all authors. If you miss this window of opportunity, you may be left with self-publishing or vanity as your only remaining option. *We want you now*!
>
> Notice: This publishing contract offer will be voided and revoked thirty days from the post-mark of this letter.

So there it was, the limited time offer, the old one-day-only sale. The technique worked well on furniture, carpet, and car buyers and was an effective tool for bagging aspiring writers chasing a dream. In fact, it had worked so well, *Writer's Market* was advising its readers not to "bow to pressure from any subsidy publisher who claims that you must 'act now' or the offer to publish may be withdrawn."[2] This advice, however, pertained to *subsidy* publishing, and as such would have been missed by a writer who bought the idea that joint venture was different. There was nothing in *Writer's Market* about the hazards of joint venture.

Richardson figured a lot of writers out there would jump at the chance to be published if they had the money. Not that many folks had six thousand dollars lying around. Very few people had enough money to buy a car, but everybody had one. That's what installment plans were for. Pay a little down now and the rest later. If General Motors could do it, why not Sovereign? For writers who happened to be strapped, Richardson suggested the following:

If the reason you are declining is a financial one, why don't you give our finance department a call to inquire about a payment plan?

Please call me to secure your future as a published author.

When a caller asked for the "finance department," Carolyn Thue would alert Bill Richardson, who would stop what he was doing and get right on the line. With the pitch book in front of him, he'd recite the joint venture spiel, then offer the following plan: two thousand dollars down, with the balance, six thousand dollars, spread over eighteen months. Now, if the writer wanted to save big money, Richardson would publish the same book for just five thousand dollars. But there was a catch—that deal required a lump-sum payment. Richardson didn't make this offer to very many people, but he had a feeling this book was going to be very hot. Whatever the writer wanted to do was fine, but there wasn't much time. Richardson couldn't hold these offers open very long. There were just too many writers out there who wanted Sovereign to publish their manuscripts.

Daniel Craig Deering, the literary agency's hottest joint venture salesman now that Dorothy was devoting all of her time to Sovereign, didn't have a problem with Bill Richardson signing up writers who were not clients of the Deering Literary Agency. But when he started nailing Deering clients, denying Daniel his joint venture kickbacks, the trouble started. Daniel considered such behavior poaching and highly unethical. While the agent waited for the appropriate passage of time before presenting the newer clients with the Sovereign offer, Richardson short-circuited the process with the following letter:

Congratulations! It is with great pleasure to inform you that [title] has been accepted by the editorial department and approved by the publishers. Your manuscript is creative, original and, we believe, a highly marketable work. We are delighted that you have chosen to join the ranks of such co-publishing authors as:

Thomas Hardy	Henry Thoreau
T. S. Elliott [*sic*]	Tolstoy
Walt Whitman	Rod McKuen
Elizabeth Browning	Edward F. Fitzgerald
Edgar Allen Poe	James Redfield
Nathaniel Hawthorne	Rudyard Kipling

These first-time authors decided to take control of their literary destiny and paid to have their novels in the public eye. With proper marketing, artwork and editing, every book has the opportunity of being a best seller.

At Sovereign, we take the author on a journey from raw manuscript to finished book. Sovereign policy dictates that no accepted manuscripts will languish on the desk of some obscure editor, but be valued as a future work that will make its own mark in the literary field.

Being accepted by Sovereign was like getting into drunk driving school. Congratulations. Richardson's statement that "no accepted manuscript will languish on the desk of some obscure editor" was true. Sovereign's own obscure editor, Stephanie Baker, was buried under a mountain of the unread books "accepted" by the "editorial department." Instead of languishing on her desk, they were stacked against the walls of her office. Millions and millions of words, each carefully considered, were lying on top of each other in an office in Nicholasville, Kentucky, while their authors waited anxiously for them to be read and commented on by Sovereign's unobscure editors. They might as well have been waiting for a bus to Mars.

That summer, Ted Nottingham published his book, *The Final Prophet.* Although it bore the Sovereign imprint, it would be marketed by its author. Sovereign's marketing director, Shane Centers, having no books to sell, had quit. Nottingham, having lined up a book signing in Lexington, would use the occasion to deliver copies of his books to his publisher and meet Bill Richardson. When the two men met at the bookstore, Nottingham experienced the same feeling that had hit him when he first met the Deerings several years before. What was this guy doing in the publishing business? He even looked out of place in the bookstore.

Nottingham had gone to the trouble of producing a promotional video, which he played for Richardson. It looked so good, Richardson just had to have it. During the next several months, he represented it as having been produced at Sovereign. Richardson would show it to every prospect who visited the office. That video was a deal closer.

The Indianapolis minister didn't drive down to Nicholasville that summer to visit Dorothy. Richardson told him she wouldn't be in the office. Dorothy had a bad right knee that made climbing the twenty-seven steps to her office too painful. Because of her condition, she was working out of the house in Lexington and was not in the mood to entertain guests. Richardson said she was taking strong pain medication that made her sleep a lot.

Dorothy may have been suffering from a sore knee, but it wasn't the only reason she was conducting business from her house. For one thing, the kickback feud between Daniel Craig Deering and Bill Richardson had escalated to periodic shouting and shoving matches, which she didn't want any part of. She also wanted to keep her private financial data away from prying eyes at the office. That's why she had her bookkeeper, Dedre Smith, work out of the house instead of the office. She was mainly worried about her brother Bill, who had been complaining about carrying Sovereign and not getting his fair share of the pie. Bill was a terrific moneymaker, but he was greedy and untrustworthy. It was true that Bill was doing the heavy lifting, but she was the owner and wasn't quite ready to throw in the towel. There was just too much money rolling in. William Paul Watson, a.k.a. Bill Richardson, wasn't going anywhere, especially to Georgia, where he was still wanted by the police. He was lucky to have a job, any job, and he knew it. If he weren't in Nicholasville, Kentucky, working for his sister, he'd be on the run or sitting in jail. He was as ungrateful as he was greedy.

I've built my publishing company by helping unknown authors and first time authors fulfill their dreams.

—Dorothy Deering, CEO, Sovereign Publications

12 *Gift Certificates*

SOVEREIGN'S CHIEF EDITOR, STEPHANIE BAKER, the English instructor hired by Dorothy at the inception of the company, quit shortly after the publication of Ted Nottingham's book, a project she had nothing to do with. To fill her position, Richardson hired Allison Arnold, a 23-year-old University of Kentucky graduate student with no experience in editing. As his new marketing director, Richardson brought on a 19-year-old girl named Jessica Johnson, a part-time student at Lexington Community College. Johnson, of course, had no idea how to market anything, but since there were still no books to sell, it didn't matter. Late that summer, Richardson changed Johnson's job designation to publication coordinator. Her main responsibility was mailing form letters to jittery authors to assure them their books were coming out on schedule.

Arnold and Johnson, as a condition of their employment, had signed confidentiality agreements. This was Richardson's way of ensuring that his employees, once they realized they were helping Dorothy bilk writers, wouldn't spill the beans to victims. It was hardly necessary. These young women, having no concept of publishing, would be slow to pick up on what was really happening. Because Richardson was so vulgar and bullying, they would quit before they had any notion that things weren't right. Having clerical employees of a publishing company sign confidentiality agreements, while intended as a measure to protect the enterprise from exposure, revealed more than it hid.

Richardson promoted his personal secretary, Carolyn Thue, to the position of office administrator. Thue would be the one nonfamily clerk who would stick it out to the very end. As Sovereign's office administrator, it was Thue's job to help Richardson slip joint venture deals past Daniel Craig Deering and to get on the telephone and calm authors who were starting to suspect they had been swindled. To these writers, the message was always the same: their books were moving slowly but surely through the pipeline. Be patient, and all will be well.

Richardson, in September 1997, hired Ronald Spriggs, a 57-year-old African American who was looking for a part-time job that would hold him over until he became eligible for social security. Spriggs had lost his middle-management job with IBM in 1993 when its facility in Lexington had been downsized. After IBM laid him off, Spriggs self-published *Amazing Management Styles,* a booklet he hoped to sell at his business planning and management workshops. He had paid ten thousand dollars for the printing of two thousand copies, most of which were still in his garage. Richardson, realizing that Spriggs's book would come in handy, named him head of Sovereign's graphic design department.

Allison Arnold, Sovereign's only editor, couldn't make a dent in the huge mound of manuscripts growing in her office. She needed help. Bill Richardson really didn't want to hire more editors, but to placate Arnold and to keep up appearances, he placed a help-wanted ad in the Lexington paper that resulted in the hiring of assistant editors Michelle Mueller and Jim Russo. Mueller had recently graduated from Louisiana State University and Russo was a graduate student at the University of Kentucky. Thinking they would be receiving valuable experience in publishing, they were willing to work for seven dollars per hour. Richardson, after hiring a succession of three young women to be his publicity directors, all of whom quit after a few weeks of envelope stuffing, soon would reverse the practice and start laying people off.

Jim Russo had been on the job less than two weeks when he witnessed one of Richardson's fights with Daniel Craig Deering. The two men were screaming, cursing, and pushing each other around Richardson's office. The fracas came to an end when Chuck Deering put himself between his son and his brother-in-law. Russo later learned they had not been fighting over artistic differences. It was all about money; who was entitled to Dorothy's joint venture kickbacks—the publisher or the agent. Although Bill Richardson, Chuck Deering, and his son Daniel seemed poorly educated and unpolished for people in publishing, Russo never even considered the fact that they were phonies or, worse, criminals. For all he knew, it was like this up in New York City, or perhaps it was just publishing, Kentucky style.

Dorothy couldn't control her brother or her stepson, so she had to separate them before somebody took a punch or a bullet. If open warfare broke out between her literary agency and her publishing company, it would not be good for business. She should have known not to put a pair of ruthless predators into a situation that might encourage competition for the same money. She didn't want to fire either man, not because they were relatives but because they were both bringing in the dough.

In the middle of October 1997, Dorothy and Chuck leased a suite of six spacious offices in a two-story brick building on the corner of two busy streets in Lexington's strip mall–franchise district a few miles south of downtown. Sovereign publications and Bill Richardson were moving out of Nicholasville. Describing herself to the landlord as being in the religious publishing business, Dorothy signed a two-year lease, agreeing to pay $1,450 a month for rent. She would also have to rent office furniture. Sovereign's new world headquarters, at 128 E. Reynolds Road, was near Dorothy's house and only a ten-minute drive from Nicholasville where she'd continue to operate the literary agency. Richardson and Daniel Craig would still be competing for the kickback money, but they wouldn't be doing it under the same roof. The chances of someone getting plugged had been lowered considerably.

Of more than 250 Sovereign books under contract, only six had any chance of actually being published. Ted Nottingham had another book he was about to publish, Dorothy's thirty-page children's book, *Freddie the Firefly,* was in the works, and four novels written by friends of the Deerings were in the pipeline.[1] No other books were on the horizon. Richardson, who was using the covers of these books as sales exhibits, didn't need any more.

When Allison Arnold decided not to follow Sovereign to Lexington, Richardson promoted Jim Russo to the position of senior editor and gave him a raise of two dollars per hour. He also informed his new head editor that he couldn't afford to bring the editorial staff back up to three. Russo said that he and Michelle Mueller were overwhelmed. They couldn't handle 250 manuscripts. *Three* editors hadn't been enough, already causing a serious bottleneck in the production of books. Even if they had six or seven editors, there would be delays in publication.

Richardson said this was not a problem; he wanted Russo to just run the manuscripts through the spelling and grammar software and call them edited.

It was no secret that Richardson, contrary to how he sounded on the phone with authors, had no interest in the books themselves. No one had ever seen him reading a manuscript, and to anyone's knowledge, no manuscript had ever been rejected for publication. Since none of the books had been editorially screened, it was reasonable to assume that many of them needed serious work. Russo had come across manuscripts that were virtually unreadable. He couldn't see how a publisher could bring out unedited books and stay in business. He explained to Richardson that editors did more than check spelling and grammar. Many, if not most, manuscripts needed to be cut or thinned out, plots didn't always hold together, characters had to be fleshed out, and parts of the book usually required some degree of reorganization. And what about material that was libelous? Unedited books could get a publisher into trouble. In this business, you had to be careful.

Richardson said he knew all of that, but the matter was out of his hands. Dorothy Deering called the shots, and she had decided they couldn't afford three editors. Russo would just have to make do.

Jim Russo had an idea. Maybe he could set up an internship program with the University of Kentucky. Students would get real-life work experience in publishing, and Richardson would obtain a steady supply of free editorial help. Richardson, who didn't have a problem with a bunch of college girls running around his office, said he liked the idea. He liked it a lot.[2]

One Saturday, while in the office catching up, Jim Russo came across a box of manuscript evaluation reports that had been issued by some literary agency in Savannah, Georgia, called A Rising Sun. He noticed that several of the forms had been filled out by an agent named Dr. Blake Richardson. Remembering that Bill Richardson had worked in Georgia, Russo wondered whether the two men were related. A few days later, Russo mentioned Dr. Blake Richardson to his boss and was surprised to learn that Bill Richardson and the doctor were one and the same. Richardson said his real name was Blake and, yes, he had been a literary agent with A Rising Sun.

Russo and Mueller had always been curious about Bill Richardson. Here was a guy who had a Ph.D. but didn't call himself doctor, had been a literary agent, and then a publisher, but had no interest in books. The mystery deepened. Who was this man?

On October 25, 1997, Dorothy Deering underwent surgery in a Lexington hospital to have her right knee replaced. She had been recuperating at home for a couple of weeks when Bill Richardson, while conversing in his office with Ron Spriggs and Jim Russo, complained that Dorothy and Chuck were spending too much of the joint venture money on themselves. He resented it because he was the one doing all the work and making all of the money. Even before her operation, Dorothy rarely came to the office. Now Chuck was staying home all day taking care of Dorothy. The literary agency was essentially in the hands of Chuck's uneducated son, Daniel Craig Deering. With Chuck talking about having his hips replaced, the kid could be running the agency for some time. If the Deering Literary Agency, Sovereign's biggest manuscript supplier, hit the skids under Daniel Craig, they would all be looking for work.

The future of the literary agency, Dorothy's medical condition, and her reckless spending put pressure on Bill Richardson to keep the money flowing into Sovereign. To make himself less dependent on Daniel Craig Deering for manuscripts, and to establish a fresh supply of joint venture money, Richardson sent letters to a hundred agents who charged fees, offering them a "finder's fee" for every client who signed with Sovereign. The joint venture kickback had been the brainchild of Jim Van Treese, but the joint venture *gift certificate* was pure Bill Richardson. Going back to his trusty mailing list, Richardson started sending fifty writers a week a one-thousand-dollar certificate that could be applied to the publication of their books. Designed by Ron Spriggs, the certificate itself, a cross between a dog food coupon and a payroll check, contained the writer's name as the payee, Richardson's signature as the payor, and an expiration date. There was also a space to type in the one thousand dollars and the title of the writer's book. The letter that accompanied the gift certificate read,

> Great news! Sovereign Publications is fulfilling the dreams of our authors with incredible success. Publisher, Dorothy Deering has created a few additional openings for publication in her next publishing season. Dorothy wants to bring your dream to Sovereign Publications to be published under her prestigious imprint of Appaloosa Press. Please apply this gift certificate of $1,000.00 toward your publishing contract. Join Sovereign Publications' other authors

who are becoming successfully published with Dorothy Deering's help. Please call me immediately to apply this gift and secure your publishing contract and publication date with America's fastest growing publishing house, Sovereign Publications.

Richardson closed the gift certificate cover letter with a message from Dorothy Deering herself.

Please accept my offer and let me help you with your publishing. I've built my publishing company by helping unknown authors & first-time authors fulfill their dreams. I will help you!

In his letter, Richardson used forms of *publish* or *publication* fourteen times, while forms of the word *dream* made three appearances and *help* or *helping* appeared four times. Dorothy was giving away a thousand dollars because she wanted to help writers realize their publishing dreams. Richardson had not been choosy in deciding who would receive Dorothy's gift; therefore the responses to it were varied. Ex-clients who had seen the light before losing more than their reading and contract fees got a good laugh out of it. Former clients who had been victimized by either ADP or NPI, or both, or were now fretting about CPI, were not so amused. Recipients of the gift certificate who already had a book with Sovereign were scared senseless by the proposition. Had Richardson and Dorothy Deering lost their minds? What kind of Mickey Mouse operation was this? Of course, a few writers treated the certificate as real money and took the bait.[3]

Early in November, Richardson heard that Dorothy had fired Dedre Smith, her bookkeeper. Curious to know why—and worried that Dedre had refused to cook the books—Richardson pressed his sister for an explanation. Any disagreement must have been about money; otherwise Dorothy wouldn't have fired the forty-year-old woman who was fighting cancer. Richardson didn't care that she had lost her job; he didn't get along with Dedre. He just wanted to know whether the reason for the firing involved money, because if it did, it involved him.[4]

Dorothy denied that Dedre's dismissal had anything to do with bookkeeping or company finances. Dorothy and Dedre were in the house working when the maid accidentally knocked over and broke an expensive lamp. Dedre didn't like the way Dorothy yelled at the maid, and that disagreement led to an argument. Not one to have her authority questioned, Dorothy fired the bookkeeper and the maid on the spot. That was according to Dorothy.

Dorothy's life began to unravel. Michael Helm, her adopted son, was shot to death in Kennesaw, Georgia, on the night of November 25, 1997, one month after her knee operation. The thirty-year-old drug dealer and former Deering employee died in the parking lot outside Cherokee Billiards. The autopsy revealed that shortly before his death, Helm had taken a large dose of cocaine. The police arrested Mike Foster, who claimed that Helm had been the aggressor and had come at him with a gun. The two men fought, and the firearm discharged, accidentally killing Helm with a bullet to the heart, a case of self-defense.[5]

With 1998 a month away, Richardson looked down the road and didn't like what he saw. The publication dates of fifty books had come and gone, and by spring, at least a hundred more were supposed to come out. Most of these manuscripts were still unread. Even if Richardson knew how to publish books, there wasn't enough time left to produce more than a handful of copies of a dozen titles. Ron Spriggs had designed six covers, and only four or five manuscripts were camera-ready. If something wasn't done, if someone didn't come up with a plan, Dorothy would have to deal with an author's revolt. Maybe it was time to call in the bankruptcy lawyers. Decisions had to be made that were bigger than Richardson. In December, just before Christmas, he called for an emergency meeting at Dorothy's house. He asked Jim Russo to attend.

With Michael Helm's death only a month old, Dorothy, addicted to the pain medicine she was taking for her knee, was in bad shape. But she pulled herself together and proposed a solution. Authors whose books were due, past due, or soon to come out would be told that the publication dates of their books were being *strategically* delayed for an indefinite period. These paperbacks were being kept off the market until the climate for bookselling improved. This was a marketing decision made in the authors' best interests.

Jim Russo, who was only two months into his four-month career with Sovereign, couldn't believe what he had just heard. Why had Richardson invited him to a family conspiracy to lie to clients and authors? His question was answered when Dorothy asked him whether he knew of any writers who would raise an unusually big stink over the delays. Russo replied that he had no idea how anyone would react. With that, the meeting came to an end.

The first time Russo ever heard anyone at Sovereign actually discuss the marketing of books, it was in the context of lying to authors about why their books weren't coming out. There was no marketing. Sovereign's marketing director, 19-year-old Jessica Johnson, wasn't working in Lexington. Richardson had transferred her to the literary agency, where she was keeping the client files updated now that Chuck was at home so much with Dorothy. Chuck's son, Daniel Craig, had essentially taken over the agency. Russo didn't know much about Chuck's boy except that he shared Bill Richardson's indifference to books. They were an odd bunch, the Deerings. A real mystery.

The sudden death of Michael Helm, although it had nothing to do directly or professionally with the Deering Literary Agency or Sovereign Publications, would significantly affect both companies. Genuinely distraught over the loss of her son and the impending loss of her life as a literary figure within the genteel racket, Dorothy, while fading deeper into the background, would use Michael's death and her ailing knee to keep the sham going as long as she could.

13 *Canadian Sunset*

CRAIG ANDREWS HAD BEEN A DEERING CLIENT for seven years. In 1993, he paid Dorothy one thousand dollars to have two of his novels published on disk. After the collapse of ADP, she talked the automobile engineer from Michigan into a $6,125 deal with Jim Van Treese and Northwest. That book never came out. Believing that Dorothy had also been a victim of NPI, Andrews sent her a $125 check to help pay her cost of going after Van Treese in court. In March of 1996, shortly after Dorothy had affiliated herself with Donald Phelan, Andrews signed a three-book deal with Commonwealth totaling $8,250. Borrowing from his 401(k) pension fund, he paid two thousand dollars down and the rest in eighteen monthly payments of $305. It was now December 1997, almost four months since the payment of his final installment and three months past the publication date of his fantasy-horror novels.

Andrews had been worried about the fate of his books since the "storm warning" alert in the October 1996 issue of *Writer's Digest* magazine. Since then, it had grown increasingly difficult to get anyone at CPI to return his calls. Having lived through the NPI nightmare and recognizing all the signs, Andrews was trying not to panic.

Craig Andrews had been a loyal Deering client. Over the years, he had paid the agency five thousand dollars in reading and contract fees and, knowing how busy Dorothy was, tried not to make a pest of himself. From Dorothy's point of view, he had been the perfect client.[1] Since she had talked him into the CPI deal and he had been such a good and patient client, he felt it appropriate to call her office and ask for help in sorting things out with Donald Phelan and CPI. A young woman he

90

didn't know answered the telephone and informed him that Dorothy Deering, because of a personal tragedy, was unavailable. Craig asked whether he could he speak to Chuck Deering. No, Mr. Deering, because he was caring for Mrs. Deering, was not taking calls, either. He would have to speak with Daniel Craig Deering, but Mr. Deering was not presently in the office. If Mr. Andrews would leave his number, Daniel Deering would return his call.

When it became apparent that Daniel Deering was not getting back to him, Andrews called and caught him in the office. Well, Daniel said after listening to Andrews's concerns and his request to have someone from the agency speak to Donald Phelan on his behalf, this was not a good time to ask for this kind of service. You see, Dorothy's beloved son, Michael, was murdered last month and everybody at the office was still in shock. As for CPI, it was true, the publisher was in trouble. Donald Phelan didn't know what he was doing and in all probability was going under. There was nothing anybody at the Deering agency could do about that. Andrews would just have to keep his fingers crossed and wait. Publishing was a rough business.

On October 16, 1997, nine days before Dorothy had her knee replaced, the attorney general of Utah filed criminal charges against her former mentor and business partner, Jim Van Treese. Van Treese, his son Jason, and a pair of former NPI executives were charged with numerous counts of communications fraud, securities fraud, tax evasion, and racketeering. According to the complaints, Van Treese and his accomplices had taken $10.5 million in joint venture money from as many as twenty-one hundred writers. Van Treese had filed for bankruptcy, but the trustee for NPI's creditors had filed suit asking that he be held *personally* liable for the money he had taken from the writers. The suit was based on the concept that one who uses a corporation to commit fraud cannot hide behind the corporate veil or take advantage of bankruptcy protection.

Donald Phelan, already under attack from a growing number of authors, former employees, writers' organizations, and *Writer's Digest* magazine, was not helped by Van Treese's arrest and the taint of criminality now associated with joint venture publishing. A disgruntled CPI author named David O'Neal established a Web site that functioned as sort of a support group for joint venture authors. The O'Neal site featured CPI updates, writers' "tales of woe," and a venue for the exchange of information. Unlike the propaganda issued by Phelan and the Deerings, these accounts were well written. One writer who contributed his tale of woe wrote,

> I'm in limbo; two books are virtually lost in the morass of Commonwealth chicanery. They won't talk to me; they won't correct the problem with the ISBN number; they aren't putting the book out where people can buy it. Sadly, almost daily, I get a note or message that somebody tried to buy my book and couldn't.[2]

According to his tale of woe, another Commonwealth author knew he was in trouble when

> I received my galleys and there were 1,136 typesetting errors; 500-plus of these were in one chapter alone. A chapter that was dialogue and typeset as one huge paragraph with quotation marks going every which way.[3]

Some of the CPI authors turned their anger inward, ashamed of themselves for letting their fantasies interfere with their reason. One such writer put it this way:

> Just as there is no quick road to riches, there is no quick road to literary success. Those of us who, in belief to the contrary, signed with CPI, have no one to blame but ourselves, our inflated egos and unproven sense of value of what we'd written. We turned to CPI because it was the easy way to get published. . . . As writers, we all tend to live in worlds of our own creation, but God help all of us when we can't recognize the difference between fantasy and reality.[4]

Most Commonwealth authors who told their stories on the O'Neal site directed the bulk of their wrath at CPI's owner, Donald Phelan.

> Because of the false promises of CPI, I am now forced to work two jobs to pay for the loan I received to pay my joint venture contribution. . . . The crook is free and living in the high lifestyle he is accustomed to while the victims are in "financial prisons" working to pay off the money he stole from them.[5]

None of these "Tales of Woe" authors, with the exception of writers who had been clients of Phelan's Canadian Literary Associates, had anything bad to say about literary agents, like Dorothy Deering, who had led them into the hellish world of joint venture publishing. Now it was becoming clear that joint venture publishing had never been a viable option and that legitimate literary agents would have known it, but that information wasn't enough to tarnish the kickback artists who had led so many of them to the slaughter. It looked as though these agents would escape the scandal unscathed.

In an attempt to stem the rising tide of suspicion, bad feeling, and panic, Phelan issued the following memo to his CPI authors:

> Over the past several weeks, an extraordinary chain of events has been the source of tremendous concern to Commonwealth Publications and to many of its authors. On the basis of the information we have been able to gather to date, it is clear that a consolidated and very well coordinated effort is currently underway to undermine the interests of our authors and those of Commonwealth itself. Motivated by a variety of goals ranging from the potential for personal monetary gain to the establishment of a competitive entity designed to seize our existing market share, a handful of industrious individuals have made it plain that it is their ambitious intent to disrupt Commonwealth operations to the point whereby we are no longer able to function.
>
> The industrious efforts of these individuals have included carefully choreographed interference with our communications, production, marketing and distribution capabilities. Their campaign has also extended into certain elements of the media, blending some of our existing internal difficulties with an imaginative array of rumor, innuendo and out-right fabricating as a means of conjuring up the most twisted portrayal of Commonwealth possible.
>
> We trust you will not be deceived by these nefarious tactics or by the slanted reports they may generate. As with any new business, we have encountered many challenges and difficulties. However, our accomplishments to date cannot be dismissed or ignored. Although Commonwealth is little more than three years old, our achievements in various market segments have far exceeded those of some of the more established publishing companies within the book trade.[6]

Donald Phelan didn't identify the people conspiring to bring him down. Perhaps he was thinking of Steve Esrati and David O'Neal, two of his more active and vocal detractors. Moreover, he didn't reveal what it was they were saying about him and his company that wasn't true. And he didn't name Sovereign Publications as "the competitive entity designed to seize our existing market share." By blaming these unnamed enemies for his problems, Phelan diverted attention from the real reason CPI was failing. CPI, like NPI before it, and Sovereign after it, was nothing more than a pyramid–vanity publishing scheme that never had a chance of succeeding for the coinvesting author.

One of CPI's authors published his reaction to Phelan's letter on the O'Neal Web site.

> What a shock to receive Phelan's form letter attributing our problems to a dark conspiracy to take over his company. He rambled on long enough to wind up saying that the authors had clogged up his communications system and it was our fault![7]

Three weeks after he tried to clear the air with his all-author letter, Phelan watched in horror as three of his former employees and three CPI authors blew the whistle on the nationally televised Canadian Broadcast Corporation program *Marketplace*. The episode, entitled "Paying Companies to Publish Books," aired on January 13, 1998. The host of the fifteen-minute segment introduced the exposé as follows:

> This is a story of promises made but not kept. We spoke to dozens of authors from Victoria, B.C., to Deming, New Mexico, to Ridgefield, Connecticut, to the United Kingdom, to New Zealand. All shared the same complaint—"Show me the book. Show me the money."

The former employees, three attractive women in their twenties—an account executive, Phelan's personal secretary, and the publicity manager—reported that none of the manuscripts were read until after the joint venture contracts were signed. According to the secretary, when Phelan still owned Canadian Literary Associates, he would send his clients fake rejection letters from Dell, Fawcett, and Bantam to soften them up for his joint venture pitch. The ex-publicity manager declared, "I had no finances, no money. Basically, I had to tell authors to try to get publicity locally. I couldn't do anything for them." The former account executive said that because Phelan owed a printing and graphics company $194,000, it was hard finding anyone to do that work. No one at CPI wanted to answer the telephone because most of the calls were from angry authors. All three of the former employees said they had quit because they got tired of lying to writers about their books.

One of the authors on the show, Craig Etchison, the West Virginia English professor who, as one of Phelan's literary clients, paid thirty-three hundred dollars to have his fantasy novel published, said that only 250 copies of *The World Weaver* were ever printed, 9,750 fewer than the contract promised. Referring to Phelan and CPI, he said, "They are liars. They are cheats. They are not legitimate."

Dave O'Neal published a transcript of the show on his Web site, and one could purchase a video of the program from CBC. Eighteen days after the airing of the show, the *Edmonton Journal* ran a story featuring a seventy-year-old author from San Diego who had filed a complaint with the Writers' Union of Canada. Referring to the San Diego man, Phelan was quoted as saying, "The people who complained the most are those who have literally harassed our staff."

In a last-ditch attempt to buy a little time, Phelan mailed a nine-page letter to more than a thousand writers, outlining how he planned to save the company.

> Although the original intent of this letter was to address the various internal and external problems that have confronted us over the last few months, I feel obligated to first respond to the barrage of rumors that have been circulated regarding Commonwealth—particularly those appearing on the Internet. As a publisher, I naturally have the opportunity to review all types and styles of writing on a daily basis. But I have never before witnessed such an explosion of creative fiction in one venue as that generated by those individuals who have elected to educate the general public as to the inner workings of our company. Suggestions that Commonwealth is a front for a terrorist organization or that we are actually a subsidiary of the now defunct Northwest Publications [*sic*] or that our General Manager, Ken Malloy [*sic*], is in reality my own brother, are simply beyond belief. No less utterly fantastic is the remark that Commonwealth is on the verge of bankruptcy. Quite the contrary. We continue to press forward, steadily opening up new markets that are proving beneficial to all concerned. . . .
>
> P.S. I deliberately withheld this letter until the airing of CBC MARKETPLACE so that I might comment on it. Suffice to say that I have difficulties in the extreme with statements made by each and every individual on the program.[8]

Working with a skeleton crew composed of his top assistant, Ken Molloy, his son Ryan, his sister Carol, his brother Michael, and three or four others, Phelan pressed forward. Writers who queried CPI in February and March received, shortly thereafter, a form letter response and a joint venture contract. These contracts were going out at a time when Phelan knew CPI had no future.[9]

In mid-April, on the day NPI authors learned that Van Treese's preliminary hearing had been postponed to July, Don Phelan, in a memo faxed to hundreds of writers, declared that Commonwealth Publications had "ceased doing business." He concluded his announcement this way:

I realize that many of you are asking for a return of your author contributions. This is simply not possible as Commonwealth lacks sufficient funds to do so. I am concerned that if Commonwealth Publications, Inc. is placed in bankruptcy, that I will be unable to offer a return of property to authors and that authors will have to reclaim their rights and manuscripts from a trustee.

That spring an Edmonton attorney filed a class action suit against CPI on behalf of fifty authors. The plaintiffs sought relief from their joint venture contracts and the return of the publishing rights to their books.

Phelan's house, in Sherwood Park, a suburban community outside Edmonton, was up for sale. He was living in Great Falls, Montana, where he was operating his new business, a book distribution company called Redmoor International.

An investigation of CPI by the Commercial Crime Section of the Royal Canadian Mounted Police fizzled out. According to a spokesman for the agency, there wasn't enough evidence of fraud to support a criminal charge.

Jim Van Treese was in jail, Donald Phelan was in Montana, and Dorothy Deering, the owner of Sovereign Publications, was in trouble.

*She [Dorothy Deering] operates under strict guidelines of Morrow
character and values.*

—Bill Richardson

14 Sovereign Digest

IN JANUARY 1998, about the time Phelan's ex-employees and three of
his authors were blasting him on TV, Bill Richardson called the Sovereign editorial staff into his office to lay them off. With Jim Russo and
Michelle Mueller out the door, there were no more editors or college
graduates on the payroll. There was no longer any need for an editor or
a person who had gone to college at Sovereign Publications.

Dorothy had a new housekeeper, a fresh bookkeeper, a physical thera-
pist, and an automatic lift that carried her up and down her stairs. In
February, after Chuck had his hips replaced, Bill Richardson told Carolyn
Thue that it wouldn't be a bad idea for her to start looking for a new job.
He suspected that the Deerings were about to declare bankruptcy, then
flee to Florida where they could hole up with Chuck's mother until the
storm passed. But until they got used to their new body parts, Dorothy
and Chuck weren't going anywhere.

In the meantime, Dorothy had to figure some way to beef up her dwin-
dling cash flow. She was attracting writers through the Sovereign Web site,
but she wanted something more tangible. This need led to the February
1998 publication of the first and last issue of the *Sovereign Digest*. The
six-page publication, designed by Ron Spriggs, looked like a scaled-down
version of a weekly newspaper. A photograph of Sovereign's new world
headquarters in Lexington dominated the front page. The caption beneath the photograph of the building at 128 E. Reynolds Road read,

> The new facility offers a more professional appearance and fulfills Sovereign's
> needs more efficiently. The addition of our Cover Design and Graphics Arts

Department and the Development of our newly reorganized Editorial and Submissions departments were also critical factors.

Assuming that "reorganized" meant "eliminated" and the Cover Design and Graphics Arts Department meant Ron Spriggs, the above caption wasn't that misleading. That the new location gave Sovereign Publications "a more professional appearance" served Dorothy's interests more than it did her authors'. The writers would have been better served with a less impressive building that housed a few editors and equipment to publish books. But you can't have everything, and in Dorothy's business, after the *Sovereign Digest,* the building came first.

Recipients of Dorothy's digest were given the opportunity to use the order form on the last page to purchase books from a list of "Sovereign's Top 10 Best Sellers." The list consisted of two books by Dorothy (her children's book and a pamphlet she had self-published years ago), Ron Spriggs's booklet on management styles, Ted Nottingham's two books, a Sovereign western that never came out, and four paperbacks that included a novel by a New Orleans lawyer named L. D. Sledge who was trying to regain the rights to his book.[1]

By showing the building and a list of Sovereign "best sellers," Dorothy had set the stage for the real reason behind the *Sovereign Digest:* to attract new joint venture authors and to milk more money out of the writers she had already hooked. Under the front-page heading, "Authors Request Upgrading," Bill Richardson pitched a shameless new scheme that arose from Dorothy's desperate need of cash.

In the past several months, many Sovereign authors have requested upgrade sizing of their books. These authors wanted to increase the size from mass-market to the larger trade size editions because they thought their books would look better and make more money at the larger size. After some research with our production, editing and accounting departments, Dorothy and I decided that it would be possible.

The cost of such an upgrade is considerable when you account for the cost of paper, binding, shipping and redesigning of the blue line pages. Dorothy and I asked these authors to share part of the burden with us and they agreed without hesitation. The author's share of upgrading from mass-market size papers to the larger size editions is two thousand dollars. . . . Dorothy and I believe that this upgrade would be more profitable for the author. Considering that the larger trade-size editions sell at a price of almost twice that of a small mass-market book, you can imagine the increase in revenue for yourself. This two thousand dollar investment will almost double your book profits for the entire life of your book.

The upgrade con was brilliant because it not only raised a lot of money quickly (about one hundred thousand dollars), it provided an excellent excuse to delay the production of fifty books. Dorothy had outdone herself.

In another *Sovereign Digest* article, "Publish or Perish," Richardson tried to talk Sovereign authors into having him publish their second and third books.

As more and more authors seek the esteemed career goal of being *published* authors, medium-size independent publishers like Sovereign Publications have successfully evolved to offer these people a very valuable opportunity. Previously published authors are experiencing difficulty finding a chance to have a second or third book published by the same publisher. Their first book must sell a minimum of 25,000 copies to receive duplicate treatment from their existing publisher. Even at Sovereign, we are very deliberate about decisions on second and third publishing contracts to previously published authors. The publishing offers you receive today are few and far between and may be the only opportunities you ever see.

I receive at least 1,000 new submissions per month at Sovereign Publications. Every one of these authors believe that they are the next John Grisham. They are seeking publication for their work and actually believe they should be treated on the same level as John Grisham. For those of you that want to hear my thoughts, I have too many authors wanting our lucrative publishing contract as it stands.

The Sovereign contract pays higher royalties and includes an abundance of features to market your book. Remember, for Sovereign's success to continue, I must sell your book. I cannot leave the success of your book to chance, neither can you. You have decisions about the future of your unpublished manuscript and your family's legacy.

So please dust off your potential best seller and live the dream. I have always said, *"successful authors do what unsuccessful authors don't."*

It's hard to imagine anyone reading this article and not thinking that Richardson was either nuts or crooked. From this letter, it wouldn't be unreasonable to conclude that he was both. And if anyone had questions about Dorothy's integrity, professionalism, or emotional stability, her article about the death of her son should have settled the issue.

> First of all, I would like to thank all of you for the letters, cards, flowers and kindness shown to me and my family after the tragic death of my son, Mike, on November 25, 1997. . . . We again thank you from the bottom of our hearts for your kindness.
>
> Please, if you intend to send flowers, we ask that you make a donation to our grandson's memorial college fund in the name of Michael Orry Helm Memorial College Fund and addressed to the Sovereign office.

Apparently, there was no occasion Dorothy wouldn't exploit to raise money from her clients and authors.[2] If that didn't make her writers cringe, then her second *Digest* piece, "My Knee Hurts," should have done the trick.

> I feel like I've fallen and can't get up. On October 27, 1997, my right knee was replaced. I thought I had made the wrong decision. I would have done anything to have my old knee again. My husband, Chuck, had his hands full. I even heard him mumbling in a low voice. I didn't quite hear what he was saying. I must have been terrible to live with during my recovery. I didn't even want to hear about exercising my new knee. I hid under the covers when I heard the doorbell ringing, hoping it wasn't the physical therapist. Just the thought of some perfect stranger bending my knee into positions that it wasn't ever able to do prior to the surgery sent shock waves all the way through Chuck's body.
>
> Poor Chuck, I don't know what I would have done without him. But if he calls me the bionic woman one more time, I am going to show him what a real knee feels like. Just kidding, honey.
>
> To everyone, I want to thank my darling, thoughtful husband, Chuck, for all the care he rendered. I found the real meaning of through thick and thin. I love you, Chuck. I just want to tell the world that when you go to the hospital for both of his [*sic*] hips to be replaced on the 13th of February, 1998, I will be there for you, Darling. I just want you to know that I will be mumbling loud enough for you to hear what I'm saying. Good luck, Honey.

Other than being in the throes of some weird, sociopathic seizure (one out of every ten words in Dorothy's article was "I"), there is no explanation why she would punish her clients and authors with this puerile love letter to herself. If she published drivel like this, she'd publish anything. Dorothy was better off just telling lies.

In his unrelenting quest for joint venture prospects, Bill Richardson discovered in early 1998, in boxes of A Rising Sun papers, a cache of manuscripts that had been under representation by Vicki and Chris Scott when their agency went under. Ellen Brazer, a client from Miami, Florida, had called the agency in January 1997 to check on her novel, "Hearts of Fire." Instead of talking to Vicki or Chris Scott, she found herself speaking to some guy named Michael Helm who said he worked for the literary agency in Nicholasville, Kentucky, that had taken over A Rising Sun. Dorothy Deering, the agent who now represented Brazer until her contract with the Savannah agency ran out, was not in the office. Helm said he would have Ms. Deering return her call. That call never came, and because Michael Helm sounded spaced out, Brazer didn't bother getting back in touch with her new agent. She moved on and, in a sense, dodged a bullet.

A year after she had spoken to the guy who sounded like he was high on something, Brazer received a call from a man who said he was Bill Richardson, the head of Sovereign Publications in Lexington, Kentucky. He had just read her novel, "Hearts of Fire," and absolutely *loved* it. In fact, he wanted to publish it as a mass-market paperback. Brazer had no idea how this publisher had gotten his hands on her novel, but she was thrilled.

A few days after that exciting phone call, Richardson sent Brazer a form letter that read,

> Congratulations! It is with great pleasure to inform you that "Hearts of Fire" has been accepted by the editorial department and approved by the publisher. Your manuscript is creative, original, and, we believe a highly remarkable work.

Richardson enclosed the one and only issue of the *Sovereign Digest* and a complimentary copy of Ted Nottingham's novel, *The Final Profit*. He also sent a joint venture contract calling for a five-thousand-dollar author's contribution. Brazer looked over the material Richardson had sent and gave him a call.[3]

> *Brazer:* Okay. I got your contract in the mail, and I have some questions to ask you. First of all, I'm incredibly excited, and I'm feeling vulnerable, too. I mean, a lot of years of my life went into this book and I wanted to ask you a couple of things. . . . I wanted to ask you, on page two, what does this mean when it says the author agrees that the publisher prevails in any dispute over editing, design or cover? My biggest concern right now is my

ability to protect my work as far as the editing is concerned. Not if you change a word or a sentence but, I mean, chapters from being cut or, you know, that kind of thing from happening.

Richardson: Well, my basic philosophy of the editing department, and I can hire a lot of editors, but it's rare that I find one, and you can't buy this trait. And what that trait is being able to edit in the author's words. And that is what my editing department is, that's their rules, and that's how they operate. So they have to edit in your words.

Brazer: Which means what?

Richardson: That they're not going to—you're not going to be at some arbitrary whims of some editor. . . .

Brazer: But, I mean then they don't cut out characters, they don't . . .

Richardson: Absolutely not. . . . They do line editing. One of the things that we do—we don't offer contracts to somebody that's needing re-writes. We don't want to re-write anything. We want the author's book to stand as is. So we take that into consideration in the evaluation before we send a contract to them.

Brazer: Okay. . . . The other thing, one question I have is um—I have another connection—with a major motion picture studio. I don't know if it's gonna help, and when I talk to your public relations people, I'll talk to them about that. But you get fifty percent of the proceeds. Is that standard?

Richardson: Standard in all publishing houses.

Brazer: Okay.

Richardson: Uh, we're very active in Hollywood. Dorothy, the publisher, she had dinner with Sydney Pollack during the summer. He wants to see everything that we are producing. She sold things—we're in negotiations with Disney right now, and we're actively seeking movie rights to the book, that's our goal.

Brazer: Okay, that's wonderful. . . . Now, how are you connected with Morrow?

Richardson: Uh, Dorothy Deering is the granddaughter of the original Morrow who started the Morrow Publishing Company.

Brazer: So that's the only connection, the family line?

Richardson: Plus, she was involved with the company somewhere along the way. And she was originally going to go out and open her own publishing company but her grandfather stopped her—she wouldn't have his blessing or his money if she did that first. She had to go to become a literary agent. She started a literary agency and became the third largest literary agent in the world, and that was over a ten-year period of time and took her two years to set this publishing house up. The doors have been open for a year and a half now.

Brazer: Oh, so you're new?

Richardson: Yeah, very new, but very well connected, and very well financed. We have a very scholarly staff here.

Brazer: Somebody asked me—when you tell somebody you're paying five thousand dollars to a company people are not familiar with, you know, you get a lot of comments, and somebody said to me—how do I know you'll print five thousand books? I mean . . .

Richardson: There's a couple publishers that are out of the country. Say, for instance, Canada maybe, there's nothing you can do with that, no matter what they do. We operate by United States laws.

Brazer: Okay.

Richardson: You have Dorothy, who, as a Morrow, she operates under strict guidelines of Morrow character and values. We don't print pornography, we don't do anything such as that. Thirty percent of what we do is all Christian work out of *Christian Writer's Market.*

Brazer: How have you done with your books since this new company?

Richardson: We've had movie offers on the first two.

Brazer: All right!

Richardson: If that tells you anything.

Brazer: That's very exciting . . . okay, great. Terrific. Wonderful, Bill. All right, well then I guess I'm going to sign this contract and we are going to be in business, my friend.

Richardson: Okay.

Brazer: I have . . . what?

Richardson: I've got a couple spots still open in the catalogue that we're producing, and that's a very good place to be in.

Brazer: Okay.

Richardson: Because all the books that we've had so far—they get in the catalogue—and we're taking back orders on books we don't even have designed yet.

Brazer: People buy them without knowing what they are about?

Richardson: Yeah! I mean, they send checks!

Brazer: You're kidding. Really?

Richardson: People send checks, bookstores start ordering them. . . .

Brazer: That's interesting.

Richardson: Sometimes our distributor says, "Hey, what's this book about? You know, we want to move on orders for it right now if that will help you spur it along."

Brazer: Let me ask you something. You said you were a year and a half old. So, the capitalization of the company and all, you guys are pretty strong?

Richardson: Dorothy was the third largest literary agent in the world. She sold 550 books to publishers and 130 screenplays to Hollywood.

Brazer: Okay.

Richardson: Plus she has some Morrow money behind her.

Brazer: Okay. All right, that sounds good enough for . . .

Richardson: She's not connected to the Morrow family, but she's inherited some.

Brazer: All right, kiddo, well I guess we're set.

Richardson: The first year in business we were operating off her investment, but we're totally on our own, we're making money now.

Brazer: Okay, terrific.

Richardson: We're very solvent . . . and, if you can rush that contract I, I'll make sure you get a good spot in this catalogue.

Brazer: Okay, that sounds like a deal there. . . .[4]

Ellen Brazer, on the strength of a form letter, a sample book, and one phone conversation with a man she didn't know, sent a five-thousand-dollar check to have her book published by a company she had never heard of. If Sovereign Publications was so solvent, so well financed, so connected to Hollywood with directors and distributors thirsting for their books, why did Bill Richardson need her five thousand dollars? That simple contradiction should have, by itself, short-circuited the deal. As a con man, Richardson was not particularly slick or well schooled. Brazer, an intelligent and talented person, had been victimized by her own excitement, and belief in her book. Selling writers to themselves was a lot easier than selling carpets.

Per your contract, this was an act that was out of our hands, and in God's hands as I pray my son is.

—Dorothy Deering

15 The Act-of-God Defense

BY JANUARY 1998, WRITERS WHO HAD BEEN WAITING months for some evidence—edited manuscripts, galleys, cover art—that their books were being published, were screaming bloody murder. The telephones at Sovereign and the literary agency were constantly ringing, and no one wanted to pick up the phone and catch hell from another crazed author. Richardson and Daniel Craig Deering had to make their telephone sales pitches from home. Something had to be done to quiet these writers; they were interfering with business, which consisted of talking more writers out of more money.

Dorothy had been into this kind of trouble back in 1995 with ADP. Before she dumped the company, she had used illness and the death of a brother-in-law to gain sympathy and buy time. Back then, however, most of her authors were out a mere five hundred dollars. Her Sovereign victims had invested ten times that amount, and there were more of them. But this time, in the areas of death and illness, she had a lot more to work with.

On the last week of February, four months after her knee surgery and three months after the death of her son, Dorothy sent a letter to Sovereign authors that announced a six-month delay on the publication of every book, including those that had been already delayed due to "market conditions." In justifying this action, she wrote,

> I am sure you know by now about the loss of our son and the serious operations both Charles and I are going through. I am recovering from knee replacement and have another one to go, and Charles just had both hips replaced Friday,

February 13. We cannot be at work on any sort of a regular basis and still have the care we need. Therefore, regretfully, we are forced to push back all of our titles approximately six months. I am very sorry about this inconvenience but losing my son, Mike, was a tragedy I am having to recover from somehow, and I will get through it but grief is a personal thing for everyone and I need care currently. Charles cannot walk at this time and is trying to help take care of me. Our other children are helping take care of us but it is understandably a very difficult time. The holidays were especially hard for me because Mike and I were Christmas lovers in this family and always made special plans for the rest of our family.

I ask for your understanding now. You know us and know that we set this company up to take better care of our authors, especially our first time authors and authors who have been abused by other publishing companies in the past. We just need this healing time and no one else can do our specific jobs. Please help us by giving us this time to recuperate. I cannot work and get through this. When Charles is healed, I go for my other knee. The healing process is long and difficult as I found out with my knee and I think he is very brave getting two hips done at the same time.

Personally, I did not know there were so many tears within a human being as I have shed for my son. I cannot even go out because I start crying wherever I am but I am having counseling through my church and it is a help. Also, if you have been through this, please get counseling for the grief so you can utilize some of the healing tools they teach you. I am trying to learn them but Mike's death was just two months ago and it is still so hard to keep focused on anything, even to writing this letter to you.

You can rest assured that when we are well, things will get back to normal and we will publish the books in the order in which we received your contracts.

Per your contract, this was an act that was out of our hands, and in God's hands as I pray my son is. Thank you for your consideration and prayers.

The letter didn't work. In fact, it made things worse. Dorothy's authors had run out of patience before she ran out of knees to cry about. Two weeks after the tear-soaked kiss-off, Bill Richardson, in an effort to restore good order and get his phones back, distributed a memo instructing these crazy writers to stop calling the office. In case they didn't get the message, he issued a warning:

I will be monitoring the calls in the future, and ask that you please wait until you are contacted by the various departments. For the most part, our authors demonstrate great professionalism and patience. If you are in this group, please ignore this letter. If you are of the other group, we will likely be having a conversation that could jeopardize your publication date.

With Dorothy tied up with her Sovereign problems, and Chuck at home recovering from his hip replacement surgery, the Deering Literary Agency had fallen into the hands of Chuck's twenty-two-year-old son, Daniel Craig. Dorothy's clients were demanding to know what they had received for their contract fees. Without Chuck, the files were in disarray, and without Dorothy, there was no one in the office to artfully lie to clients. Daniel Craig Deering, who was only interested in making joint venture deals, didn't have time to fool around with Dorothy's crybaby clients. The agency, crumbling from within, was no longer of any use to Dorothy, so she "sold" it to Daniel Craig for one dollar. That March he moved out of the office in downtown Nicholasville and set up business in his house at 120 Davis Drive in the Orchard subdivision at the edge of town. He had one employee, a young woman who worked part-time answering the phone and keeping track of files. He liked to tell writers he had purchased the agency for two hundred thousand dollars. Besides charging reading and contract fees, he now offered a line-editing service for which writers were asked to pay three dollars to five dollars per manuscript page to have their books polished up for publishing. A hustler with a drug habit who never finished high school was doing business in Kentucky as a freelance book editor and literary agent. Only in America.

In March 1998, after dumping the literary agency she had owned and operated for ten years, Dorothy and Chuck began seriously considering bankruptcy for Sovereign Publications. They began meeting with an attorney in Lexington named Charles Grundy who didn't know the history of the company or anything about the Deerings. As Dorothy and Chuck made arrangements to protect their assets from their pain-in-the-neck writers, Bill Richardson kept the gift certificates circulating, pushed trade paper upgrades, and ran magazine ads soliciting manuscripts for Sovereign Publications. The money kept coming in—sixty thousand dollars in upgrades alone—but no books would be coming out. Having been bled dry since the day it was created eighteen months earlier, Sovereign staggered on, victimizing writers who had no idea they were feeding a zombie.

16 Death Heads Units

DIANE GOSHGARIAN WAS OUTRAGED WHEN SHE RECEIVED Dorothy's letter about not calling Sovereign. The forty-five-year-old nurse from Brookline, Massachusetts, who had worked three years on an historical novel based on her grandmother's struggle to survive the Armenian genocide during World War I, had been greatly influenced by Dorothy's promise to treat every Sovereign author as though they were well-known writers. She had signed on with Dorothy after seeing the Deering ad in *Literary Market Place.* Six months later, Dorothy talked her into paying $6,425 to have "Arbitrary Sword" published. Less than a month earlier, after reading the *Sovereign Digest,* Goshgarian had paid another two thousand dollars to have her book, already six months past its publication date, upgraded to trade paperback. Now she was learning that her book was going to be pushed back another six months. She was not happy.

Diane didn't understand why Dorothy's bad knees, the death of her son, and Chuck Deering's new hips had delayed, again, the publication of her book. Was there something wrong with Bill Richardson, too? In a letter to Dorothy in which she expressed sympathy for the loss of her son, Goshgarian wrote,

> It makes me very uneasy that you accepted more money from me ($2,000) to upgrade the book to a trade size at a time when you knew you were not going to be able to meet your current obligation. You did not inform me that there were problems with production prior to accepting this money and I have learned through my bank that the check I sent was cashed. If this money is truly

to be used for an upgrade, wouldn't it be more appropriate to request the money when the book is actually going to print?

I have invested my share (a total now of $8,425) in the publication of this book. Now I need to know from you that you will do your part to ensure that I get what we mutually agreed to, i.e., the publication of my book, *The Arbitrary Sword*.

Although Goshgarian had written to Dorothy, Bill Richardson was the one who replied to her letter. The reason the publication of her novel had been delayed, he said, had nothing to do with Dorothy's personal tragedies. The book was being held back because Dorothy had decided it needed further editing — this from the man who had fired all of his editors, and told Ellen Brazer that at Sovereign "we want the author's book to stand as is." Richardson, after rambling on about the high costs and difficulties of publishing, including insulting remarks like "How could you possibly know any of this information, you're just the author," concluded his letter this way:

> Dorothy is not only recovering from total knee replacement, but she is struggling to survive everyday. Your letter upset her so much that she sat and cried all over again. She needs our love and kindness so she can return and help the rest of us survive. Please refrain from being so emotional over this situation.

As a coinvestor in her own book, Goshgarian didn't like being told she was "just the author," and she had used up all of her love and kindness for Dorothy, and the knucklehead who had written her this ridiculous, disgusting, and insulting letter. Did they take her for a fool? It was time to call a lawyer.

A week after Bill Richardson tried to put Diane Goshgarian in her place, Dorothy received, at her house in Lexington, a certified letter from an attorney in Boston demanding, within ten days, the return of her client's money. By not publishing Goshgarian's book within the time frame promised, Dorothy Deering had breached the contract, rendering it null and void. Because Dorothy had solicited the so-called upgrade money when she had no intention of publishing Goshgarian's book on time, the author was charging her with "unfair, false, misleading and deceptive conduct" in violation of Kentucky's Consumer Protection Act. The attorney, making reference to Bill Richardson's "threatening and incoherent" letter, made a threat of her own: If Goshgarian didn't get back her $8,425, a complaint would be filed with the Kentucky attorney general's office.

The last thing Dorothy needed was her own version of Steve Esrati, the writer who had stood up to Donald Phelan. She was furious with her brother for stirring up the hornet's nest with that insulting letter. Writers like Goshgarian had to be finessed, not threatened and humiliated. How could he be such a thug? Having decided to handle this problem herself, Dorothy, being as sweet as she could be, picked up the phone and called her author.

After apologizing for her brother, and the embarrassing misunderstanding, Dorothy said she would push forward the editing of "The Arbitrary Sword." Goshgarian had Dorothy's solemn promise that in three months, ten thousand copies of her upgraded book would be in the stores selling like hotcakes. When the first printing sold out, and it would be because Dorothy planned to market the book aggressively, another fifteen hundred copies would be rushed into print. How did that sound?

Still smarting over Bill Richardson, and no longer able to trust Dorothy, Goshgarian said she wanted all of this in writing. She would ask her lawyer to incorporate these new terms into a side agreement Dorothy would have to sign. After sending Dorothy a letter confirming the substance of their phone conversation, Dorothy called back and left the following message on Diane's answering machine: "I don't answer to any pissant lawyers."

When Bill Richardson received a copy of the modified publishing agreement drawn up by Diane Goshgarian's attorney, he too was furious. This writer had a lot of nerve making a deal with Dorothy behind his back. He felt this was a direct challenge to his authority, and he wouldn't stand for it. He was upset not only with his sister but also her husband, Chuck. While he was out there raising money and doing battle with a growing mob of self-deluding, egotistical whiners, the Deerings were behind the front lines indulging themselves with new body parts and living in the lap of luxury.

To make sure that Goshgarian understood that Dorothy Deering was no longer in control of Sovereign Publications, Richardson faxed this letter to her attorney:

> Rewriting our contract is not within your powers as an attorney. In fact, I don't
> believe you have any experience in entertainment law or copyright law or pub-

lishing law. Your claims are contrary to the publishing laws of this country and industry. The contract will stand as is, without exceptions. This contract is a legal document and was signed by your client. We will not change any part of this contract.

Diane is only a first-time author and really doesn't understand anything but harassment. She's tried to circumvent the process of publishing by harassing my employees. Diane created so much termoil [*sic*] within our editing staff that she affected the whole publishing schedule for the company. She's been put on communication probation and only allowed to speak to me.

Not content to merely portray himself as an unschooled, chauvinistic jackass, Richardson proceeded to document the fact he had suffered some kind of emotional breakdown that plagued overwrought swindlers.

If you wish to debate in front of a judge our contract, section B.1. "*unless prevented by circumstances beyond it's control,*" please be my guest. We will be up to the task. We will have death certificates, a grieving mother, testimony from surgeons about Dorothy and Charles [*sic*] major surgeries and two publishers in wheel chairs in this courtroom.

The courtroom image of Dorothy and Chuck sitting long-faced in their wheelchairs with enlarged photographs of Michael Helm held against their broken hearts, must have sent chills through the attorney. The lawyer must have wondered how someone like Diane Goshgarian had gotten tied up with people like this. She had written a serious book, tried to get it published, and ended up having her money stolen by a guy who had put her on "communication probation."

The attorney, referring to Richardson's letters as "foolish, condescending and factually inaccurate," restated her client's demands and threatened to file a formal complaint with the Kentucky attorney general's office. Richardson, his wrath now directed at the attorney, came back with this:

Your emotional, insulting nature will undoubtedly work against you in court. It won't take much effort on my part for you to lose control. You're already highly irritated and out-of-control over the first rounds of dialogue. You're [*sic*] quick response to my fax shows an aggressive and impulsive character flaw. You'll be able to blend into the Kentucky legal system should you pursue this course of action.

Without explaining what it was about Kentucky's legal system that rewarded character-flawed attorneys, Richardson listed thirteen reasons why Diane Goshgarian's complaints against Sovereign Publications were not only groundless but mean-spirited. Three of these reasons incorporated the Deering's surgeries and the fact that "Dorothy's son was murdered while she had just came [sic] out of surgery." Under reason number 10, Richardson wrote, "I am sure a court will have mercy on the Deerings, even if a lawyer from Boston doesn't. A delay is a delay and is not the end of the world. Why act as if your client has been murdered?"

Who said anything about murder? Was this some kind of Freudian slip, or had this guy turned homicidal? Goshgarian wondered whether she was supposed to take that as a threat.

Goshgarian realized that she would not be getting her $8,425 back, and that suing Sovereign Publications would be throwing good money after bad. So she did what she could to protect other writers from becoming victims. She wrote a long letter to the attorney general of Kentucky in which she told and documented her story, describing Sovereign as a troubled and deceitful operation. A few days later, she received a form letter stating that her complaint had been forwarded to Sovereign for reply and for a possible resolution to the dispute. If her problem with the company in question required legal action, she was advised to obtain the services of an attorney. This was not the response Goshgarian had hoped for. She already had a lawyer, and had she been able to resolve her problem with Sovereign, she wouldn't have written to the attorney general.

Goshgarian, having been on the receiving end of Bill Richardson's wrath, braced herself for his reaction to what she had done. She didn't have to wait very long, and when it came, it took her by surprise. She received a thousand-dollar gift certificate toward the publication of her next book. On the coupon itself, in the place where the title of the manuscript was identified, someone had typed, "Death Heads Units."[1] Goshgarian had not written a book by that name. Having already concluded that Richardson was emotionally unstable, she took this as a threat. Her battle with Bill Richardson entered a new and frightening stage.

A week after she received the gift certificate, the attorney general sent Goshgarian Richardson's official response to her complaint. It was enclosed with a form letter that read, "This information is being provided so you may have an opportunity to know the company's position regarding your complaint." Richardson's two-page letter revealed more about his deteriorating personality than it did his side of the dispute. Since he didn't have a valid defense to Goshgarian's complaint, he attacked her personally.

> I must tell you that Ms. Goshgarian is an accomplished, but unknown first time author. She is able to paint vivid, realistic pictures with her writings and have the reader believe any fictional untruth that she wishes to create. Ms. Goshgarian is Armenian and believes that the whole world persecuted her family for generations and owes her something of which I'm not prepared to give. She has taken this aggression out on my employees and at times, I have had to limit her phone calls and communications to my office only. She has shown an overwhelming desire to have her book published without consideration of fundamental business practices. She has gone behind my back and begged, manipulated my employees to move her book up on the list in front of authors that were contracted before she was contracted. When I found out about this, I put her in her correct place in line. She immediately began to lash out at my position as vice president and as a man. There will never be a day when a first time, unknown author tells me how to run this publishing company.

It was no wonder Bill Richardson was so distraught. He had two women trying to tell him how to run Sovereign Publications. One was a fake literary agent hooked on pain pills and the other a lying Armenian out to destroy his manhood. Having accused Goshgarian of possessing a persecution complex, Richardson revealed that he had one.

> Dorothy's son was murdered two weeks after her surgery. She has been totally devastated and probably will never be the same. Ms. Goshgarian says she doesn't care about any of Dorothy's problems. She is cold hearted and very cruel to anyone else's but her own problems. Maybe the torture and misfortunes of her race of people has caused her to treat others without much understanding. That's a shame.

> Ms. Goshgarian signed a publishing contract that protects the publisher as well as the author. The contract says, "Publisher agrees to publish the Work within eighteen months after receipt of signed contract, provided it is not hindered by conditions out of it's control." I think that two major surgeries and the unplanned murder of her son qualify as circumstances out of her control.

The *unplanned murder?* What did he mean by that? Was this another Freudian slip? Was Richardson implying that Diane Goshgarian thought Dorothy had planned her son's homicide as a breach of contract defense? On July 15, 1998, Goshgarian, convinced that Richardson possessed an unstable, perhaps criminal personality, wrote another letter to the attorney general's office. This time she made it clear her problem was more than a consumer-type dispute over the terms of a publishing contract. She wanted an investigation of the "Death Heads Units" threat as well as a fraud investigation of Sovereign Publications.

> I believe that Sovereign will continue to make false claims as to the work they are doing on behalf of the clients and the money they have spent doing it. I think they will even sporadically release a few books to make it appear that their business is legitimate. I can't force them to substantiate their claims, but your office can. Since a large number of people are affected by this, I again urge you to take immediate steps and conduct a thorough investigation of this company.

Goshgarian wrote a similar letter to the FBI in Boston, noting that Dorothy Deering was using the post office to defraud writers while Bill Richardson had employed the U.S. mail to attempt to threaten her into silence. Weren't these federal offenses? She also wrote another letter to the attorney general's office in Kentucky and two weeks later received another form letter telling her that the complaint had been forwarded to the company in question. Down in Kentucky, they were running her around in circles.

Goshgarian's second letter to the attorney general brought yet another response from Sovereign Publications, but this time it wasn't from Bill Richardson. The latest answer to her complaint came from Chuck Deering, who identified himself as Sovereign's CEO. What had happened to Bill Richardson? According to Sovereign's new leader, he had been fired. "Mr. Bill Richardson has been dismissed from his position in our company for the harsh letter he sent, without the knowledge or approval of myself or my wife Dorothy."

Blaming the unfortunate flap entirely on Bill Richardson, Chuck renewed Dorothy's offer to quickly edit and publish Goshgarian's novel. Denying any knowledge of the "Death Heads Units" business and shrugging off Goshgarian's charges of fraud, Chuck assured the attorney general that Dorothy loved her writers and treated every one of their manuscripts as a "mental labor of love." Chuck concluded his letter to the attorney general with a condescending, personal attack on the complainant.

> I am asking you to try to understand the obvious ATTACK tone of her letter as one of a disappointed first time author.

When an author goes out of their [*sic*] way to crucify a hard working small publisher, such as we, the motive is strictly REVENGE!!!

I would be most agreeable to come to a reasonable solution with Ms. Goshgarian, but her actions have demonstrated that she does not want a solution, just a head on a platter.

In conclusion, Ms. Goshgarian has taken a simple contractual matter and made an issue of vengeance [*sic*] toward us personally.

Diane Goshgarian realized it would take more than a handful of writers to bring Dorothy and her accomplices to justice. She had done everything in her power to alert the authorities to a situation that was likely to get worse. Eventually someone in law enforcement would have to take notice of what was going on in the name of publishing. She just didn't know how bad things had to get before that happened.

If Bantam comes up with an offer before Harper Collins does, and then, you know, we'll have two to negotiate by.

—Daniel Craig Deering

17 The Ammerman Experience

IN THE FALL OF 1996, AFTER DOROTHY HAD LAUNCHED her joint venture company, John Kirk, an attorney with offices in Paintsville and Inez, Kentucky, ran across Sovereign Publications on the Internet. Shortly after submitting two chapters of his novel, he received a letter from Dorothy Deering praising what he had written and asking to see the rest. In March of the following year, Kirk, in Bill Richardson's office on East Reynolds Road, signed a Sovereign contract. He left Lexington that day minus $4,625 in his bank account. Thirteen months later, his book had not been published as promised, so Kirk drove across the state to visit Bill Richardson and find out why. He took with him the novel he had written in the interim.

Richardson, at first a bit nervous, explained that because of Dorothy's health and the murder of her son, the publishing dates of all books had been pushed back six months. He promised, however, to put Kirk's manuscript on the fast track for publication and presented him with a complimentary copy of Ted Nottingham's new book, *The Curse of Cain,* the untold story of John Wilkes Booth. Kirk also viewed a promotional video about Nottingham's book that had been produced, according to Richardson, by Sovereign's marketing department. The offices that day looked abandoned, and when Kirk asked Richardson where all the employees were, Richardson said he had given his editors the day off as a reward for months of hard work. Because the editors and the graphic arts people were enjoying a well-earned vacation, it was a bad time to discuss the progress of Kirk's upcoming book. Richardson did want to talk about publishing Kirk's second novel and, in that regard, had terrific news. Since

Dorothy Deering was so excited about having Kirk as a Sovereign author, she had authorized a major discount for his new manuscript. Before heading home that day, Kirk signed another joint venture contract and wrote another check, this time for $6,175.

During the next few weeks, every time Kirk called Sovereign to talk to an editor, he got a different excuse as to why that wouldn't be possible. Suddenly he realized he had been defrauded and began thinking about how he was going to get his money back. He called Bill Richardson and said he wanted to set up a meeting with Dorothy Deering to discuss the possibility of publishing his third book. Richardson called back to say that Dorothy looked forward to seeing him at Sovereign headquarters on the last day of May.

On the big day, Kirk and his wife, Loyce, made a point of arriving at Sovereign two hours early. When they arrived, Richardson was the only person on the premises. Since they were early, Kirk asked Richardson for a tour of the operation, and after that, Richardson could show Kirk the progress they were making on his first book. Visibly uneasy, Richardson led the Kirks around the abandoned facility where Kirk saw no evidence whatsoever of publishing or any other activity. All he saw were manuscripts, hundreds of them. Finally, Kirk asked Richardson where he was hiding all of his employees. Well, as things would happen, everybody in the place except Richardson had come down with the flu. They were all at home sick. As for Kirk's upcoming book, the galleys and cover art were currently at the facility in Nicholasville. Kirk suggested they jump in his car and take the fifteen-minute drive south. He had plenty of time. Before signing a contract for his third book, Kirk wanted to see what they had done with his first. As Richardson was explaining why his schedule prohibited him from leaving Sovereign headquarters, Dorothy and Chuck walked into his office.

Dorothy, walking without the aid of her crutches, looked like a bag lady off her medication. Chuck, housing a pair of hips less than three months old, was getting around with a cane. This was the first time Kirk had seen either one of them in person, and he was not favorably impressed. Like a pair of windup tragedy dolls, they immediately unleashed a litany of despair and woe that would have brought tears to the eyes of an IRS agent. But Kirk and his wife weren't buying any of it.

Kirk told Dorothy that he was in Lexington for two reasons. He had come to see what they had done with his first book and, if he liked what he saw, was ready to sign a third Sovereign contract. Since Bill Richardson didn't have the time to take him to Nicholasville, he was hoping Dorothy would accompany him there. Without making eye contact with Kirk or his wife, Dorothy said she simply wasn't up to making the trip. It seemed that Dorothy wanted to talk about everything but his books. The more Kirk tried to engage her on that topic, the more attention she paid to Kirk's wife, Loyce, changing the subject to grandchildren, cooking, shopping, and the like. Ignoring Dorothy's futile efforts to charm his wife, Kirk kept the pressure on, asking Dorothy whether she had actually read his manuscripts. Of course she had; she loved his books. Could she remember their titles? No, but that didn't mean she hadn't read them. When Kirk asked Dorothy to simply identify the genre they were in, she turned to Kirk's wife and, amid bouts of crying and giggling, began talking about her son Michael and how she couldn't get over his death. Although increasingly angry with himself for being hoodwinked by people of this ilk, Kirk was able to extract a little revenge.

After an hour or so of toying with Dorothy Deering, Kirk grew tired of torturing the scoundrels who had ripped him off. He offered Dorothy a proposal: forget the first book, return that money to him, then concentrate on the second book. If that went well, they could talk about the third. Kirk, of course, had no intention of ever doing business with these people again. He figured he would have a better chance of getting his money back piecemeal than all at once. He would hold that third book over their heads as an incentive.

Chuck Deering, other than to console his wife when she broke into tears, hadn't contributed much to the conversation until Kirk suggested the return of some of his money. He and Dorothy had dragged their recently operated-on bodies to this meeting with the intent of picking up another joint venture check. Instead of cash from this guy, they were getting a load of his crap. Now he was talking about getting his money back! That was not how the Deerings did business. They were not big on giving back. Once they had the money, it was theirs.

Before anyone could respond to Kirk's proposed plan of action, Chuck got slowly to his feet and announced that he had business to attend to in Dorothy's office. Cane in hand, he hobbled out of the room. A few minutes later, he returned to the group and said to Bill Richardson, "Barnes and Noble just called; they want another five thousand copies of Nottingham's book." Kirk didn't know whether to laugh or to cry. He had wasted his time and his money on these con artists. How could he have been fooled by such clowns?

John Kirk and his wife left Lexington that afternoon with a signed copy of Dorothy's self-published booklet, *Freddie the Firefly,* and Dorothy's promise to send him a check covering the joint venture amount of his first book. He knew he would never see his money or his name on the cover of a Sovereign paperback. He knew he'd been had, but he'd had his fun. Kirk could imagine Dorothy Deering giving Bill Richardson hell for wasting her time on a mark who had wised up.

The next day, John Kirk called the FBI office in Lexington to report what he believed were scam artists passing themselves off as publishers. He didn't know this for a fact, but after seeing all of these manuscripts piled around the office, he suspected that Dorothy Deering had victimized a lot of writers. During the next month, Kirk called the FBI several times, adding new details to his complaints. He wanted the FBI to know that if the Deerings were ever prosecuted, he would be willing to testify against them.

Dan Ammerman was smart, talented, and ambitious. He had been a CBS anchorman, a journalist, an actor for eight years in the TV series *Dallas,* and the founder of a Houston-based communications consulting firm called the Ammerman Experience. He had also written a book and was looking for a literary agent. Not accustomed to failure or rejection, Ammerman had been stunned when only one agent of the sixty he had queried showed any interest in "My Mother's Secret," a work described by Ammerman as a Christian novel. That agent was Daniel Craig Deering.[1]

One of sixty wasn't the response Ammerman had hoped for, but at least the agent who did respond was interested enough to call him on the phone. In the course of their conversation, Ammerman learned that Dorothy Deering, the owner of the agency, had just had her knee replaced, and until she got back to work, Daniel was handling all the clients himself. Because he was so overworked, the agency wasn't taking on many new writers. However, if Ammerman didn't mind paying $175 to have "My Mother's Secret" evaluated by one of the college professors who did this work for the agency, he could send it in. If the professor liked the manuscript, Daniel would consider representing the book. They were busy, but Daniel simply couldn't resist the opportunity to help yet another unpublished writer realize his dream. That is what the Deering agency was all about, helping writers.

Ten days after sending in the $175 reading fee, Ammerman received, in the form of a seven-page boilerplate evaluation sheet, his manuscript critique, filled out by a Cristina Cowart. The review was positive, and Ammerman was thrilled. Along with the evaluation, Daniel had sent the "It is with great pride that I invite you to join the group of prestigious authors" letter in which he informed Ammerman that he had "already spoken to some publishers who are willing to review your work." Ammerman signed the one-year agency agreement and sent it back to Nicholasville with the five-hundred-dollar contract fee. Finally, he had himself a literary agent.

Ammerman, prepared to wait at least a month before hearing from his agent, was surprised to get another letter from Daniel just one week after he'd signed the agency contract. Daniel had more:

> Great News! After extensive research, the Deering Literary Agency has developed an on-line Internet web site for a select group of Deering authors. This will be sure to give your book or screenplay the maximum exposure to publishers and producers. We welcome you to join this select group of authors and reserve your space on the Deering Internet home page.
>
> Publishers and movie producers are on-line and surf the net on a regular basis. They are looking for the next best seller, and yes, maybe even their next movie to produce. Our staff has been working diligently to develop this revolutionary new web-site, just in time for the 1998–1999 literary season. If you would like a FRONT LINE FEATURE on our new aggressive web-site, the price is small. The exposure and results will be greater than you can imagine!

Ammerman could purchase six months of Web-site exposure for $375 or pay $575 for a year's worth. He bought the $575 package, bringing his total investment in the Deering Agency to $1,250. To determine what his $575 had bought him, Ammerman kept checking the Deering Web site. Not only wasn't his or any other manuscript featured, the Web site itself was a mishmash of misspellings and bad grammar. This site would hardly impress publishers and movie producers. Each time Ammerman called his agent to ask about his Web-site feature and to point out the misspellings, Daniel blamed the situation on the Web-site service and assured him the problem was being corrected. He was not to worry.

But Ammerman was worried, and by 1998, the problem still left unfixed, he intensified his efforts to have his agent address the situation. Finally, in the middle of January, Ammerman had become such a pest Daniel had no choice but to write him a letter asking his client not to call the office for at least twelve weeks.

On June 4, 1998, two months before Chuck Deering gave up Bill Richardson to the U.S. marshals and three months after he and Dorothy began meeting with the bankruptcy attorney, Ammerman, after waiting the prescribed twelve weeks, called Daniel Deering.[2] The agent assured his client that during the past three months he had done everything in his power to place "My Mother's Secret" with a publisher. In Daniel's opinion, the manuscript hadn't sold because it was in need of professional line editing. The conversation continued:

> *Deering:* There's going to be some revisions that's probably going to have to be made so you're gonna have to be able to have a little bit of free time in order to be able to correspond back with the editor.
>
> *Ammerman:* I've got all that.
>
> *Deering:* Okay.
>
> *Ammerman:* I own a corporation and I've got plenty of people to run it and I'm sitting in a big office and I've got a computer and . . .
>
> *Deering:* Right.
>
> *Ammerman:* A telephone line and I can do just about anything if somebody would give me the instructions on how to do it.
>
> *Deering:* Well, I tell you what. Let me have your number and let me call you back and see what kind of price range I can get you under because if you go outside it's gonna run you between six to eight dollars a page.[3]
>
> *Ammerman:* Oh, God.
>
> *Deering:* I want to see my editor; he does things for me fairly cheap, because we're backed up as far as the agency goes but I can always get him to do it on his own time. And it would be a lot cheaper that way for you.

The conversation ended with Deering promising to get back to Ammerman with the in-house editing price. A month passed and Deering didn't call, so Ammerman called the agent. Deering had good news: his editor had agreed to do the job at the low price of $3.25 per page. Since the manuscript was only 375 pages long, that didn't involve an enormous amount of money.

Ammerman: Wonderful.

Deering: Okay. So I mean, I have done everything I *possibly* can do for you there. Okay?

Ammerman: How do I pay him?

Deering: Okay. Now, I'm gonna have to stand responsible to him for the fee, the reason being we've had people say—now don't take me wrong, Mr. Ammerman—say they want it done and then I go ahead and say, "Okay, go ahead and grab it," and take off—and then—I know you will, so what I do, I'm gonna go ahead and give him a check to do so, but I want to figure exactly how much this is gonna cost so you know right off the bat.

Ammerman: Okay.

Deering: Okay. This way we have no hidden anything; I don't like surprises.

Ammerman: Now, he [the editor] will be in touch with me as to . . .

Deering: Yes. He's gonna start on it this weekend. Okay? And so he said you'll probably hear from him around Wednesday. His name is Jim Stafford.

Ammerman: Jim Stafford?

Deering: Yes.

Ammerman: Okay. Excellent.

Deering: Not Stafford—Stanford.

Ammerman: Stanford?

Deering: Yes. He just corrected me himself. Okay. So let's get down to bare line here, bottom line. All right, so we have 375 pages times $3.25 comes to $1,218.75.

Ammerman: Piece of cake.

Deering: Okay. $1,218.75.

Ammerman: Okay. It will probably run more than that but I'll send you that to get you started.

Deering: Okay. I don't think it's gonna run any more than that. Once I tell you it's a price, it's a price.

Ammerman: You got it.

Deering: Okay, so what do you . . . I'm gonna go ahead and allow him to take the manuscript out actually this evening 'cause he's not in tomorrow. Now, you're going to send the check out to what address?[4]

A month later, when Ammerman called to ask how the work was progressing (he had not heard from the editor), Deering had incredibly good news. Not only had the novel been line edited and retyped, Harper Collins wanted to publish it!

The conversation:

Ammerman: Oh, boy.

Deering: They're gonna put you in their catalogue and they're gonna publish your book.

Ammerman: Now you're kidding.

Deering: No, sir. It's gonna be on a standard royalty contract. Now I know for a fact they're gonna print probably thirty thousand copies to begin with.

Ammerman: Oh, my God.

Deering: Yeah, so have a happy, happy, happy weekend. So, I will probably know the logistics part—he said he can't get with me next week—but the week following we'll start our negotiations, and then after thirty days probably after that you'll sign a contract.

Ammerman: All *right!* Okay!

Deering: Yeah.

Ammerman: That's what I like to hear!

Deering: Well, I'm, I got CHILLS—actually I'm sittin' on my front porch drinking a glass of tea here . . . Okay, now the process we're having—the editing process—was done and it ran up to, brought your book to 597 pages.

Ammerman: Okay.

Deering: That was as low as we got it so you paid for 375 [pages].

Ammerman: Yeah.

Deering: The other $3.25 a page, that's something you owe her because like I said I was having her do that for you. [Deering had forgotten that the phantom editing job had been done by a Jim Stanford.]

Ammerman: What he [Ammerman had not forgotten] needs to do is tell me how much.[5]

Deering: Okay. So you need to go to your bookstore and start looking around at what they have out as their best sellers and things like that. Do that little research for yourself. This way you'll know where you fall.

Ammerman: Okay.

Deering: If Bantam comes up with an offer before Harper Collins does, and then, you know, we'll have two to negotiate by. They're just as interested, but they haven't said "We want it" yet. What I'm gonna do is I'm gonna call my editor there. I'm gonna call up to Harper Collins in New York and just tell them, "Okay, I got the message, we're ready to go," and all that good stuff.

Ammerman: All *right*.

Deering: Congratulations, Mr. Ammerman.

Ammerman: Thank *you.*

Deering: After a long haul, you finally did it.

Ammerman: Congratulations to you.

Deering: I told you I smelled it in the air. But I only get fifteen percent of what you get.

Ammerman: Let's hope it's fifteen percent of a lot.

Having been successful in the media and as a businessman was nothing compared to the euphoria Ammerman experienced when he got off the phone with his agent. He was walking on air, and the feeling lasted for weeks. He told people that a major New York City publisher was excited about his book. He fantasized about life as a best-selling novelist. It was wonderful.

On September 4, 1998, about a month after receiving the good news, Ammerman phoned Daniel Deering to find out how the negotiations with Harper Collins and Bantam were coming along.

Deering: They're having a few problems. There's a few inserts in it [the manuscript] that they say at least were from [taken from] another manuscript, another copyrighted manuscript, and they're supposed to highlight that for me and send it to me so I can send it to you and have it revised. I tried to call you and tell you that. Other than that, it looks like you're gonna be a published author, buddy.

Ammerman: Okay, pal.

Deering: I'm trying to do everything I can to get the process hurried up, so I know how people are; they wanna see an end result.

Ammerman: If they want me to revise it, I will revise it. I can't understand where that . . .

Deering: I don't, either, and I really don't.

Ammerman: Okay, now, are they talking about *my* manuscript or the one your people revised.

Deering: They're talking about the one my people revised.

Ammerman: Okay.

Deering: So what I have done, yesterday, I sent them the original manuscript that before we did our editing process on it and see if it's still there, too, and he said he'd have it back to me at least by Tuesday of next week.

Ammerman: Okay, now you told me, the last time we talked, that you were gonna send me a disk with the revised manuscript on it.

Deering: I know. I know. I know. I know. Once I write something down on the little stick note, put it on the file and send it over to have it done, I'm lost from there if it's not done. I just usually have to wait for the client to call and tell me it's not done. But I will make sure I will get that out to you today.

Ammerman: Okay. And as soon as they respond to you, you send it to me quick.

Deering: I will; it will be overnight as just as soon as I get it in my hand.

Ammerman: They said a whole page; it was that significant?

Deering: That, they didn't get into. They said it was significant enough to send it back to me to have it revised. I know that.

Ammerman: Well, I'll be damned. Huh. Okay. I haven't received the disk and I was wondering whether it may have come in when I was traveling or something like that.

Deering: [A clicking sound comes over the phone.] Hear that right there?

Ammerman: Pardon me?

Deering: That's your disk. The editor just handed it to me. She's going—"Sorry, sorry" [laughs]. Yeah, I'll get that out to ya today. Okay?

Ammerman: Thank you, partner.

Deering: You have a great weekend, sir.

After waiting ten days for the computer disk containing his revised manuscript, Ammerman called Nicholasville to determine why he hadn't received it. A young woman he had not previously spoken to answered the telephone. In response to Ammerman's inquiry as to the status of "My Mother's Secret," the young woman blurted, "Oh, that must be one of the books erased by the new girl."

Ammerman felt like he had been hit in the face with a bucket of cold water. The reality of the situation came to him in a flash; he was the victim of a scam. He had paid $3,352.75 for nothing. It wasn't about the money as much as it was about the anger, the disappointment and, yes, the shame. His manuscript had not been revised. There were no interested publishers, and he was not going to be a published author. It had all been a cruel and cold-blooded lie.

After he had recovered from the shock of having his hopes dashed in a sudden flash of insight, Dan Ammerman began looking for another agent, the kind of agent who carries a gun and works for the FBI. Instead of his novel, he'd be submitting a bit of tape-recorded nonfiction, starring Daniel Craig Deering. It was time Mr. Deering got his own dose of reality.

18 The Mob

BILL RICHARDSON WAS NO LONGER EMPLOYED at Sovereign
Publications, but he hadn't been dismissed by Chuck Deering. On a dog-
day afternoon in mid-August 1998, when Richardson and his only employee, Carolyn Thue, were alone at Sovereign's world headquarters on
East Reynolds Road, two men in dark suits strode into the building.
Obviously not a pair of novelists, they identified themselves as U.S. marshals. Where was William Paul Watson? they asked. Thue said she had
no idea who they were talking about. One of the men asked whether she
knew who owned the Nissan parked outside. "That belongs to my boss,
Bill Richardson," she replied.

"Where is Mr. Richardson?"

"He's back there," she said, pointing toward his office.

Not waiting to be announced, the two men went straight to the office. A few minutes later, they came out with Watson. When Thue saw
the handcuffs and the look on her boss's face, she got the picture. Suddenly Thue was alone with her thoughts, without a goodbye from the
cops or their prisoner.

Watson, a few days after his arrest, called Thue from the jail in
Kennesaw. He was furious. He said that Chuck Deering had turned him
in to the feds because Dorothy was about to shut down the business and
didn't want to pay him his share of the money. Now that Dorothy didn't
need him anymore, she had thrown him to the wolves. The following day,
Sovereign's last employee started looking for another job.

In November 1997, Kimberly Reese, an unpublished writer from west
Texas who had dealt with a series of fee agents she believed were bogus,

126

created a Web site called the Write Connection. Reese wanted to protect writers like herself from unscrupulous agents, book doctors, and publishers. In addition to providing general information and advice, she hoped to compile a list of literary enterprises aspiring writers should avoid. To help her with this roster of bad apples, she turned to published novelists Ann C. Crispin and Victoria Strauss, members of Science Fiction and Fantasy Writers of America (SFWA). Through SFWA, Strauss and Crispin had been collecting and cataloguing written complaints about a growing group of fee agents, book doctors, and joint venture publishers such as Northwest, Commonwealth, and Sovereign. Using this SFWA data and information she had collected directly through her Web site, Reese posted her "Questionable Agent" and "Questionable Publisher" lists. These features immediately became wildly popular centerpieces of the Write Connection. Finally, an aspiring writer could ascertain whether a specific agent, book doctor, or publisher had been the subject of writer complaints. Better Business Bureaus (BBBs) were no help, and writers were learning that advertisement of an outfit in a writer's magazine or the *Literary Market Place,* or listing in a publishing directory, did not mean that the company was legitimate. The Write Connection quickly became a safe harbor for aspiring writers.

Members of the genteel racket who found themselves on Reese's roster of questionable agents had to find some way to get themselves off the list. A few listees denied that they charged contracts fees, dealt with vanity publishers, had no manuscript sales, or were essentially in the line-editing business and demanded to be removed from the Web site. Most, however, simply objected to the list. Many of these practitioners accused Reese of violating their constitutional right to conduct, without interference, their lawful businesses. Being on a disapproval list, exposed for what they were, hurt their businesses. The truth was killing them. Therefore, if Reese didn't shut down her Web site, they would have to take her to court.

Thanks to the efforts of Reese, Crispin, and Strauss, aspiring writers across America were beginning to see the outline and scope of the genteel racket. Among the first to join in the movement to expose literary charlatans were Dorothy Deering's more vocal detractors, writers like Tom Mahon, the Florida ADP and NPI victim who had been blowing the whistle on the Deerings since the summer of 1996. After receiving a thousand-dollar gift certificate from Bill Richardson in the spring of 1998, Mahon sent a long, detailed, and documented letter of complaint to the BBB in Lexington.[1] Mahon posted his letter on the Write Connection.

> In 1992 I started working on an idea I had for a novel. By the summer of 1993 I had found an agent who was thrilled with the work, telling me I definitely had a "winner here." She claimed my novel was "one of the best" to ever come into her agency. In fact, a producer with Paramount Pictures in Hollywood wanted a treatment of my manuscript immediately. I was flying high! I was going to get published. Soon I'd be the guest of honor at signing parties and I'd be collecting royalties. My many hours of research, writing and editing had paid off. Soon I would forever be known as an author.

To the Lexington BBB and users of the Write Connection, Mahon declared that Dorothy Deering was a literary fraud who was enriching herself at her clients' expense. He questioned her claim to William Morrow lineage and accused her of being "too cozy" with Jim Van Treese and Donald Phelan. As for the Deering "manuscript express," her trips to New York City and Hollywood, Mahon called them writer-paid vacations for Dorothy and Chuck. Mahon also pointed out, quite correctly, that the recent sale of the Deering Literary Agency to Daniel Craig Deering was merely a scheme to get angry clients off Dorothy's back. Mahon concluded his BBB and Internet letter as follows:

> I regret to inform you of such despicable business practices taking place under the fair skies of Kentucky. But dishonest business practices abound everywhere, unfortunately. From 1993 to 1996 it was "send us $500 for this, $300 for that, another $300 for this, and yet another $500 for that." I was never published. One author I know of shelled out over $15,000 for deals Dorothy Deering urged her to take. Disgraceful.

The BBB in Lexington simply forwarded Mahon's letter to the Deering Literary Agency, now owned by Daniel Craig Deering. Mahon could have done that himself. The real damage to the Deerings came from the fact Mahon had posted the letter on the Writer Connection, where it was being read by hundreds of aspiring writers, many of whom were fellow victims of the Deering agency.

Chuck Deering, who had been working behind the scenes with Dorothy, could not let this public attack on his wife go unanswered. Responding online, he came out of the shadows swinging. Chuck wanted to assure everyone that Dorothy was in *fact* Betty Morrow's daughter. This was true, but *that* Betty Morrow, born and raised in Lima, Ohio, had never been married to William F. Morrow, a distinction Chuck elected not to mention. According to Chuck, Dorothy had sold 450 manuscripts, an outstanding record of achievement. This was also true, if by "sold," Chuck meant talked her clients into vanity deals with Northwest, Commonwealth, and Sovereign, most of which had not and would never be published. Lest anyone question Dorothy's legitimacy, her agency, at one time, had been featured in twenty-eight publishing directories, referral guides, and other writer-oriented venues. Dottie, with a long list of satisfied clients, had worked very hard for her writers. It wasn't her fault Mr. Mahon had written a book nobody wanted to publish (that is, except ADP and Jim Van Treese).

Mahon, in a follow-up letter to Chuck also published on the Write Connection, asked him to identify a few of the contracts Dorothy had negotiated with publishers other than NPI, CPI, or Sovereign. He also wanted Chuck to comment on the widely held suspicion that Daniel Craig Deering was nothing more than Dorothy's front man, that she was still pulling the strings. Mindful that Mahon was challenging him in front of a large audience of Deering clients, Chuck felt compelled to post his response online.

> Your letter is as I expected from "one of the mob." I will not answer any more of your ranting and threatening letters, moreover, if a war is what you want? [*sic*] Join the Army. We did our work in a professional manner and tried to help all our clients. I hope that you find some peace in your obviously confused life. Deering Literary is now and has been totally under the control and ownership of my son Daniel since shortly after the murder of our son Mike.

The Write Connection had become a rallying point for Deering clients who were fed up and willing to join the fight. Mahon, the point man in the client-Deering skirmish, picked up, through the Write Connection, a comrade-in-arms named Carole Fox-Breeding. The romance novelist from Las Vegas had started out with A Rising Sun, then wound up with the Deering Agency and a joint venture deal with Commonwealth. Refusing to be handed off to Chuck Deering's son, Fox-Breeding, in her online letter to Dorothy and Chuck, hit hard.

> Dorothy Deering has always intimated, by her advertising, that she had an "inroad"—connections because her family, purportedly, founded William Morrow

Publishing Co. This may or may not be true, but Dorothy certainly had no connections whatsoever. One publisher told me in confidence that they don't even open the Deering submittals. Many come slopped together in a box, which is utterly unprofessional to say the least. Throw it all at the wall AND HOPE SOMETHING STICKS. To me, the writing on the wall appeared very early, but not early enough to save me from disastrous shenanigans.

You didn't care about individual authors, you just wanted to amass these collective exorbitant agency fees, charging neophytes large sums to be a part of the prestigious Deering organization. Believe me, there's nothing prestigious, professional or businesslike about your group. Why would you have to knock yourself out to legitimately sell a book when you were probably making more on your agency fees?

Why, indeed. It seemed that more and more writers, albeit too late, were on to the Deerings and the genteel racket. Two days after Fox-Breeding's Write Connection posting, Chuck, sounding like a man about to be run out of town, replied,

> I am in receipt of your hate mail. It looks as though you have decided to join the "mob" against us. So be it. We have never deceived or mislead [*sic*] our clients in any way. Moreover we went the extra mile to try to help our authors. You and the rest of the "mob" are intent on ruining the reputation of my family and our businesses. I strongly advise that the fervor of the "mob" is misdirected and taking a very dangerous course of revenge toward my family and our businesses. It is time for the "mob" to "cease and desist in all defamation of character and public slander" toward my family and our businesses. If the attacks do not stop as of now, I will be forced to seek legal council [*sic*] to stop the problem. I do not want to do this as it is expensive and time consuming. The only winners in this type of action are the lawyers. But if that is what it takes to stop the intentional and purposeful attacks to destroy our business and reputation, not to mention the crude references to our dead son and our credentials to operate our businesses, so be it!!!

A few days after his threat to sue people like Tom Mahon, Diane Goshgarian, and Carol Fox-Breeding, Chuck, using the Write Connection as his venue, threw in the towel.

> To whom it may concern:
> Be advised that there will be no further correspondence in reply to the

malicious mail addressed to us. Daniel C. Deering is [*sic*] the owner of record of the Deering Literary Agency since December of 1997.

With that, Chuck Deering slipped back into the shadows to console his embattled and ailing wife. After ratting on her brother and handing the literary agency over to her quasi-literate stepson, Dorothy, with more time to plan her bankruptcy, had washed her hands of clients. As far as she was concerned, they could all go to hell, or worse, deal with the agency's new owner, Daniel Craig Deering.

19 *September Surprise*

IN JUNE 1997, CAROLYN STEINMETZ, a Deering client from Essex Junction, Vermont, received a call from Dorothy Deering she would never forget. A publisher had made an offer on her novel, "Crossroads." It was a joint venture offer, but the good part was this: because Dorothy owned the publishing company, she could cut Steinmetz a special deal. Instead of the standard ten-thousand-dollar investment, Steinmetz would have to pay only six thousand dollars. Dorothy was extending her this favor because she knew how badly Steinmetz had been treated by her previous agent, Chris Scott of A Rising Sun.

Steinmetz was thrilled, but there was a problem. She wasn't sure she could get her hands on that much money. Dorothy said she realized this was a lot of cash, and if Steinmetz couldn't take advantage of the deal, she would understand. In fact, it was such a bad deal for Sovereign, Steinmetz's decision not to sign the contract would save Dorothy a lot of money. She had only extended the offer out of the goodness of her heart.

The day after receiving the big call from Dorothy Deering, Steinmetz called the Better Business Bureau in Lexington. According to the person she spoke to, there had been no complaints on file against the Deering Literary Agency or Sovereign Publications. Having established that she was dealing with a legitimate person, Steinmetz and her husband discussed the money and decided that they could borrow only four thousand dollars. They were fretting about this money when Dorothy called to inform her client that time was running out. Steinmetz told Dorothy that because she and her husband could raise only four thousand dollars, she would have to decline her generous offer. Dorothy said she hated the idea of

Steinmetz's book, with its commercial potential, not getting published. She had a plan. She would take the four thousand now, and Steinmetz could pay off the two-thousand-dollar balance in hundred-dollar monthly payments. The debt would be paid in twenty months, coinciding with the February 1999 publication of the book. This kind of deal was why Dorothy had gotten into the business: to help writers get their start.

Steinmetz and her husband borrowed the money, signed the Sovereign contract, and over the next six months, made their monthly payments on time. During this period, there had been no word from Dorothy or anyone else at Sovereign Publications. Just before Christmas 1997, Steinmetz called to check on her book. Chuck Deering answered the phone. He had bad news but was sure she would understand. The publication of all Sovereign books had been delayed six months. It was Dorothy; she was in crisis. First, the knee operation, then the shooting death of her son, Michael.

Carolyn Steinmetz was not an uncaring person, but she wasn't sure she understood why Dorothy Deering's personal problems had delayed the publication of her book. Had she missed one of her monthly joint venture payments due to illness or personal tragedy, would Dorothy have understood? Business was business; hadn't they entered into a business agreement?

Steinmetz decided not to complain. She didn't want to appear ungrateful to the woman who had given her such a good break on the publishing deal. Sovereign was a small, family-owned company, and losing a son was indeed tragic. A six-month delay was disappointing, but in the scheme of things, no big deal.

In February 1998, a month before turning the literary agency over to Daniel Craig Deering, and just weeks before she initiated a series of meetings with a bankruptcy lawyer, Dorothy called Steinmetz to propose another deal. For the lump-sum payment of three thousand dollars, she would publish Steinmetz's other novel, "Planned Death." Both books would be out in one year, the original publishing date of "Crossroads." That brought Steinmetz's investment to nine thousand dollars, one thousand less than it cost most authors to have one book published. Dorothy asked Steinmetz not to tell anyone about the proposal; if word got out, the other authors would demand the same deal. The Vermont writer would also have to make her decision quickly. This wasn't a one-day sale, but it was a limited-time offer.

Carolyn didn't know why Dorothy was being so nice to her and didn't ask. She did ask, however, if the three thousand dollars could be paid in monthly installments like the two-thousand-dollar balance for "Crossroads." Steinmetz didn't want to appear ungrateful, but having already invested four thousand dollars and still obligated to pay a hundred a month on her first novel, money was tight. What did Dorothy think about a down payment and the rest spread out over a year? That was possible, Dorothy replied, but if that's the way it had to be, she would have to charge five thousand dollars for the second novel. To save two thousand, Dorothy suggested that Carolyn ask a member of her family to lend her the money. "We believe in you and your books," Dorothy said. It was a darn good investment.

Carolyn borrowed the three thousand dollars from her mother, signed another Sovereign contract, and sent Dorothy the check. A week later she received, from Sovereign Publications, a pair of certificates (suitable for hanging) announcing the upcoming publication of her books. The diploma-like certificates were signed by Dorothy Deering. Once again, Steinmetz waited and worried. Six months went by without a peep from her publisher. In the middle of June 1998, she picked up the phone and called. The last time she had phoned after a six-month wait, Chuck Deering told her that the publication of her book had been delayed. Once again, Chuck Deering took her call. It seemed the only time she spoke to Dorothy was when money was the topic of discussion. Carolyn asked Chuck whether he had any problem with her coming to Lexington and taking a tour of Sovereign Publications. Maybe she could speak to an editor and check out her cover art. In August she and her husband were driving their daughter to Kentucky, where she had enrolled in a college not far from Lexington. Chuck said that he and Dorothy would be there to welcome them. Bill Richardson would also be on hand to discuss her two books. He looked forward to her visit and assured her she would leave Kentucky quite impressed with Sovereign Publications. There was nothing Dorothy liked better than to visit with her authors.

Carolyn and her husband pulled into Sovereign's parking lot just days before the company ceased to exist. Bill Richardson was on ice in Georgia, Daniel Craig Deering was running the literary agency out of his house in Nicholasville, and Dorothy and Chuck were holed up in south Florida with Chuck's mother. They had moved out of Lexington and had no immediate plans to return.

Daniel Craig Deering just happened to be at Sovereign's world head-quarters when Carolyn arrived with her husband. He was in the office rifling files for prospective victims. The visitors from Vermont pulled up and parked their car next to his BMW. Inside, boxes, files, cabinets, desks, office equipment, and chairs were stacked against the walls. It looked as though the place had been abandoned, and in a hurry. Carolyn was about to leave when Daniel Craig Deering came out of one of the offices carrying a box of manuscripts. Carolyn introduced herself as a Sovereign author from Vermont who had stopped by for a tour and a check on her books. Where was everyone? Had Sovereign moved? Daniel laughed and said he could explain the mess, and why nobody was there to greet the author and her husband.

"I know it looks bad," Daniel said. "We had a big storm and the roof leaked. We're getting new carpets and new office furniture. Insurance is paying for everything." Because of the disruption, Dorothy had given everybody a few days off. Chuck and the publicist were in New York City negotiating a big book deal, and Dorothy was home with the flu.

Okay, so they weren't going to meet Dorothy or Chuck. Since they were there, however, maybe Daniel could show them what progress had been made on Carolyn's books. Oh, Daniel said, he couldn't do that. For one, he didn't work for Sovereign; he was the owner of the Deering Literary Agency. Second, all of the manuscripts and galley proofs were packed away in boxes. He wouldn't be able to locate Carolyn's file even if he were authorized.

Carolyn wasn't the suspicious type, but something about all of this smelled fishy. Maybe Daniel could call Dorothy and ask her where the Steinmetz material was packed. "You know," he said, "you have to be patient. These are just books we are talking about; it's not a life and death situation." Just in case Carolyn didn't know what a real life and death situation was, Daniel gave them a personal illustration. Shortly after his wife had triplets, deemed in good health by their doctor, the babies died. If Daniel could forgive that doctor, surely Carolyn could cut Dorothy a break on having a leaky roof and temporary disorganization. Dorothy didn't control the weather. Was it her fault she had the flu? Daniel also reminded Carolyn of Dorothy's operation and the killing of her son. Floods, murder, surgery, dead babies, and the flu—what could Carolyn say to that, except that some people weren't very lucky. It sounded like the Deerings were definitely snakebitten.

After her second Sovereign contract was signed, Carolyn had sent Dorothy her third novel to represent after Dorothy promised to sell it to a royalty-paying publisher. Since Dorothy no longer owned the literary agency, Carolyn wanted the manuscript back and said so to Daniel. Maybe she could find an agent who wasn't so unlucky. Fine, Daniel said, the moment that he returned to his office in Nicholasville he'd mail the book back to her house in Vermont. That would, however, be quite a shame because he had just finished pitching the novel to an editor in New York City who *loved* it and was ready to make an offer. "I want to represent your book," Daniel said. "I can get it published by a major house."

Carolyn, while wary of Chuck Deering's son, was, in spite of herself, excited by the notion of a big-time editor liking her work. She was intrigued enough to be drawn into a discussion of her novel with the agent. She noticed that when referring to the editor, Daniel didn't reveal this person's name. When she asked for the editor's identity, Daniel said, "If you're making me send back the manuscript, I can't do that."

"Why not?"

"Then you won't need an agent. I want you to sign a contract with me. I can sell your book."

Carolyn didn't know what to think. First the disappointment of not seeing what Sovereign had done with her books, then this. It was all so sudden, too much to sort out all at once. Sensing her indecision, Daniel pushed harder. If Carolyn signed up with him, he'd use his influence with his father to guarantee that both of Carolyn's books would be published on time. With him as her agent, she would have an inside track at Sovereign *and* see her latest book published by a New York publishing house. In fact, if she wanted, he could get her Sovereign books published *ahead* of schedule. What did she think of that?

Choosing to be optimistic and trusting rather than pessimistic and skeptical, Carolyn, hoping to protect her Sovereign investment, wrote Daniel a check for three hundred dollars, his price for a year's representation. An hour later, back at the hotel room in Lexington, Carolyn had second thoughts. Why hadn't the agent, when he heard from the New York editor, called her at once with the good news? Why had he submitted her novel in the first place? She wasn't his client. And why, if he was on the verge of such a big sale, did he need her three hundred dollars? Although the thought scared her to death, she had to admit there was something wrong with Daniel Craig Deering and his story, including that bit about the leaky roof. The more she thought about it, the sicker she got. It was all a sham; she had been conned by a family straight from Hollywood casting who had sold her a pair of your-book-is-coming-out certificates for nine thousand dollars. Before heading back to Vermont, she called Daniel Craig's office several times but no one answered the phone. He was probably out spending her three hundred dollars.

On September 1, 1998, shortly after Carolyn Steinmetz had returned to Vermont, people calling Sovereign Publications received a taped message from Chuck Deering sadly announcing, on the second anniversary of its formation, the death of Dorothy's publishing house. Due to "a terrible set of circumstances" brought on by their "rapidly declining health," Sovereign was about to go into bankruptcy. Charles wanted to assure Dorothy's authors that she had been working hard to publish their books right up to the very end. Unfortunately, returning anyone's joint venture money was out of the question, but if writers had any other questions about reacquiring the rights to their manuscripts and so forth, they could call the law offices of Cunningham and Associates in Lexington and speak to attorney Charles Grundy. In parting, Chuck wanted everyone to know just how devastated Dorothy was over the loss of her publishing company. In time, perhaps, she would recover.

Writers hit the hardest by Dorothy's September Surprise were the ones who had signed Sovereign contracts within the previous six months. These people were not aware of the growing discontent among writers who had figured her out, authors like Diane Goshgarian, John Kirk, and Carolyn Steinmetz. Of course, it wasn't easy for any of her victims.[1] Having accused Dorothy of being a fraud, and being proven right, did little to soften the blow.

I told my dad not to marry that gold digger.

—Daniel Craig Deering

20 Class Action

BAD NEWS TRAVELS FAST, and it wasn't long before Sovereign authors around the country got word of the impending bankruptcy. Some had listened to Chuck's heart-tugging phone message, others dialed into a disconnected line, and many, like Carolyn Steinmetz, were notified through the Write Connection. Although she wasn't completely blindsided by Sovereign's sudden demise, Steinmetz was badly shaken and furious. As far as she was concerned, Dorothy Deering had stolen nine thousand dollars from her family. Dorothy had taken that money from a family she knew couldn't afford it with no intention of publishing Steinmetz's books. If that wasn't fraud, there was no such crime. Thanks to the Write Connection, Steinmetz realized that Dorothy had swindled hundreds of writers out of millions of dollars. Once she regained her composure, she picked up the phone and called Daniel Craig Deering.

Steinmetz asked the agent why, when she and her husband walked into the gutted offices of Sovereign Publications, didn't he tell her the truth? Why all the folderol about using his influence to get her books published ahead of schedule when he knew the company was belly-up? Was he that desperate for her three hundred dollars? What kind of scam were they operating down there?

Daniel said he understood why Carolyn was so upset. But if she thought *she* had been victimized by Dorothy Deering, listen to this: Before his father married Dorothy Deering, as the son of John Deering, the inventor of the John Deere tractor, Chuck had been a wealthy man. Dorothy, through her various business fiascoes, including Sovereign Publications, had squandered all of Chuck's money and had even lost $660,000

Daniel had given her out of his own Deering inheritance. All that woman knew how to do was spend other people's money. "I told my dad not to marry that gold digger," he said, "but he didn't listen."

Daniel assured Carolyn that he was just as shocked and surprised at Sovereign's collapse as she and the other authors were. But Carolyn was luckier than the others because he still considered her a client, and business at the literary agency was booming. So here was what he was prepared to do for her: First, he would sell her latest novel to that major publisher in New York. Then he would publish her two Sovereign books himself. Just because Dorothy Deering was a crook didn't mean that he was. Two weeks later, when Carolyn called his office, his line had been disconnected.

Ron Howell, a retired and disabled New York City longshoreman who lived with his wife, Maureen, in Naples, Florida, had been one of the first to sign a joint venture contract with Sovereign Publications. In 1993, after finishing his forty-five-thousand-word novella "Broadway Joe," Ron, as a birthday gift to Maureen, gave her the copyright to the book. But when he tried to acquire literary representation, Ron couldn't find a literary agent who shared his assessment of his work. Of the forty-four agents queried, only one agreed that "Broadway Joe" was a potential best seller. That agent was Dorothy Deering. In December 1995, having paid her reading and contract fees, Ron sat back and waited for Dorothy to do her thing. A year passed, and then one afternoon the phone rang; it was Chuck Deering, and he had great news. Dorothy had found a publisher for Ron's book! It was a joint venture house called Sovereign, and because "Broadway Joe" was only forty-five thousand words, Ron's share came to only $3,375. Ron had reservations, but after talking to Chuck and having faith in his judgment, Ron decided to sign the contract.[1]

A year after making the deal, about the time "Broadway Joe" was scheduled to come out, Ron called Sovereign to coordinate his plans for promoting the book. He spoke to Carolyn Thue, who told him about Michael Helm and how devastated they all were over his death. Having suffered a similar tragedy, Ron called Dorothy to express his deepest sympathy and to say he fully understood why she had delayed the publication of his book.

In February 1998, six months before the new publication date of "Broadway Joe," and six months before William Watson was hauled off to jail, Ron received a call from Carolyn Thue. She was phoning on behalf of Bill Richardson, who thought Ron might be interested in upgrading "Broadway Joe" from mass-market to trade paperback. As a trade edition, the book would certainly look better, carry a higher cover price, and have a much better chance of being reviewed by newspapers like the *New York Times*. Upgrading would also accelerate the publication of the book by three, maybe four months. Ron could make all of this happen for only two thousand dollars. Was he up to the challenge?

Ron had been retired for years and was living on a fixed income. Two thousand dollars was a lot of money, particularly when it had to be paid in one lump sum. But the way Ron figured it, you had to spend money to make it, so he scraped together the cash and went for the deal.

Three months slipped by and "Broadway Joe" still wasn't out, so Ron called Dorothy to see whether there was a problem. When Daniel Craig Deering answered the phone, Ron learned that Dorothy was no longer involved with the literary agency. She still owned Sovereign, but because of her knee and Michael Helm's death, "Broadway Joe" wouldn't be coming out for another six months. Ron was getting tired of these delays; every time he called it was one thing or the other. But there was nothing he could do to hurry things along. He'd just have to continue trusting Dorothy Deering and her Sovereign staff.

A month after speaking to Daniel Craig Deering, Ron and Maureen decided to drive up to Lexington and pay Bill Richardson a surprise visit. That afternoon in June, Carolyn Thue, looking more like the janitorial help than the cute thing in her *Sovereign Digest* photograph, escorted the couple into Richardson's office. There, surrounded by shelves of file folders like those you see in a doctor's complex, Ron and Maureen were greeted by a tall man with a head the size and shape of a basketball, sporting a smile as big and bold as the diamond on his pinky. The big guy seemed truly pleased to see them, and immediately apologized for the delay in publication of "Broadway Joe." Richardson hated to say this, but just between them, they were having a problem with Dorothy. She had been out of the loop for months, the knee operation and all, and until she got back in the office, everything would remain on hold. If she didn't snap out of it soon, he was taking over. But either way, "Broadway Joe," a dynamite book, was coming out and coming out big. Richardson was aiming for the first of next month.

Over lunch at a nearly restaurant (Bill's treat), Richardson went on at length about how he was going to *personally* promote Ron's book right to the top of the best-seller list. Before they left Lexington that day, Richardson presented the Florida couple with complimentary copies of Ted Nottingham's books and a signed copy of Dorothy's *Freddie the Firefly*. As they drove back to Naples, Ron couldn't help feeling a bit ashamed of himself for doubting Sovereign Publications. Thank God for Bill Richardson.

Soon after Ron and his wife got back to Florida, Ron began arranging a series of book signings in and around Naples. In August he started checking with bookstores to see if his books were in stock. They weren't. The books still hadn't arrived by the middle of the month. Worried that he'd have to start canceling events, Ron called Bill Richardson. Chuck Deering answered the phone, and the news wasn't good: His book wasn't out, and Bill Richardson, the man who was going to promote the hell out of it, was no longer employed at Sovereign Publications. Bill Richardson, according to Chuck, had returned to Georgia.

The news wasn't all bad. Ron had Chuck's promise that "Broadway Joe" would be in the stores, flying off the shelf, in three to six weeks. Ron would have to reschedule a couple of book signings; otherwise, no harm done. Chuck, to make sure Ron realized he was a man of his word, said, "If I'm lying, you can come to Lexington and beat me up."

September came, and still no sign of "Broadway Joe." One of Ron's friends, also waiting for the book to come out, asked a Barnes and Noble employee why they didn't have the title. The bookseller checked the computer and announced that the publisher was no longer in business. The friend called Ron, and Ron called Sovereign to hear Chuck Deering's recorded message.

Ron and Maureen spent the next three weeks in a stupor. As one of Dorothy Deering's most loyal and trusting authors, Ron was crushed by the cold-hearted efficiency of the swindle. He had no idea there were people like this in publishing. You couldn't trust anyone.

Diane Goshgarian, the nurse from Brookline, Massachusetts, had been trying to get her joint venture and upgrade money back since March of 1998. In May she had tried, without success, to arouse the interests of the FBI and the attorney general of Kentucky. The angry letters between her and Bill Richardson had culminated in his "Death Heads Units" threat. In the wake of the September Surprise, she sent follow-up letters to the FBI and the attorney general.

Despite Goshgarian's efforts, the authorities remained uninterested in Dorothy Deering's ten-year impersonation of a literary agent and publisher. Having struck out with the crime fighters, Goshgarian began discussing, with a Lexington attorney, the possibility of a class-action civil suit brought by Sovereign victims against Dorothy Deering. Before going any farther, the lawyer hired a local private investigator to determine whether the Deerings had anything of value to recover. The PI, after a check at the courthouse, reported that the Deerings had no "visible assets of record." Financially speaking, they had left the state without a trace.

Although there wasn't a good chance of winning damages from the Deerings, Goshgarian decided to go ahead with the lawsuit anyway. Communicating through the Write Connection, she urged other Sovereign victims to join the class action. Eventually, twenty-five other authors would sign on as Deering plaintiffs.

In November, two months after Sovereign bit the dust, Kimberly Reese, under a blistering attack from dozens of agents on her Web site's disapproval list, shut down the Write Connection. She couldn't afford to hire a lawyer to fend off the threatened lawsuits. That she held on so long under such hostile conditions revealed her commitment to helping writers spot the charlatans. She was a pioneer and, in the world of the aspiring writer, a hero.

Science fiction writer Ann C. Crispin and fantasy novelist Victoria Strauss incorporated the data Kim Reese had accumulated into a Web site they had been operating called Writer Beware. As a service for members of Science Fiction and Fantasy Writers of America, writers could analyze the available data and decide for themselves whether they wanted to do business with a listed agency or publisher.[2]

Now that the Deering name was mud, Daniel Craig Deering, to wash off the stink of fraud, decided to call himself the Daniel Craig Literary Group. In an all-client memo dated December 18, 1998, he wrote,

> It is with great pride that I introduce the merge of the Deering Literary Agency into the Daniel Craig Literary Group. However, with this merge the Daniel Craig Literary Group must deny any responsibility for any perceived errors of the Deering Literary Agency.

About the time Daniel Craig Deering was desperately trying to separate himself from the people who had taught him the genteel racket, he was interviewed by phone by a reporter doing a story on the Deering-Sovereign scandal. In support of his contention that "I do run things completely differently," Daniel noted that while Dorothy had two hundred to three hundred clients at a time, he worked with only eighty. He also denied charging his clients up-front fees. When asked to describe his current relationship with Dorothy and Chuck, Daniel said he was "not in the best standings" with them.[3]

Dorothy and Chuck were now living with his mother in her double-wide in Davenport, Florida. William Paul Watson, a.k.a. Bill Richardson, was out on bail in Georgia, and Daniel Craig Deering, under his new name, was fleecing writers from his house in Nicholasville. Bill and Daniel hated each other; both couldn't stand Dorothy; and Dorothy blamed Bill for everything. Like a pack of wild dogs, the only things that had held them together so long were their hunger and the availability of easy prey.

Now they were the ones about to be hunted.

I sensed, but could not prove, that the reason that books weren't going to the printer was because the money had already been spent or diverted for the Deerings' personal use.

—Jim Russo, former editor, Sovereign Publications

21   The Hunter

AS SOVEREIGN AUTHORS ACROSS THE COUNTRY LISTENED to Chuck Deering's prerecorded kiss-off, FBI agent Clay Mason settled into his new office in Frankfort, Kentucky. He had spent the previous thirteen years assigned to the field office in Washington, D.C., where he had specialized in the investigation of government fraud and public corruption. His last case, a six-year investigation of Pentagon fraud, had resulted in the imprisonment of several bigwigs, including an assistant secretary of the Navy. It was one of those cases important enough to have a title, "Ill Wind," and to become the subject of a book.[1]

The two-agent FBI outpost in Frankfort, the state capital, twenty-five miles west of Lexington, was operated as a branch of the Louisville field division. Mason, born and raised in central Kentucky, had returned home. While a business administration major at the University of Kentucky, Mason had been fascinated and impressed with the FBI's role in the famous Abscam sting investigation in which U.S. congressmen and other high-ranking officials were caught taking bribes from a bureau undercover informant. After graduating in 1985 from law school at the University of Louisville, Mason realized his dream by becoming a special agent with the Federal Bureau of Investigation.

Tall, with sandy graying hair combed back in the style of a business executive, the neatly mustached, bespectacled agent cut the figure of a careful and dogged investigator capable of unraveling complex conspiracies composed of deception, corruption, and trails of phony paper. While most FBI agents chased after bank robbers, car thieves, mobsters, and drug dealers, Mason went after the white-collar criminal, the crook who picked your pocket while shaking your hand. Over the years, Mason had fine-tuned his ability to detect the scent of fraud and to follow it to its source. Married to Jane, a veterinarian turned teacher, and the father of three, Mason had the demeanor of a professional man in a southern town where people spoke with a drawl and took pains to be polite. He was a man who seemed at home with his environment, his job, and himself.

Six months after being transferred from the Washington field office, Mason, while talking with a supervisor in the Lexington resident agency, noted that the caseload in Frankfort had been light. With time on his hands, Mason asked whether there were any cases in Lexington he could work on. As it turned out, there was a case—well, just a complaint—that was right down Mason's alley. A local publishing company had just gone under, and in the wake of its collapse, a number of authors who had paid to have their books published were alleging fraud. No one in the office knew anything about publishing or how a such a business could entail fraudulent behavior. As a result, the writers' complaints had not been investigated.

Mason had never investigated or even heard of a case of fraud involving a publishing company. His only brush with the literary world had to do with a children's book he had written, which had caused him to read a couple of how-to manuals on query letters, the role of literary agents, and who published what. Having failed to interest a literary agent in his work, he also knew the sting of rejection and how frustration and desperation could cloud a writer's thinking and make him vulnerable. That wasn't much, but at least he would be able to see things from the writer's point of view. Yes, he was willing to look over the complaints against the Lexington publisher.

When he leafed through the file on Sovereign Publications, a firm that had been doing business on East Reynolds Road, Mason was immediately struck by how detailed, documented, and well articulated the complaints were. They were, in essence, mini investigative reports. This quality was particularly true of the material sent to the FBI in Boston by a Diane Goshgarian. The file also contained letters and documents sent over by the Kentucky attorney general's office.[2] A writer named Thomas E. Mahon had provided an enormous amount of information, along with his own analysis of how and why he and hundreds of other writers were victims of fraud. Mason was both impressed and intrigued. One thing was obvious; victimize a writer and the story gets told.

The central villains in these accounts were Dorothy L. Deering and her husband, Charles F. Deering. Dorothy owned the publishing company and a literary agency headquartered in Nicholasville. Playing supporting roles were bad guys Bill Richardson and Chuck' son, Daniel Craig Deering. Richardson, while a fugitive from the law, had been Dorothy's chief publishing operative, whereas Daniel Craig had worked in her literary agency. Mason was amazed that all this literary activity—writer representation and book publishing—had taken place in central Kentucky. Coming across words and phrases like *contract fee, joint venture,* and *upgrade to trade paper* and references to ADP, NPI, and CPI, Mason realized he would have to bone up.

The core complaint against Dorothy Deering, doing business as Sovereign Publications—the allegation that had the strongest whiff of fraud—was that she had taken money from writers under the false pretense of publishing their manuscripts. After she had enriched herself with funds earmarked for the production of paperback books, she had closed shop to avoid paying back the money. If this allegation were true and could be proven, Mason would have a case. To establish this case in a criminal court, Mason would have to present evidence that Dorothy had solicited money with no intention of producing any books. In other words, he would have to provide evidence of criminal intent. Was Dorothy Deering a crook or just a lousy businesswoman? If the complaints were to be believed, she was a criminal.

Special Agent Mason, back in his office in Frankfort (surprisingly cluttered for a man with such an orderly mind), began studying the supporting documents supplied by the complainants. He read five editions of *News & Notes,* material that had been published on the Deering and Sovereign Web sites, the first and only issue of the *Sovereign Digest,* correspondence (including e-mail) between Dorothy and her employees and various authors, and the terms of joint venture contracts issued by Northwest, Commonwealth, and Sovereign Publications. He also took the time to consult a number of New York City literary agents and publishing house editors. He read material published by the Association of Authors' Representatives and spoke to scam hunters Ann C. Crispin and Victoria Strauss. The more he learned about the world of legitimate publishing, the more he could see the outlines of the genteel racket and Dorothy Deering's place in it. Mason had learned, for example, that there was nothing wrong with subsidy publishing as long as it was presented honestly. But when offered as a commercial alternative to nonvanity publishing, it was bogus. Joint venture, as marketed by Jim Van Treese, Donald Phelan, and Dorothy Deering, was a scam.

Mason's interest in the case intensified when he learned that about fifteen years before, Dorothy had pleaded guilty to embezzlement in Tennessee, and that Bill Richardson was William Paul Watson, a fugitive from the law who was being harbored in Lexington by his sister. That Dorothy had employed Daniel Craig Deering as a literary agent was also revealing. Not only did he lack experience in the field, he was a ninth-grade dropout with a drug addiction. Her husband, a former car salesman, had been running the literary agency while Dorothy was busy with Sovereign. Mason doubted, under the circumstances, Dorothy's claim that she was the daughter of William F. Morrow. He could check that out easily. If she had lied about it, she had probably lied about everything.

A few weeks into his investigation, the general counsel for the Morrow Company reported to Mason that probate records related to William F. Morrow showed that he had never been married to a Betty Morrow nor did he have a daughter. Dorothy Deering was not in any way related to the publishing magnate. She had lied about a matter she knew would greatly influence the decisions of her authors.[3]

On March 3, 1999, six months after Chuck Deering lowered the boom on Sovereign authors everywhere, Special Agent Clay Mason of the Frankfort resident agency officially opened a case of wire and mail fraud schemes against Dorothy Deering and Sovereign Publications.[4] The investigation would also include the related activities of Charles Deering, William Paul Watson, and Daniel Craig Deering. Before making his decision to utilize his time and the resources of the FBI to probe this matter, Clay Mason had gathered more than enough evidence to convince himself he was going after the right people. In this investigation, he didn't expect to be drilling a dry hole.

Pat Sullivan, the owner of the office building at 128 East Reynolds Road, was one of the first people interviewed in Mason's freshly opened case. In October 1997, Mr. Sullivan met with Dorothy and Chuck Deering to discuss the leasing, to Sovereign Publications, of six unfurnished offices. Walking with the help of a cane, Dorothy said that her company, the publisher of religious books, was in good financial shape. She handed

Sullivan a sheet of paper containing a list of her company's assets. That day, Dorothy and Chuck signed a two-year lease in which they agreed to pay monthly rent of $1,450. Six months after moving in with their rented furniture, the Deerings fell behind in their rent. Sullivan sent them a notice, and when they didn't respond, he called Dorothy. Blaming the delinquency on personal tragedies, her recent knee surgery and the murder of her son, Dorothy promised to take care of the problem. For a while, the rent came in on time; then it stopped. Eleven months after the Deerings signed the lease, Mr. Sullivan, while having lunch at a nearby restaurant, ran into another one of his tenants. "My neighbors just moved out," he said. He was referring to Sovereign Publications. Mr. Sullivan had no idea they were leaving.[5] The Deerings, having paid rent for only ten months of a two-year lease, would end up owing Mr. Sullivan $20,300, money he would not recover.

To learn more about the Deerings and the man everyone knew as Bill Richardson, Mason started interviewing the people who had worked at Sovereign Publications. Since they had all been written about in the *Sovereign Digest,* identifying them was not a problem. Mason found Jim Russo, the young college graduated hired in September 1997 to do editorial work. He was the most articulate and helpful.

A couple of weeks after Jim Russo was fired by Bill Richardson, he wrote an eight-page letter to a Sovereign author named Paul D. Shackelford.[6] One of the initial FBI complainants, Shackelford had included Russo's January 13, 1998, letter with other documents attached to his complaint. Russo's letter, a virtual investigative report, detailed everything the editor had learned about Dorothy Deering, Bill Richardson, Daniel Craig Deering, and Sovereign Publications during his four-month employment there. It provided the FBI agent with a thorough overview of Sovereign's operations and thumbnail sketches of the people who ran the company. Russo's description of Sovereign's methods of acquiring manuscripts helped Mason understand how Dorothy had lured so many writers into her trap.

> Potential Sovereign authors came into contact with us in several ways: 1) they saw our ads in various magazines; 2) they were steered to Sovereign via Deering [Literary Agency]; 3) other agents referred them to us. (I'm fairly certain that Bill Richardson had Jessica and Carolyn contact several agents via a mass mailing to offer them commissions for steering clients to Sovereign); or 4) old Deering files were combed through for names of past/inactive clients.

When it came to witnessing, from the inside, the infamous publishing delays that led to the erosion of Dorothy's credibility and, ultimately, to the demise of Sovereign, Jim Russo had a front-row seat.

> In a meeting with Bill Richardson, a former carpet salesman who ran the day-to-day operations, and his sister Dorothy Deering at her house, I witnessed them reschedule the publishing dates of numerous books. (I do not remember the exact date of this meeting, but it was after Dorothy's knee surgery and her son's murder, because Chuck and Dorothy argued about paying attorney fees for her son's friends.) ... The rescheduling was done with the understanding that Bill would notify the authors and obtain their consent. He later did so by telling the authors that the rescheduling was being done for marketing considerations (i.e., "timing" for optimal publicity). Yet, no such considerations were ever discussed in that meeting with Dorothy. Instead, she seemed to make her decisions on whether or not she liked the authors.... [A]t least once, Dorothy rescheduled books by coming into the office and pointing out manuscript boxes with her cane. Her decisions seemed to be made on the spur of the moment. Many of the books that were delayed were in fact ready to go to the printer. I never did discover the true reason for the delays.

It didn't take Russo long to see through Dorothy's pretensions of being a player in the publishing and film industries. He must have been wildly amused by what he considered a bit of her false advertising.

> Dorothy had the walls of the agency covered with signed photos of movie stars, many of which she claimed to know personally. She also claimed to spend a good deal of time representing her clients to the top publishers and producers in New York and Hollywood each year.

Russo had also noticed that Dorothy and Chuck were not above flaunting their wealth, and that this did not sit well with Bill Richardson.

> The Deerings took frequent, expensive vacations, owned a large home in the Rabbit Run subdivision of Lexington (at least it was my impression they owned the home) and sported expensive jewelry (Chuck Deering showed me a 7 carat diamond ring that Dorothy recently had purchased for him), and paid all of Bill Richardson's housing and utility expenses (according to Bill). Yet, I once heard Bill Richardson complaining that the Deerings were spending Sovereign's money as fast as it came in.... Bill complained that they had taken too many trips and that we needed to bring in some more contracts. Toward the end of

my tenure there, I was prohibited from working overtime (at the rate of $15/hr.), and we were all forced to take time off without pay.

Russo, while he got along fairly well with Bill Richardson, found him, as a publisher, out of his element. He was also a liar.

I often overheard Bill telling prospective authors on the phone that we received a thousand submissions per month and only contracted a tiny fraction of those. The truth was that we probably received one hundred submissions per month (and that is a generous estimate) and accepted at least 90% of them. We tracked all submissions with a database; I do not know if the records are still available.

It seemed as if Bill devoted almost all of his time to securing contracts and very little to marketing/publishing. Carolyn [Thue] often complained that the only thing he cared about was selling contracts. He prided himself on his sales ability, and on more than one occasion, he told me not to worry because the books would sell, even though he was apparently making no effort in that direction.

That Daniel Craig Deering was an even odder fit than Bill Richardson hadn't escaped Russo's attention, as well as the fact the two men didn't get along.

When I began working at Sovereign Publications, we were located across the hall from the Deering Literary Agency in an office in Nicholasville. Sovereign later moved to Lexington, apparently because Bill and Dan Deering were struggling for control of the company. One day, early in my tenure, I walked by Dan's door and observed Bill and Dan angrily shoving each other back and forth yelling at each other.

Dorothy and Chuck were allowing Chuck's son, Dan, to take over the business, despite the fact that Dan (to my knowledge), never even graduated from high school. (I recall Jessica Johnson telling me he dropped out in ninth grade.) On a trip to the printer in Illinois, Dan asked me if I would give him basic grammar lessons.

Russo's letter not only provided Special Agent Mason with a wealth of information and dozens of productive leads, it contained, in the following, one of the elements he would need to prove a case of fraud.

I sensed, but could not prove, that the reason that books weren't going to the printer was because the money had already been spent or diverted for the Deerings' personal use.

This revelation, and the fact that Bill Richardson had fired his editorial staff eight months before Dorothy and Chuck cut and ran, indicated to Mason that, for at least eight months, Dorothy Deering was taking her authors' money under the false pretense of publishing their books.

As word spread that the Deerings and Bill Richardson were subjects of an official FBI investigation, information in the form of letters and documentation began pouring into Mason's office. The more Mason learned about his subjects and their victims, the more hooked he became on the case. Every night he lugged papers home, where he'd work on the case after hours. It had become a labor of love. And no one loved it more than Dorothy's victims. Finally, someone was listening; someone who carried a badge and could make arrests.

22   Poor Dorothy

SPECIAL AGENT CLAY MASON'S INVESTIGATIVE INTEREST IN
Dorothy Deering had expanded beyond her doing business as Sovereign
Publications. He was now interested in her operation of the Deering Literary Agency and Atlantic Disk Publishers and her relationships with
joint venture publishers Jim Van Treese and Donald T. Phelan. To establish a decade-long pattern of deceit and unmet promises, and associa-
tions with other practitioners of publishing shams, Mason, armed with
a long list of victims, asked fifteen FBI field divisions to interview Deering
clients and Sovereign authors. Agents in those offices were also asked to
collect correspondence, contracts, and other documents pertinent to
Mason's investigation. An agent assigned to the Portland, Maine, office
questioned Vicki and Chris Scott, who were living in Booth Harbor.
Dorothy's sister and her husband, having themselves been practitioners
in the genteel racket, were not particularly forthcoming about the
Deerings.[1] Chris Scott did confirm that he was in fact the son of Randolph
Scott. Their agency, A Rising Sun, had gone under a couple of months
after Dorothy launched Sovereign. They, therefore, had little knowledge
of that aspect of Dorothy's business.

In addition to Mason's leads being covered in the other FBI offices,
he decided to call around the country and interview many victims himself. This practice saved a lot of time and, because Mason was so familiar with the case, produced better results. Conducting a nationwide investigation from his office in Frankfort, Mason heard story after story of
how Dorothy Deering, with the help of her family, had taken her authors'
money, strung them along with excuses, then kissed them off after they

had been bled dry. These writers were angry, heartbroken, and ashamed. They still couldn't believe what had happened to them. They were suffering, and they wanted Dorothy to pay for what she had done. She was a monster with a soft, little voice and a sweet line of bull. They wanted justice; they wanted revenge; they wanted to stop thinking of themselves as fools. People got stung by auto mechanics, home repair contractors, funeral directors, stockbrokers, and used car salesmen. But what kind of fool let himself get nailed by a goddamned literary agent? Mason knew the answer to that: an aspiring writer. Mason believed that Dorothy's victims were too hard on themselves. They had done nothing wrong. Mason was convinced they were victims of a cold-blooded swindler. Who would expect that their literary agent was a serial thief?

Pushing his investigation forward from the initial complainants, Dorothy's former employees at Sovereign, and a wide array of her victims, Mason sought out and questioned the half dozen or so women who had served brief stints as her personal bookkeeper. They had all left her employ when they realized she was cooking the books by treating joint venture money as income instead of debt.

Piecing together Dorothy's financial picture from assorted documents and records, public and private, Mason determined that Dorothy had a lot of money to spend. During the calendar year 1997, one of her best years, the Deering Literary Agency brought in ninety thousand dollars, and Sovereign Publications $992,000. Of that money, $677,000 went straight to Dorothy and Chuck in the form of personal expenses, "profits," bonuses, and salary. This amount didn't include twelve thousand dollars for "travel" and thirty-one thousand dollars for "housing." Most of what was left over went to Bill Richardson and Donald Craig Deering. None of it went for books. This was the year Dorothy and Chuck went on extended vacations, furnished a home, and purchased their new body parts. The only activity in 1997 that even came close to publishing involved creation of the *Sovereign Digest,* a tool they would use to steal more money.

Having done his homework, Mason was ready to talk to the subjects of his investigation. If they lied to him, he would know it; if they tried to con him, he would know that, too. He didn't want to grill anyone; it wasn't the time for a full-scale, give-them-their-Miranda-rights interrogation. He wanted to size them up, get their story, and perhaps get them rattled. He knew there were rifts in the family, hostilities he could exploit. He knew that among thieves, there was no such thing as honor. Mainly there was greed, cunning, and, when things get hot, self-interest. And there was a lot of stupidity. Unlike their portrayal in the media, most criminals are in fact stupid.

Mason decided to start with Daniel Craig Deering. No longer bilking writers as a phony literary agent and book doctor, Daniel was still living in Nicholasville with his wife and young daughter. He had moved out of the house on Davis Drive and was renting a more modest place in a less suburban neighborhood. He was now dabbling in the home improvement business.[2]

On the last day of March 1999, the FBI agent paid Daniel Craig Deering a surprise visit at his home. Mason informed Deering that he was gathering information relative to a mail fraud investigation of the Deering Literary Agency and Sovereign Publications. Seeing Daniel as he was that day, no one in the literary world would have believed he had managed to impersonate even a fee-based agent. Had it not been for the telephone and Dorothy's form letters, he never would have made it in the genteel racket.

Keeping his cool and acting friendly and a little puzzled as to why the FBI would be talking to him, Deering said he knew very little about Sovereign Publications other than the fact that Bill Richardson, a grossly incompetent man, had run it into the ground. As for the literary agency, he had taken it over after Dorothy had disgraced the family name by spending all the money on herself instead of the business. At the time he purchased the agency and tried to save it, Dorothy was so hooked on pain medicine from her knee operation and so distraught over the murder of her son, she had no idea what she was doing. The woman was a basket case. Daniel had done all he could to save the agency, even changing its name, but the damage had been done. When Dorothy used Sovereign Publications to give her brother a job and to hide him from the police, the company was doomed. Richardson had treated his employees like dirt and lied to his authors. Dorothy and her brother had ruined a pair of very good companies. Chuck Deering, a decent and honorable man, never should have married that woman.

Daniel, perhaps in an attempt to gain a little sympathy, mentioned that he had recently hurt his back in a car accident, an injury that would require major surgery. "What was it about these people and their bodies?" Mason wondered. Daniel's back; his dad's kidney, then hips; and Dorothy's knee—when things got tough, the Deerings got surgery.

During the course of the interview, Daniel Deering made reference to boxes of manuscripts and other papers stored in his basement. He said he had thrown out a ton of agency paper when he moved out of the house on Davis.[3] What was left of his literary files, the boxes in the basement, he had no use for and would be throwing away. If Mason was interested in this material, it was his. The agent took up Deering's offer, and when he drove back to Frankfort that day, he had a back seat and trunk full of what was left of the Deering Literary Agency.

In his desire to appear cooperative and aboveboard, Deering had given the FBI a treasure trove of evidence. Once again, Mason was reminded of how stupid most criminals were. Even the white-collar kind.

When they learned they were the subjects of an FBI investigation, Dorothy and Chuck sold Chuck's diamond ring and hired a lawyer in Lexington to arrange a sit-down with the agent in charge of the case. Dorothy would represent herself as a literary agent and publisher who had been highly respected and hardworking. After working ten years to establish herself, she had lost everything through bad luck and tragedy. She would tell the agent that if her brother, Bill Watson, had made criminal allegations about her, it was out of spite and not true. He was the criminal in the family and was getting even with Chuck, whom he thought had turned him into the authorities in Georgia. She and Chuck were coming to Lexington to straighten out this misunderstanding. They would be staying with her old friend and Bill Richardson hater, Mary Layne. Layne was now married to David Brannon, the employee Richardson had forced out of Sovereign after he fired his girlfriend.

The meeting with the FBI agent had been set for Tuesday, April 13, 1999, in the attorney's office. Mason had only one condition; he wanted to speak with the Deerings separately. He would start his interview with Dorothy at ten in the morning and question Chuck in the afternoon. Mason would not try to persuade either one to confess. He simply wanted to draw them out and record what they had to say for themselves. If they lied, he could prove it. He was confident he would eventually be able to make his case with or without their cooperation. In cases like this, there wasn't blood or other physical evidence connecting the suspects to the crime. Dorothy hadn't spilled any blood, but she had spilled a lot of ink, and it was her published writings that revealed her method of operation and documented her deceit. Dorothy's paper trail was Mason's best evidence. He'd confront her with her own words. He would also impress her with his knowledge of how she did business within the genteel racket. She would realize the extent of his preparations for the interview. She would know he had her number by the detailed nature of his questions. He wouldn't have to raise his voice or accuse her of anything. He would, with her lawyer looking on, psychologically apply the rubber hose. Compared with banging heads with some low-grade street thug, this meeting would be interrogative ecstasy.

The Dorothy Deering that Mason had come to imagine through her letters, press releases, newsletters, and Web page, the manic merchant of the writer's dream, was nothing like the woman who walked into the lawyer's office. Disheveled, plain, squat, and wrapped around a pair of arm crutches, she looked like a farm woman who had been kicked by a horse. Instead of a brassy, fast-talking sociopath, he was confronted by a soft-spoken, drug-addled melancholic. Mason had his game, and Dorothy had hers, and she was good. He wasn't the only one who had prepared for the interview.

Mason introduced himself and said that in light of the numerous allegations of fraud made against her, he appreciated the opportunity to hear what she had to say about her ten-year career in the literary business. Mason suggested that she start by outlining the key events in her life—how she met Chuck, got into the business, and so forth—then chronicle her career as a literary agent and publisher.

Dorothy, without reference to William F. Morrow, said that when she couldn't get her science fiction novel published through a literary agent, decided to become one herself. Things were tough at first—it's not an easy business to succeed in—but slowly she built a client base. In 1990, she moved the agency from Nicholasville, Kentucky, to Acworth, Georgia. A few years later, she started an association with Northwest Publishing of Salt Lake City. In describing her business with NPI, Mason noticed that Dorothy failed to mention the 10-percent "finder's fees" or that Jim Van Treese had paid to become a *silent* partner in the Deering Literary Agency, details she had also kept from her NPI authors. NPI went under, and Dorothy began doing business with a Canadian joint venture publisher called Commonwealth Publications. In talking about NPI and CPI, Dorothy never used the words *vanity* or *subsidy*. In describing her relationship with these two publishers, Dorothy carefully pointed out that

Van Treese and Phelan simply had the right of first refusal on her clients' manuscripts. She didn't say, but she and Mason knew, that in joint venture publishing, there is no such thing as a manuscript refusal.

In 1996, with Northwest in bankruptcy and Commonwealth in trouble, Dorothy started Sovereign Publications, her own joint venture company. She had always dreamt of helping aspiring writers realize their dreams of being published. And she was doing just that until November 25, 1997, the day her son, Michael Helm, was shot to death in Kennesaw, Georgia. After that her businesses spun out of control. Her brother, William, in the wake of her personal devastation—she was also recovering from knee surgery—took control of Sovereign and ran the company into the ground. She sold the literary agency to Chuck's son, Daniel Craig Deering. She had trained the young man herself, but for some reason he was unable to make a go of the agency. Daniel Craig had personal problems of his own and wasn't ready for the responsibility of all those writers, some of whom could act like children. Whatever happened to the agency after she had sold it was not her responsibility.

Dorothy was amazed that after all she had been through, she was being investigated by the FBI. She had lost everything; wasn't that punishment enough? Ten years of hard work, a decade of devotion to the unpublished writer, was down the drain. She had lost her livelihood, her businesses, and her life's work. This was a tragedy, not a federal crime.

Dorothy informed the agent that over the past ten years, she had learned a lot about writers. As creative people, they had big imaginations. They also tended to be self-centered and, when they didn't get what they wanted, could be unreasonable and even cruel. Diane Goshgarian and Thomas Mahon were good examples of that. Many Deering clients and authors had taken their anger and frustration out on her. They wanted blood, blaming Dorothy for events that had been out of her control. The writers weren't the only ones who were suffering. They hadn't lost everything. Dorothy said she had always tried to help her clients and authors. Sovereign was built on Christian principles, as reflected in the company motto, which was to "represent and publish for the good of mankind." It's too bad some of her writers couldn't show a little more understanding, forgiveness, and mercy.

Special Agent Mason was a little short on forgiveness and mercy, but he had plenty of understanding. His investigation had led him to understand that Dorothy Deering represented and published for the good of Dorothy Deering. To hell with mankind. Now that Dorothy had recited her spiel, performed her role as the misunderstood victim, it was Mason's turn. Because her entire enterprise was founded and operated on deceit, the agent hardly knew where to begin.

23 The Genteel Grilling

MASON DECIDED TO START HIS QUESTIONING by getting Dorothy Deering to admit that she was not related to William F. Morrow. He called her attention to the July 20, 1993, Atlantic Disk Publishers press release in which she had written, "Mrs. Deering is the daughter of Betty Morrow of the original Morrow publishing family." Five years later, she was still making the claim on the Deering Web site. To make sure prospective clients realized the significance of her family ties, she had written, "Her background as the daughter of Betty Morrow from the original Morrow publishing family, gave her an edge in the industry." Mason pointed out that Dorothy had used the Morrow family connection to acquire joint venture money by referring to Sovereign Publications as a "Morrow family publisher." Since the Morrow affiliation was obviously important to her business, Mason wanted to know exactly *how* her mother, Betty Morrow, was related to the famous publisher. When Dorothy didn't respond to his pointed question, Mason pressed the issue. He said he had asked this question because many of the writers he had spoken to had told him that the Morrow connection had influenced their decisions to sign on with her agency and her publishing company.

Well, Dorothy replied, it was hard for her to control what went on in an author's mind.

But wasn't that the point? Mason asked. By making such a big deal about William F. Morrow, wasn't she doing just that? Wasn't she trying to control what they thought about her and her enterprises?

No, not really. She dealt with intelligent adults who were capable of making their own decisions.

They were going around in circles, so Mason decided to lay his cards on the table. He said he had spoken to the attorney in charge of the William F. Morrow estate and there was no reference to a Betty Morrow in the probate records. In fact, Mr. Morrow was not married to a woman named Betty, his mother was not named Betty, he had no sisters with that name, and he had only one child, a boy. What did Dorothy think of that?

Dorothy asked how she was supposed to think of it.

But wasn't she, by falsely representing herself as a member of the William F. Morrow family, using deception as a means of getting writers to pay her fees? Why else would she lie about something like this? What Christian principle was she applying here?

Dorothy seemed taken aback by Mason's challenge to her integrity. She insisted she was not a liar. It was true she couldn't explain exactly how she was related to William F. Morrow, but since childhood she had been told there was a relationship. In business, in advertising, everybody exaggerated. They had a term for it: puffing. To suggest some kind of fraudulent behavior here was unfair and uncalled for. She was simply trying to make it, for herself and her clients, in a very tough industry.

Mason asked Dorothy to describe the education, training, and experience that had prepared her for a career in literary representation. Wasn't this a field that required specialized training and experience within the publishing industry? And didn't most, if not all, literary agents learn their trade in and around publishing centers like New York City?

Dorothy said there were hundreds of agents, like her, who were self-taught, and who did business outside New York City and other metropolitan areas. If it weren't for these agents, first-time writers would never find representation. Just because she didn't have a fancy education didn't mean she couldn't help aspiring writers. Mason asked Dorothy how far she had gotten in school. She had graduated, she said, from Fairmont High School near Dayton, Ohio, in 1962.

Mason, with a copy of the May 1995 issue of *News & Notes* in front of him, asked Dorothy if she had ever advertised herself as having degrees from Ohio State and Brigham Young universities. Did she recall telling a client named Vernon Mallow that she had degrees from these schools?

Dorothy replied that she had represented thousands of writers and had no way of recalling what she might have said to any one of them. As to what was printed in one of the newsletters, anything was possible given that her husband Chuck was the editor in chief. As a former salesman,

Chuck was capable of a little puffing himself. When did they start putting people in jail for hyping their resumes?

Mason prefaced his next set of questions by reading from a Deering form letter sent to prospective clients: "It is our agency's standard practice to 'test the waters' before we even suggest a representation contract. We will only be accepting a few new manuscripts for representation in the next few months and would like you to respond within the next week so we can fill one of these limited openings." By "testing the waters," a phrase also used by Donald Phelan, was Dorothy implying that a publishing house editor had read the prospective client's manuscript and was interested in the book?

It meant, Dorothy said, that she had contacted an editor about the manuscripts and that the work was on its way. She never said the editor had *read* the manuscript and wanted to publish it.

Mason asked what Dorothy meant by "contacting" the editor. Had she spoken to this person when in New York City on one of her manuscript selling trips? Had she talked over the phone with this editor? Could she name a few of the New York City editors she regularly talked to about prospective clients' manuscripts? Perhaps she could describe a few of her success stories regarding these books. Mason said he wanted to write down the author's names, the titles of the books, and the identity of the publishers. Having been a literary agent for ten years, she must have had plenty of success stories. Mason needed only a few.

Dorothy said she was in no condition to provide Mason with that kind of detail. She was ill and had been under tremendous stress since her knee operation, the murder of her son, and the collapse of the publishing company. By "testing the waters" she had simply meant that the market conditions for a prospective client's manuscript were good and that the work would be submitted to a group of carefully selected editors. There were no guarantees in this business, and her writers knew that.

In addition to implying publishing interest in the prospective client's work, wasn't Dorothy, in that letter, creating a false impression of exclusivity? Wasn't it a fact that no prospective client willing to pay the contract fee was ever turned down? Wasn't "we will only be accepting a few new manuscripts for representation" a lie?

Dorothy wanted to make it clear that some prospective clients were in fact rejected. For example, she would never represent pornography.

How many pornographic manuscripts came into the agency?

Dorothy said she would have no way of knowing that.

What percentage of nonpornographic manuscripts were rejected for representation? Fifty percent? Twenty percent?

Dorothy couldn't answer that question, either. Who had time to keep records like that?

Mason asked Dorothy whether she read every manuscript her agency represented.

She said yes, she read every one.

How many clients did she represent, say, in 1995 or 1996?

Dorothy said she couldn't answer that. Her husband Chuck kept track of that kind of information.

Was it one hundred, two hundred, seven hundred?

Whatever the exact number, Dorothy replied, there is no question they were running a successful business. That was something she was quite proud of. They worked hard, maybe too hard.

Was it true, Mason asked, that the Deering Literary Agency was the third-largest company of its kind in America?

Dorothy allowed that this was possible, but she didn't know that for a fact.

But didn't you tell that to people?

No, of course not.

Did Chuck tell people that?

He could have. She had no way of controlling what her husband said.

Could her brother have told authors the agency was that big?

Yes, that sounded like something Bill might say. He sometimes got carried away.

Questioning Dorothy was like grilling someone who was either very stupid or mildly schizophrenic. It was like herding cats. So you had a big agency with a lot of clients?

Yes.

How many agents did you employ?

Dorothy said that she and Charles, with the help of their children, did all of the work.

You were successful.

Yes.

In what way were you successful?

We had a good business.

What does that mean, "good business"?

We had a lot of clients.

Did you sell a lot of manuscripts?

Yes.

To royalty-paying publishers?

Yes, many.

Then why did you have to charge up-front fees?

Because, Dorothy explained, it cost a lot of money to market a client's manuscript.

But didn't you get that back in commission?

Not if there was no commission.

So how much did it cost to market a client's manuscript to Northwest or Commonwealth or, for that matter, to Sovereign?

Before she presented joint venture offers to her clients, she had marketed their manuscripts to publishers that offered standard contracts.

What about Sovereign?

Same story.

Who paid to have the manuscripts copied?

The client.

Who paid to have their manuscripts pitched in New York and Los Angeles?

The client.

Mason asked Dorothy to break down the cost of marketing one manuscript for one year. He said he needed help in understanding how that cost Dorothy five hundred dollars. In other words, how much of that five hundred went to pay rent, how much to paying the phone bill, and what percentage to postage? Could she give him a cost breakdown?

Absolutely not. She wasn't an accountant.

But didn't her clients demand that kind of financial accountability?

Of course not. They knew how difficult it was to sell a manuscript. They knew how hard she worked for them.

So they trusted you?

Yes.

They trusted you with their manuscripts and their money?

Yes.

Did you feel any responsibility or remorse when Northwest and Commonwealth collapsed? The failures of those companies cost your clients more than $2 million. How would you feel if you had paid an agent five hundred dollars to be hooked up with a publisher that cost you another five thousand dollars or so?

Dorothy said she couldn't understand how the failure of a couple of publishing houses had anything to do with her. As an agent, it was her duty to pass on every publishing offer to her clients. They were adults; they could make their own decisions about their books.

Yes, Mason countered, but you were more than just a conduit; you *sold* your clients on those deals. You were able to talk them into these contracts because they trusted you. Had they known of your financial interest in these companies, would they have trusted you enough to gamble their money?

Financial interest? What financial interest?

The kickbacks. Did your clients know about the kickbacks?

They were finder's fees, standard in the business. Dorothy said she was as shocked as her clients when things went bad at NPI and CPI. She wasn't running those companies; her clients knew that. It's a tough industry. She had lost thousands in potential royalties when NPI and CPI went under. Who could blame her for someone else's bad management?

From a February 1995 form letter in which Dorothy was, with great pride, inviting a prospective client to join her group of prestigious authors, Mason read, "The Dorothy Deering Literary Agency now has agents in all book-starved Russian territories, Poland, China, Japan, all of the United Kingdom, Canada, Thailand, all of Europe and Africa. Your manuscript will be sent to all of these representatives." Mason wanted to know how many agents comprised this network of foreign Deering literary representatives.

Dorothy wasn't sure.

Fifty?

A handful. One agent represented several countries.

And did you submit manuscripts to foreign publishers?

Yes.

Mason, referring to the summer 1995 issue of *News & Notes,* read Dorothy the following: "We have managed to sell three books in Russia in the last week." Would Dorothy mind identifying those three books?

She couldn't off the top of her head furnish that information. That was a long time ago.

Mason read on. "My Russian agent who covers all Russian territories and Poland, does the translating himself for my authors free of charge upon the sale of their books." True?

Dorothy indicated that it was.

Would she please provide the name of that Russian associate?

The name escaped her. The FBI agent would find it, however, on her Rolodex.

Mason returned to the February 1995 letter. "Upon receiving your signed contracts, you will be included in our catalogue that will be sent to over three hundred publishers and every editor in those publishing houses." Regarding this catalogue, Mason made two points: first, no client he had spoken to had ever seen one, and second, Daniel Craig Deering said it never existed. What did Dorothy have to say about that?

Understaffed and overworked, she was never able to put together the catalogue. That didn't mean she didn't intend to or that she meant to mislead anyone.

Returning to a former theme, Mason asked Dorothy whether her clients, in return for their annual five-hundred-dollar contract fees, got what they paid for. He had spoken to former clients who had paid thousands of dollars in contract fees and, in return, ended up losing thousands more to Jim Van Treese and Donald Phelan. Weren't literary agents supposed to help their clients make money? All of her clients seemed to have lost money. What did she have to say about that?

Dorothy pointed out that she didn't represent writers like Stephen King. It wasn't easy representing first-time authors. You had to be in the publishing business to appreciate this fact.

Mason acknowledged that he wasn't in publishing, but he had interviewed at least six of Dorothy's former employees, who told him that boxes stuffed with different manuscripts were mailed to editors whose names they had pulled out of publishing directories available to the public. These ex-Deering employees also said there were extended periods when nothing went out of the office. Why would writers pay Dorothy to do what they could do themselves?

Because publishers didn't consider author-submitted manuscripts. Writers, particularly aspiring novelists, had to have an agent. That was common knowledge.

Not being in publishing, Mason wanted to know whether other literary agents charged their clients an extra five hundred dollars to personally pitch their manuscripts in New York City and Los Angeles. Wasn't that what the five-hundred-dollar contract fee had purchased?

Dorothy said that she and Chuck worked their tails off during those trips. It wasn't all fun and games. No one was forcing her clients to pay the extra money, and there were no guarantees.

Reciting from the December 1995 issue of *News & Notes*, Mason read: "The last trip to New York yielded four sales and the last trip to Hollywood yielded three options and two sales." Why hadn't Dorothy been more specific about these deals? Didn't literary agents like to advertise their successes? Dorothy had been much more detailed in reporting her sales to Northwest and Commonwealth. Was it possible there were no sales, no movie options? Was this a ploy to keep the travel money rolling in, another case of puffing? Maybe Dorothy could settle the issue right now by simply providing the details of those deals.

It was unreasonable to expect her to remember that kind of thing four years after it happened. They were hectic times; when she looked back, it was all a blur. That's all she had to say about the manuscript excursions to New York and Los Angeles.

Maybe Dorothy could recall something she had told Diane Goshgarian just a year ago. Diane was upset because one month after paying two thousand dollars to have her novel upgraded, Dorothy put all Sovereign books on a six-month delay. In a phone conversation with the writer during which Dorothy agreed to put her book back on schedule, Dorothy mentioned that she and Chuck were negotiating five movie deals for Deering clients. Was that true?

Dorothy didn't recall that conversation. Just because they were negotiating deals didn't mean that any of them came through.

Did Dorothy tell a client she had dinner with the movie director Sydney Pollack? If Mason called Mr. Pollack, would he know who Dorothy Deering was?

Mason was asking her questions she simply couldn't answer. She had met all kinds of people in Hollywood; whether one of them was Sydney Pollack she didn't know. She might have told someone that; she told a lot of people a lot of things. What was the harm?

Mason was wearing Dorothy down, but he couldn't make her snap. He had let her know what he knew and how he felt about the way she had conducted her business. He had documented her lies, the ten-year pattern of deception, and the shear outrageousness of her response to his pointed questions. However, without the tools of remorse, shame, and embarrassment, he would not be able to forge a confession. It was simply not in this woman to admit defeat, to acknowledge wrongdoing, or to take personal responsibility for the harm she had caused. She was as hard-hearted and cold-blooded as any swindler he had ever questioned.

Mason could have continued grilling Dorothy about Sovereign Publications, asking her why she had hired her brother, a fugitive from justice who had no experience in publishing. He could point out the conflict of interest associated with a literary agent vanity publishing her own clients. But he would be lecturing a person who could only recognize one interest—hers. When there was only one interest involved, there was no conflict. Mason knew that everything that took place at Sovereign after the death of Dorothy's son would be blamed on William Paul Watson, a.k.a. Bill Richardson. Dorothy would deny participation in the upgrade scheme, the gift certificate ploy, and the firing of the editorial staff.

Mason and Dorothy had been in the room together four hours when the FBI man terminated the interview. He didn't get a confession, but what he did acquire was a good reading on Dorothy Deering, the person. As he had suspected, she was not some hapless rube who had bitten off more than she could chew. She was a criminal subject worthy of his time and effort. In Mason's opinion, this woman belonged in prison, and he would do his best to put her there.

Clay Mason realized that it wouldn't be enough just to show that Dorothy Deering was a phony and a liar. He would have to prove with solid evidence that Dorothy never relinquished control of Sovereign Publications and that she had raked in hundreds of thousands of joint venture dollars without any intention of publishing books. He believed that he was close to making the case, that all he needed were a few more pieces to the puzzle. He didn't expect Chuck Deering to be much help, but a deal with William Paul Watson was a real possibility.

Sovereign was an organizational mess.

—William Paul Watson

24 Dishonor among Thieves

AFTER HIS FOUR-HOUR BOUT WITH DOROTHY DEERING, Mason carried to his car the two boxes of documents she had brought to the lawyer's office. He had expected more and wondered how much she had destroyed or was holding back. In Dorothy's case, the paper trail was long and twisted, and could lead to jail. Surely what was left of the Deering Literary Agency and Sovereign Publications would fill more than two boxes.

Chuck Deering—husband, caretaker, goodwill ambassador, second banana—strode into the office with a happy face and an extended hand. Casually dressed and obviously used to the new hips joint venture deals had purchased, Chuck was as open, warm, and accommodating as his wife was closed, cold, and hostile. Not only odd as a couple, they were inappropriate, even for a pair of literary phonies. How had these two pulled it off? And for so long? This was a guy who, after failing as a car salesman, had succeeded as the manager of a fee-based literary agency in Nicholasville, Kentucky. The first thing out of his mouth when he walked in the door—"I'll tell you everything you want to know"—was a lie.

As a fraud investigator, when Mason heard a suspect say, "Honest to God," or "I'm not a thief," or "I'll tell you everything," he knew he was dealing with a liar, a crook, or a person who would talk a lot and say nothing. That afternoon in the lawyer's office, Chuck did most of the talking and said very little. Mason listened, took notes, and realized early on that Dorothy and Chuck had come to their interviews well prepared. The only difference in their stories was the point of view. While trying to come off unrehearsed and spontaneous, Chuck didn't wander far from the script: After the sudden and violent death of Michael Helm, Dorothy, already reeling from major surgery, had to remove herself from the day-to-day operations of the literary agency and her publishing company. Chuck couldn't manage the literary agency and the care for Dorothy, so he took a leave of absence that was extended when he underwent surgery. After that, Dorothy, still an emotional and physical wreck, had to care for him. Without Dorothy behind the wheel, the businesses she had created from scratch veered off course and crashed, destroying everything she had worked for. The woman Mason had met that morning was not the Dorothy Deering her writers had known and loved.

Chuck wanted to be perfectly honest, and that meant admitting that mistakes had been made. Perhaps the biggest and most costly error had been putting Dorothy's brother Bill in charge of Sovereign Publications. The man knew nothing about publishing but had been hired only to manage the business end of the operation. When tragedy swept Dorothy away, Bill assumed total control of Sovereign, and the rest is history. At a time when Dorothy's authors needed assurance that publishing delays didn't mean that their contracts were being breached, Bill tried to bully them into submission. He was vulgar and insulting, and turned Dorothy's once loyal authors against her. He completely mishandled everything.

Dorothy had hired top-rated people to work at Sovereign, all of whom quit or were fired by Bill. The folks Bill had hired to replace them all quit because they couldn't stand working for him, either. You can't run a company without employees. Bill ran them all off. Out of the goodness of her heart, Dorothy had given her brother a high-paying job. He repaid her by destroying the business she had worked so hard to establish. That was it; that was the whole story. Chuck had nothing else to say. He'd be happy to answer questions.

After listening to Chuck, Mason had a little more insight into how he and Dorothy had managed to bilk so many writers. Mason didn't see the point of asking Chuck the same questions he had put to Dorothy. She had slapped enough lipstick on the pig. But just to get Chuck to lie, Mason asked him if he could name some of Dorothy's "affiliates" in places like book-starved Russia. Oh, boy, Chuck said, that was a toughie. Dorothy dealt with those people; therefore he didn't have a good memory for that. In response to Mason's questions about the Deering manuscript catalogue that was supposedly sent to every editor in three hundred publishing houses, Chuck said that project never got off the ground. It was a good idea, though. Dorothy had a lot of good ideas.

Mason replied that he was getting the impression that the Deering Literary Agency and Sovereign Publications were nothing but ideas, figments of Dorothy's imagination. She imagined she was the daughter or granddaughter of William F. Morrow. She imagined she was a wheeler and dealer in Hollywood and New York City and did business with imaginary associates around the world. Her cozy relationships with Jim Van Treese and Donald Phelan, and the publication of her newsletters, were the only aspects of her business that seemed to be real.

Having been the business manager of and a contributor to *News & Notes,* maybe Chuck could clear up a question Mason had about an item that appeared in the October-November 1995 issue. It had to do with the new arrangement Dorothy had forged with Donald Phelan and Commonwealth Publications. Reading from the newsletter, Mason said, "They—CPI—are moving us to Nicholasville, Kentucky where the literary agency began, to be close to the web press and paper company to fulfill the U.S. publishing needs." What exactly, Mason wanted to know, was a web press?

Chuck shook his head and smiled. "I have no idea," he said. "You'd have to check with Dorothy."

Mason had nothing further to say to Chuck Deering, so at five o'clock he terminated the interview. Chuck and Dorothy were quite a team; he didn't know anything, and she couldn't remember. The interviews, however, had not been a waste of time. Mason now had a sense of the people he was after, and how he might get them into prison. It really didn't matter that Dorothy had lost her memory of the Deering Literary Agency and Sovereign Publications. Her letters, contracts, company publications, and financial records would tell the story. So would her former employees, including her brother Bill, and, of course, her victims. Dorothy may have lost her memory, but her victims hadn't lost theirs. They would never forget.

Twelve days after Clay Mason took the measure of Dorothy Deering and her sidekick husband, William Paul Watson called the Frankfort office and spoke to the agent. He said he did not want to come out of Mason's investigation as the scapegoat. He wanted the opportunity to tell his side of the story. He said he was back in Kentucky, living with his wife's family near Paintsville, just across the line from Huntington, West Virginia. When could he drive over to Frankfort for a talk? Mason said they could get together on Friday, April 30, 1999.

Watson walked into Mason's office and got right to the point. "Sovereign," he said, "was an organizational mess" when he took over the operation. Because of his background in business, Dorothy had hired him to straighten things out. By the time he came aboard, Dorothy had already turned Sovereign into a pyramid scheme. To prove his charge, he showed Mason a large chart he had made showing joint venture deals created before and after he took charge. As Mason could see from the chart, more deals had been made before he accepted the position than after. As vice president in charge of operations, he was trying to turn Sovereign Publications into a legitimate publishing house when his sister pulled the plug.

The truth was, according to Watson, that Dorothy had given him an impossible job. She kept pushing back the publication dates of books because there was never enough money to print any of them up. While he was dealing every day with angry and unreasonable authors, Dorothy was sitting in front of the television set in her expensively furnished house buying jewelry and Caribbean cruises advertised on the QVC channel. Because Dorothy and Chuck were spending most of the joint venture money on themselves, he had to lay off employees. They bled the company dry, closed the operation down, then moved to Florida. What Dorothy and Chuck did to their Sovereign authors was not his fault. Dorothy was the owner, the boss, and the one who controlled the cash flow. She had the bookkeepers report to her house instead of the office because she didn't want anyone to know how she was diverting the money.

Watson concluded his spiel by making it clear it wasn't his intention to accuse Dorothy and Chuck of any criminal activity; he was simply making sure they didn't turn *him* into the bad guy. Who knows, if Dorothy's son Michael hadn't been murdered, the company might have been saved.

Mason had progressed far enough into his investigation to know that Watson had just fed him a load of crap to save his own neck. However, there was still a lot he didn't know. He hadn't completed Watson's background investigation, and he hadn't yet been given the phone conversation taped by Ellen Brazer. Watson would later have a hard time explaining why he was taking Brazer's joint venture money when he knew, beyond a doubt, that her book would never be published. That tape would be more incriminating than a confession.

In the taped phone conversation with the Miami writer, Watson had said that Sovereign Publications was backed with Morrow money. It was

William F. Morrow who had made Dorothy establish herself as a literary agent before he would finance her publishing venture. Not yet privy to that conversation, Mason, curious as to how Watson would respond, asked him how he and Dorothy knew they were related to William F. Morrow. According to Watson, Dorothy had conducted a genealogical study that revealed that they were related to Anne Spencer Morrow, the noted author and wife of Charles A. Lindbergh, the world-famous aviator. Watson's answer caught Mason by surprise. The outrageous lie that Dorothy and Bill were related to the Lindbergh baby was more than even he had bargained for.

Mason felt he was getting an accurate fix on Dorothy, Chuck, and William Paul Watson, but he wasn't sure what role Daniel Craig Deering had played in the Deering and Sovereign swindles. The young man was obviously a phony, but was he a crook and, if so, how bad a one? On the day of the Watson interview, Mason paid Daniel a surprise visit at his house in Nicholasville. The FBI agent said it was only fair that Daniel knew he had interviewed Dorothy, Chuck, and Dorothy's brother Bill. Mason couldn't reveal what they had told him, but it might be a good time for Daniel to line up a sharp defense attorney. After pounding that little bug into Daniel's ear, Mason bid him goodbye.

Having met Dorothy and her crew, Mason figured that when push came to shove, it would be Dorothy, Chuck, and Daniel Craig against William Paul Watson. That meant, in all likelihood, that Watson, being outnumbered, would launch a preemptive strike. He'd be the first, in other words, to make a deal. There was, thank God, no honor among thieves, and when it came to staying out of jail, blood was no thicker than water.

25 *Pleading Not Guilty*

MASON STAYED ON THE CASE FULL-TIME THROUGHOUT the
months of May, June, and July. By August 1999, he felt confident enough
to present his evidence to assistant U.S. attorney Kenneth R. Taylor. The
federal prosecutor not only was impressed with Mason's work but also
fully appreciated the seriousness and scope of the Deering-Sovereign
scam. In his opinion, Mason had made enough of a case to indict Dorothy, Chuck, William Paul Watson, and Daniel Craig Deering.

Mason and Taylor decided that although Dorothy, Chuck, and Daniel
Craig Deering had swindled hundreds of writers as phony literary agents,
the surest and most direct route to fraud convictions would involve es-
tablishing how much joint venture money they had taken, knowing that
it was not being used to publish books. Mason had compiled a list of two
hundred authors who together had paid Sovereign publications more
than a million dollars. There were at least fifty more victims Mason had
not yet identified by name. Of all their manuscripts, only four or five
books were ever produced. After January 1998, no books were published.

On September 2, 1999, in the federal courthouse at Lexington, Mason presented his case to a grand jury of twenty-four citizens of the eastern district of Kentucky. Through writer's accounts and supporting documents, Mason tried to establish at least a strong probability that the
defendants had used the U.S. mail to defraud, by their intentional mis-
representation, authors who had paid to have their manuscripts turned
into paperback books. The agent also discussed the upgrade scheme and
the issuance of gift certificates at a time when the defendants knew that
Sovereign had no future. Mason said he had questioned a dozen writers

who had signed joint venture contracts after William Paul Watson, a.k.a. Bill Richardson, had fired Sovereign's two editors. A couple of these victims had paid their money just weeks before Sovereign closed its doors. Mason urged the grand jurors to apply common sense to the facts of the case. If they did, they would conclude that Dorothy Deering and her accomplices had committed criminal fraud.

The grand jurors didn't make Mason and Taylor wait very long for their verdict. They unanimously returned a true bill against the defendants, charging them with mail fraud and fraud by wire. If convicted, each defendant could be sentenced to up to ten years in prison. It was a historic indictment that brought joy and relief to victims all across the country. After all of these years, Dorothy Deering had finally met her match.

Dorothy and the other defendants were spared the indignity of being arrested and hauled off to jail in handcuffs. Instead, they were issued summonses notifying them of their indictments and the date they were to be arraigned. Dorothy and Chuck were still in Florida with Chuck's mother; Watson was in Paintsville; and Daniel Craig Deering was living with his wife's family in Huntington, West Virginia.

A week later, the four, now destitute, were in Lexington, each with a court-appointed attorney, to be arraigned in federal district court. The defendants pleaded not guilty and were released on their own recognizance. Chief Judge Karl S. Forester set November 15, 1999, as the trial date.

Special Agent Mason realized that having enough evidence to sustain an indictment was not necessarily enough to support a criminal conviction. For that he would need proof beyond a reasonable doubt that Dorothy and her accomplices had intended to swindle her clients and authors. Kenneth R. Taylor, the man who would prosecute the Deerings and William Paul Watson, sent a letter to Deering and Sovereign authors updating them on the status of the case, explaining how events would unfold, and informing them about the kind of evidence he was looking for.

> One of the hardest decisions we face is whom, and how many, of the victims to call to the witness stand. Of the 250 or so known victims, well over half have contacted us. Obviously, neither our financial resources nor the court and jury's patience will countenance calling that many. We hope to put forth a cross sample, along with testimony from a summary investigator who will account for virtually every contract and the results. All testimony must be live and in person.
>
> The one real issue for the jury in this case is "intent." That is, did the defen-

dants intend to defraud, or is this simply an unfortunate business failing. . . .
We are especially interested in those of you who signed publishing contract in
1998, because the signs of insolvency and business demise were prevalent at
that time.

The prosecutor was not having a difficult time finding victims willing to testify against the defendants. In fact, his office was being flooded
with nicely written accounts of the Deering's misrepresentations and
business chicanery. Most of these writers were expressing concern over
the status and whereabouts of their manuscripts. In addressing this issue, Taylor wrote,

> Unfortunately, few if any, [manuscripts] have turned up in our various searches
> and investigations. It is my belief that they were discarded when the business
> was terminated. Those that were in the possession of the Daniel Craig Liter-
> ary Agency were seen being discarded curbside when his residence was vacated.

Mason hadn't given up hope that the Deering-Sovereign archive still
existed and that he would find it. While this vast collection of documents
would damn her, there was a good chance that Dorothy had not been able
to destroy what had taken her ten years to accumulate. She might even
have saved them to restart her business when the dust settled. In Mason's
mind, Dorothy Deering was fully capable of having thumbed her nose
at a federal subpoena.

The Deering case became national news when, a month after the
indictments, the *Washington Post* carried a front-page article about Sovereign Publications called "Publishing Schemes Prove to Be Pure Fiction."[1] The piece featured an Indiana writer named Paul Shackelford who
had paid Sovereign $4,675 only to be "snowballed" when the publisher
closed its doors. Shackelford was one of twenty-five plaintiffs in the class-
action suit against the Deerings. Prosecutor Taylor, showing empathy for
victimized writers, was quoted as saying,

> It's an emotional roller coaster. They [the writers] wondered if they were good
> writers. They find somebody who says they're a good writer. They start pump-
> ing themselves up. They get a publication date. They tell all their friends. They
> go out and schedule book signings. Then the sky falls in.

Patrick Nash, the attorney representing Chuck Deering, told the
Washington Post that the Deerings had been "engaged in a legitimate

business, and that's what our proof will be in the criminal trial." Clay Mason, not interviewed by the *Washington Post,* was busy rounding up writers who would take the stand and tell a different story.

On October 19, 1999, seven weeks after the indictments, Mason received a call from Attorney Nash. The lawyer said that Chuck and his wife, in the spirit of full compliance with the subpoena requiring the production of all Deering-Sovereign documents, wanted the FBI agent to know there were some company papers stored in a rental-space facility in Lexington. When Mason arrived at the storage location, he could hardly believe what he found. As he had suspected, Dorothy hadn't thrown away anything. Two large bins were carefully packed with four hundred boxes of Deering-Sovereign material. Dorothy had not intended to give up what ten years of fraud had produced, but Chuck, with the trial approaching, must have gotten cold feet.

The next day, Mason returned to the storage facility driving the biggest Ryder truck he could rent. After hours of heavy lifting, he drove to his office in Frankfort in a groaning truck he feared was so overloaded it would break down on the highway.

Van Treese had moved the Deering Literary Agency to Georgia, Phelan had taken it back to Nicholasville, and now Clay Mason had moved it and Sovereign Publications to the FBI office in Frankfort. This was not the place Dorothy Deering wanted her defunct companies to be headquartered, and Clay Mason was not the agent she wanted handling her files. But at this point, not too many people cared what Dorothy wanted.

We are genuinely sorry for our actions and wish to apologize to everyone we may have harmed.

--Chuck Deering

26 Dorothy's Last Deal

CLAY MASON SPENT A WEEK COMBING THROUGH, sorting, and cataloguing the mountain of material Dorothy had socked away. He found five hundred manuscripts; a hundred or so how-to books on writing, editing, and publishing; and hundreds of client and author files dating back to 1989. In digging through the remains of Dorothy's lost enterprise, Mason came upon two items that lifted his case to a higher plateau. He found the twelve-page notebook—the boiler-room-style pitch book Richardson had created and used to break down the resistance of potential joint venture authors—and a canceled check signed by Dorothy and made payable to an attorney named Charles Grundy. The check was interesting because it was made out to a lawyer who worked for a firm that specialized in bankruptcy and was dated February 1998. If this meant what the agent thought it meant, Dorothy was obtaining bankruptcy advice six months before she threw in the towel, a period during which she and her employees had solicited and received hundreds of thousands of dollars in joint venture money. This evidence was as close as Mason would get to a smoking gun.

Mason called Charles Grundy at the Lexington firm of Cunningham and Associates and asked him point blank whether, in February 1998, he had consulted with a Dorothy Deering on the subject of bankruptcy. Mr. Grundy said that because of the attorney-client privilege, he was not at liberty to divulge that information. The next day Kenneth R. Taylor filed a motion before Judge Karl S. Forester asking the court to, in this instance, waive the attorney-client privilege. Mason was not inquiring as to what was said by the parties involved; he was merely, in the context of a fraud investigation, trying to confirm that Dorothy Deering had sought bank-ruptcy advice. This information, he hoped, was not protected by attor-ney-client privilege.

After the discovery of Dorothy's literary cache, Mason was given the phone conversations taped by Dan Ammerman and Ellen Brazer. These writers couldn't have done a better job of getting Daniel Craig Deering and William Paul Watson to incriminate themselves had they been wear-ing an FBI wire. Crooks hate, more than anything, hearing themselves committing crimes on tape. Mason's case was finally coming together.

When word filtered back to William Paul Watson that the FBI had his pitch book, Dorothy's canceled bankruptcy check, the Brazer tape, and Diane Goshgarian's "Death Heads Units" testimony, he decided that maybe it was a good time to start helping the good guys get his sister, her husband, and Chuck's idiot son. Through his attorney, he sent word to Kenneth R. Taylor that he was ready to deal. If he didn't make the first move, the other three would paint him as the villain, and there was no way he was going to spend the next ten years in prison. Watson had just one question: what was the prosecutor willing to offer in return for his cooperation? The best he could do, said Kenneth R. Taylor, was to rec-ommend one year in the can and three on probation. Watson could take it or leave it because Clay Mason had him cold.

Judge Karl S. Forester, on November 19, 1999, ruled that the attor-ney-client privilege did not prohibit attorney Charles Grundy from dis-closing to FBI agent Clay Mason whether Dorothy Deering had asked for bankruptcy advice in February 1998. The judge would set a date for the parties to meet in his office and learn the answer to that question. On December 8, before Judge Forester and the FBI, Grundy confirmed that he and his client, in February 1998, had talked about the possible bank-ruptcy of Sovereign Publications. At that moment, Mason knew he was in the driver's seat. He had made an open-and-shut fraud case against Dorothy Deering.

Two days after the victory in the judge's chambers, William Paul Watson went to federal court to change his plea to guilty. Watson had already signed the plea agreement, which in part read,

In 1997, the defendant joined an enterprise, Sovereign Publications, being operated by his sister and her husband. After a period of time, it became ap-parent to the defendant that the operation was fraudulent, in that money was taken from aspiring authors with the promise of publication of manuscripts, when, in fact, it would have been impossible to perform as promised. For several months, the defendant continued to aid and abet his fraud. The use of the United States mail was a prominent part of the fraud scheme.

Before he accepted Watson's plea, Judge Forester asked the defendant, "You knew there was no legitimate way the books would be published, and you solicited manuscripts anyway?"

"Yes, sir," Watson replied.

The judge allowed Watson to plead guilty to one count of aiding and abetting fraud. He would be sentenced at a later date.

In reviewing his evidence, Clay Mason was confident that if Dorothy and Chuck didn't cop a plea and the case went to trial, the government would prevail. To prove that Dorothy Deering had no intention of publishing her authors' books, Mason had, in addition to Watson's testimony,

1. Jim Russo's testimony regarding how Dorothy had lied about the reason she was delaying the publication of all books in December 1997;
2. Watson's firing of his editorial staff in January 1998; and
3. Dorothy's bankruptcy consultation with the lawyer in February 1998.

To prove that joint venture solicitations had occurred after January 1998, Mason had

1. Diane Goshgarian's testimony that she had paid two thousand dollars to have her novel "upgraded" in February 1998;
2. the testimony of John Kirk, who signed a Sovereign contract in April 1998; and
3. the testimony of five other writers who had either paid for or were solicited joint venture deals after May 1998.

Mason also had gift certificate mailings during the summer of 1998 and the testimony of Dorothy's last bookkeeper, who could establish that the joint venture proceeds were not going toward the production of books.

Dorothy Deering didn't care what evidence of her wrongdoing the FBI agent thought he had. She did not want to admit to a crime she had not committed. She did not want to give her enemies—the FBI and those malicious, revenge-seeking writers blaming her for events that had been out of her control—the satisfaction of her defeat. These writers, people she had tried to help, wanted to make her the scapegoat for their own failures. When the jurors saw what a scumbag her brother was, and heard her tales of woe, they would find her innocent.

The prosecutor and the FBI agent were ready to go to trial and were not in the mood to recommend a light sentence in return for a plea. But as the trial date grew near, Chuck Deering blinked, and so did Dorothy. They would each plead guilty to one count of mail fraud, a crime that carried at that time, as a maximum penalty, five years in prison. As for what sentence Judge Forester would impose, all bets were off. It was not much of a deal, but the Deerings took it.

The plea hearing for Dorothy and Chuck took place on December 22, 1999, in Judge Forester's courtroom. The only people in attendance were the judge, the prosecutor, Clay Mason, the defendants, their attorneys, and John Cheves, a reporter for the *Lexington Herald-Leader*. Judge Forester, a white-haired grandfatherly man with dark-framed glasses and a reputation as being even-tempered and fair, asked Kenneth Taylor to read the indictment and cite some of the evidence against the defendants. As the clean-cut, salt-and-pepper-haired prosecutor rattled off the evidence Clay Mason had so painstakingly gathered, Dorothy sat at the defense table and cried while Chuck patted her on the shoulder. At the conclusion of Taylor's recitation of the evidence, Judge Forester asked the defendants to rise. Chuck, looking like a giant next to his wife, helped her to her feet. "Are these charges true?" the judge asked.

"Yes, they are," Chuck replied. Chuck then asked the judge whether he could read a statement to the court.

"You may," replied Judge Forester.

Reading from a sheet of paper in a shaky voice, Chuck said, "We are genuinely sorry for our actions and wish to apologize to everyone we may have harmed. We will accept the consequences of our acts."

Judge Forester, not a man to lecture or issue sanctimonious speeches, asked this of the defendants: "It was never your intention to publish those literary works. You didn't even have the means to do that. Isn't that right?"

"Yes, sir," the couple replied.

With the guilty pleas entered into the record, Judge Forester set March 31, 2000, as the sentencing date, then adjourned. In the hallway outside the courtroom, the prosecutor, in speaking to the newspaper reporter, said, "This is sad; there is nothing more vulnerable than a vain writer."

A week later, in the same courtroom, Daniel Craig Deering pleaded guilty to one count of aiding and abetting fraud. He would also be sentenced by Judge Forester on March 31, 2000. Dorothy and Chuck had returned to Florida to await their fate. Daniel Craig would head back to Huntington, West Virginia, to ponder his future. Dorothy had heard that Judge Forester was a kind man, giving her hope that he, sensing that she wasn't the criminal type, would sentence her to some kind of probation.[1] Surely he could see that she could never survive in the company of real criminals. She had made a few mistakes, but she wasn't a common criminal like her brother.

Dorothy Deering was not your ordinary swindler. She was a con artist, an impostor. That she had taken so much money from so many writers for so long, without changing her name, moving great distances, or altering the identity of her enterprise, shows how good she was at selling herself and the dream of being published. Her own dream of leading the life of a literary agent and publisher collapsed when she could no longer maintain the illusion of legitimacy. One can only speculate how much longer Dorothy could have sustained her fantasy life had she not decided to impersonate a publisher. Unlike her literary clients, her Sovereign victims had purchased more than just an illusion. Books are tangible objects. They either exist or do not exist.

Dorothy could manufacture the dream but not the book. She crept into her victims' lives and took more than their money. She stole their dreams, their confidence, and their self-respect. She was worse than the ordinary thief; she was every writer's nightmare.

Epilogue

DOROTHY, CHUCK, DANIEL CRAIG, and William Paul Watson were sentenced by Judge Karl S. Forester on March 31, 2000. They were ordered to pay, both as a group and individually, more than $2 million to the people they had swindled. Since they claimed to be broke, and the court knew of no assets to attach, this fine was essentially symbolic.[1] They were also banned from the publishing business for life, and Dorothy, Chuck, and William Paul were ordered to seek mental health counseling.

Dorothy L. Deering

Judge Forester sentenced Dorothy to forty-six months in prison to be followed by three years of supervised release. She began her sentence on April 24, 2000, at the federal corrections institution (FCI) at Danbury, Connecticut. If she entered a halfway facility toward the end of her term, she could be released in April 2003; otherwise, she would get out in August of that year.

After ten days at the facility in Danbury, Dorothy was transferred to an FCI in Forth Worth from which, five months later, she was moved to a federal prison camp near Lexington, Kentucky. Dorothy was housed in a three-story brick building at the crest of a gentle rise, one-half mile from I-64 in the heart of Kentucky's horse country. Looking like a dormitory on the campus of a small college, the building, once the medical facility for the men's prison a half mile to the west, houses 180 inmates. The prisoners wear loose-fitting blue uniforms similar to the work outfits of hospital physicians, and are bunked three to a room. With access to only three television sets, one for each floor, Dorothy rubbed shoulders with drug offenders, embezzlers, tax cheats, and a bank robber or two. Inmates met with visitors in the basement of the building on Friday evenings and during the day on Saturday and Sunday.

Dorothy earned fourteen dollars a month by mopping the chapel floor ten hours a week. Since inmates had to buy their own soap and other personal items, Charles's mother was sending Dorothy $125 a month, from which thirty dollars was deducted pursuant to the restitution portion of her sentence. Her worldly possessions were being stored at the home of Chuck's son Mark in Chattanooga, Tennessee.

In December 2001, when this writer visited Dorothy at the federal prison camp at Lexington, she walked without a limp, spoke softly, and made it clear that being in prison was a living hell. According to Dorothy, her fellow inmates were having sex, fighting with each other, or getting drunk on readily available booze. She had been threatened many times and called a racist. The only bright spots in her life were the letters she regularly received from Chuck and the periodic writing workshops she held at the prison. Her writing seminars had been so popular, she was thinking about starting a correspondence school for aspiring writers once she got out.

Dorothy also made it clear how she felt about her federal conviction. Convinced that she had done nothing wrong, legally or morally, and that she was the victim rather than the bad guy, she referred to Clay Mason's investigation as an "FBI witch hunt." Claiming that prosecutor Kenneth R. Taylor had gone back on his promise to recommend a sentence of eighteen months in return for her plea, she considered him a "hatchet man and liar." She continued to maintain that she never intended to defraud anyone. It had always been her purpose to help aspiring writers. That is what she did and, Lord willing, would continue to do.

Charles F. Deering

Before being sentenced, Chuck Deering said this to Judge Forester: "I chose the wrong road and am ready to face the consequences." As it turned out, the consequences were quite severe—forty-one months in prison followed by three years of supervised release. Dorothy's second in charge and principal supporter would serve his time in the FCI in Ashland, Kentucky, eighty-three miles east of Lexington, where he would work in the prison garage ordering parts for Bureau of Prison vehicles. Chuck would be paid eighty dollars a month minus the twenty-five dollars deducted for his victims.

William Paul Watson, a.k.a. Bill Richardson

Judge Forester sent Watson away for one year and one day. At the time of this writing, Watson had served three months of his three-year term of supervised release. He had been incarcerated at the FCI at Manchester, Kentucky. Upon release from prison, he returned to the Paintsville area in the eastern part of the state.

Daniel Craig Deering

Judge Forester was easiest on Daniel Craig Deering. He sentenced Chuck's son to five months of house arrest. When the electronic bracelet came off, Daniel was to spend five years on supervised release. Daniel violated the terms of his probation when he tested positive for drugs, and that infringement led to a six-month stretch at the FCI in Ashland, Kentucky. On August 23, 2002, having tested positive again, he was sentenced to three more months at the prison.

David Brannon

When David Brannon left Sovereign Publications in May 1997, he took with him Sovereign contracts, form letters, and lists of Deering clients and potential joint venture authors. Shortly thereafter, he started Brannon and Baker, his own joint venture publishing company. Early in 1998, Brannon signed ten writers to joint venture contracts totaling forty to fifty thousand dollars. Two years later, when it became obvious he had no intention of publishing any books, Clay Mason opened an investigation that led to Brannon's plea of guilty to one count of mail fraud. In August of 2001, he was sentenced to a year and a day at a minimum-security facility in southern Florida.

James Van Treese

On October 9, 1998, in the case of *Duane H. Gillman, Trustee of the Estate of Northwest Publishing, Inc. vs. James Van Treese and Jason Van Treese* a federal district court in Utah entered the judgment that the defendants were *personally* liable for $10.5 million, the amount they had swindled from NPI authors. These damages were determined to be a result of the defendants' "gross negligence in the performance of their duties as officers and directors of Northwest Publishing, Inc."

A state judge in Salt Lake City, on February 9, 2001, sentenced James Van Treese to thirty years in prison after the defendant pleaded guilty to four counts of communications fraud, two counts of securities fraud, and one count of failing to pay income tax. On sentencing Van Treese, the judge said that the defendant had not repaid any of the stolen money and noted his prior convictions for mail fraud and theft.

Van Treese's son, Jason, who did not contest two charges of third-degree felonies involving failure to pay income tax, pleaded guilty to the class A misdemeanor of attempted communication fraud.

Donald T. Phelan

Commonwealth Publications, Inc., ceased doing business in March 1998. Phelan did not file for bankruptcy; he simply abandoned the company. On June 18, 1998, an Alberta court, pursuant to a consent judgment, awarded CPI authors $14,455,000 in civil damages. Since there were no CPI assets, the class-action judgment was merely symbolic. The court did, however, terminate all contracts between Commonwealth and its authors and ordered the return of all manuscripts, as well as the copyrights to these works.

Although he was the subject of an investigation by the Royal Canadian Mounted Police, Phelan was not charged with any crimes connected to his doing business as Commonwealth Publications, Inc. In Canada, proving fraud is more difficult than it is in the United States.

As of February 2000, Donald Phelan's wife Lorraine owned an Edmonton company called The Write Image, a firm that, for a fee, published clients' autobiographies and memoirs. The firm employed Phelan as a "writing consultant." Clients could also pay Donald Phelan a fee to ghostwrite their life stories. The Better Business Bureau in Edmonton, after receiving eighty written complaints against CPI, issued a press release entitled "Consumers Warned of Unreliable Publishing Firm," advising writers not to do business with the Phelans.

The Victims

Thomas E. Mahon, the Florida high school teacher (now dean) who paid eight thousand dollars in contract and reading fees to both ADP and NPI, is still writing. He does not have an agent and is still looking for a publisher.

He realizes now that his novels, when submitted to the Deerings, needed a lot of work.

Ronald Howell, the retired longshoreman living in Naples, Florida, is still writing. His novella "Broadway Joe" was not published, and he doesn't have an agent. He too realizes that his book was not sufficiently polished when he paid Sovereign Publications to publish it.

Diane Goshgarian, the Sovereign victim from Brookline, Massachusetts, who believed she had been threatened by Bill Richardson after she paid two thousand dollars for the trade paper upgrade, has self-published her novel, *The Arbitrary Sword*. She still writes but doesn't have an agent.

The Money

After the September Surprise, there were rumors that Dorothy and Chuck, during their Caribbean cruises, had socked away joint venture cash in the Cayman Islands, Jamaica, the Bahamas, or the Dominican Republic. Like buccaneers of old, they were burying their ill-gotten treasure in the Caribbean Sea. When asked whether he believed this story to be true, FBI agent Clay Mason said it was possible but unlikely. As far as he could tell, from the financial records, the Deerings had spent all the money on themselves and their extended family.

Notes
Sources and Acknowledgments
Index

Notes

1. Queen of Fees

1. A directory widely used by freelance and aspiring writers to find magazine and book publishers, literary agents, and advice on how to get published, *Writer's Market* is published annually by Writer's Digest Books of Cincinnati.

2. The *Literary Market Place* is an annual directory of the publishing industry that contains a comprehensive list of publishers, writers' conferences, writing contests, and literary agents. Published by R. R. Bowker, it is available in most public libraries and is considered the bible of the industry.

3. A freelance manuscript reader paid twenty-five dollars to read and evaluate a book.

2. Atlantic Disk Publishers

1. *Writer's Digest,* October 1994. Eleven other fee agents advertised in that issue.

2. According to the *Who's Who* entry for William Morrow, his wife's name was Honore Willsie and the couple did not have a daughter.

3. Northwest Publishing

1. Interview with Dorothy Deering, December 15, 2001.

2. The July and August 1994 issues of *Writer's Digest* magazine.

4. Lies, Lies, and More Lies

1. Pigeon-dropping and the bank examiner's scam are short, hit-and-run con jobs that do not require elaborate planning or impersonation.

2. The final status report for "Apparition," dated April 1996, contained a list of twenty-five publishers and five film companies. The manuscript was never sold. In November 1994, ADP published ten copies of *Axis II,* producing a royalty of $1.96 from the sale of one disk. "Sebastian Yard" was never published.

3. There is no record of an NPI book by Terri W. Jenkins. The letter itself has no letterhead identifying this writer, and there is no reference in the body of the letter to the title of the book. Therefore, there was no way a recipient of this letter could verify its authenticity.

8. The Dead Publishers Society

1. Shia Kapos, *Salt Lake City Tribune,* April 4, 1996.

2. Dorothy would later refer to Tom Mahon as a "terrible and vile human being."

3. Kristen Moulto, "Publisher's Broken Promises Shatter Authors' Dreams of Success," *Salt Lake Tribune,* July 28, 1996.

9. Sovereign Publications

1. The other seven imprints were Appaloosa Press, Blue Jean Press, Crusaders Press, Dreamscape Press, Hippopotamus Press, Homage Press, and Stargate Press.

10. Storm Warning

1. *Writer's Digest* chose not to publish Captain Kerr's letter.

2. William Kerr's book, *Path of the Golden Dragon,* came out in the spring of 1997. Kerr told this author that twenty thousand copies were sold, causing the book to appear briefly on the *New York Times* best-seller list. Kerr, however, received no royalty payment from CPI and never saw his other book, "The Red Hand." After the collapse of CPI, Kerr received death threats from victims who blamed his *Writer's Digest* letter for allowing Phelan to take advantage of more writers. Kerr and his family had to go into hiding as a result of these threats.

3. The Rising Sun ad in the 1997 edition of *Literary Market Place* did indicate membership in the Association of Authors' Representatives. The agency, in fact, was never a member.

4. Three months after Glenda Ivey rejected Chuck Deering's joint venture offer, she received a second vanity pitch directly from Sovereign. She didn't bother to reply. Her Deering contract expired in December 1997, and she didn't re-up.

11. Little Brother

1. David Brannon and Mary Layne would start their own joint venture publishing company modeled after Sovereign. Layne's role in the venture was limited. She lent Brannon twenty-five hundred dollars to get the company started.

2. *Writer's Market,* 1996, p. 276.

12. Gift Certificates

1. *Dawn's Revenge* by L. D. Sledge, *Thunder Moon* by Larry Franklin, *Confederate Memories* by Phyllis Philips, and *Life's a Joy* by Betty Krause.

2. The internship program never got off the ground.

3. Between November 1997 and July 1998, five hundred Sovereign gift certificates were mailed to writers.

4. After the firing of Dedre Smith, Allison Arnold took her to a Lexington attorney to discuss a possible sexual harassment suit against Bill Richardson.

5. The jury agreed, acquitting Foster of the charge of criminal homicide. Michael's father, Robert Helm, agrees with this account of the case. He told this author that his son had been "living on the edge" and "hanging around the wrong places." Dorothy's version of the shooting, to the author and others, would be much more favorable to her son. She admitted he was on drugs but otherwise considers him an innocent victim. Chuck Deering attended Foster's trial.

13. Canadian Sunset

1. In 2001, when this author asked Dorothy Deering whether the name Craig Andrews rang a bell, she said it did not.

2. Tale of Woe no. 3, February 3, 1998, www.managementalternatives.com/welcome.htm, accessed February 23, 1998.

3. Tale of Woe no. 13, February 27, 1998.

4. Tale of Woe no. 13, February 27, 1998.

5. Tale of Woe no. 21, May 4, 1998.

6. CPI letter, December 15, 1997.

7. O'Neal site, December 16, 1997.

8. CPI letter, February 1, 1998.

9. This author, pursuant to a publishing sting, queried CPI on December 23, 1997. This query brought, three weeks later, a form letter expressing interest in the manuscript. On January 30, 1998, the 210-page mystery, missing sixty pages, was on its way to Commonwealth. The joint venture contract calling for a $3,850 contribution came back on February 10, 1998.

14. Sovereign Digest

1. According to Ted Nottingham, Sovereign paid him, for both books, less than two hundred dollars in royalties.

2. There is no record of how many writers sent money toward the education of her grandchild.

3. This phone conversation, audiotaped by Brazer, is reported verbatim.

4. This was the last time Ellen Brazer spoke to Bill Richardson. Beginning in the late spring of 1998, every time she called Sovereign and got someone, it was Chuck Deering who, according to her, always sounded "spaced out." Her book was not published, and she didn't get her money back. She has since found another publisher for her novel.

16. Death Heads Units

1. Carolyn Thue told this author she did not make out that gift certificate.

At the time it was sent, she was Richardson's only employee. There were no manuscripts with that title waiting for publication at Sovereign.

17. The Ammerman Experience

1. Ammerman had found the name of the Deering Agency in an advertisement in the *Literary Market Place*. According to that ad, the Deerings "specialize in new authors of fiction." *Literary Market Place* 1997, p. 618.

2. This and the three telephone conversations that follow were recorded by Dan Ammerman.

3. By outside, Deering probably meant an editing job by a company other than the Deering Agency.

4. Daniel, now the owner of record of the Deering Literary Agency, had moved the operation to his house at 120 Davis Drive in Nicholasville. Ammerman was not aware that the agency was no longer at the 106 North Main Street address.

5. This brought the editing job to $2,102.75 and Ammerman's total investment to $3,352.75.

18. The Mob

1. At that time, the BBB in Lexington had the Deerings doing business as a bookstore.

19. September Surprise

1. According to Laurie Pettit, when she heard the news, her "whole world collapsed." She had paid Sovereign $7,875 in April 1997. Four months later, she gave Dorothy five thousand dollars (a discount) for her second book. A few days before recording his phone message, Chuck Deering told the Franklin, Tennessee, writer that Sovereign was "solid." On the day she learned about Sovereign, Pettit received a three-hundred-dollar contract extension solicitation letter from Daniel Craig Deering.

20. Class Action

1. Chuck Deering told Ron Howell that Dorothy, having just purchased a big literary agency in Pittsburgh, now owned the third-largest literary agency in America.

2. The Writer Beware data bank, as of February 2002, contained complaints, court papers, newspaper articles, promotional literature, contracts, magazine ads, and published agency listings about 250 literary agents and one hundred publishers. The only people who had access to the documents behind the listings were Victoria Strauss and the five members of the SFWA Writing Scam Committee.

3. Dana Massing, "Agents Who Scam Would-Be Authors," *Erie Times News*, December 6, 1998, p. 7B.

21. The Hunter

1. *When the Pentagon Was for Sale* by Andy Pasztor.

2. Scott Sutherland, an agent assigned to the attorney general's office in Frankfort and the recipient of complaints against the Deerings, would assist Mason in his investigation.

3. To this writer, Dorothy Deering also claimed kinship to Dwight C. Morrow, the father of Anne Spencer Morrow, the wife of Charles A. Lindbergh. As the author of two books on the Lindbergh kidnapping case, I can say that Dwight C. Morrow and William F. Morrow were not related to each other or to Dorothy Deering.

4. Wire and mail fraud schemes involve violations of 18 U.S.C. sections 1341 and 1343 and carry the FBI file designation 196-D.

5. It was later learned that before moving out, the Deerings sold the rented office furniture.

6. Shackelford, a thirty-seven-year-old boiler tender from Knox, Indiana, had signed a $4,650 Sovereign contract in October 1996 for publication of his novel "Haunting Memories." In May 1998, Daniel Craig Deering sent him a Sovereign contract for his second mystery, "A Writer's Nightmare." Shackelford declined and later joined Diane Goshgarian's class-action suit. He was also featured in the September 28, 1999, article about Sovereign in the *Washington Post*.

22. Poor Dorothy

1. According to Glenda Ivey, a client of A Rising Sun, Chris Scott "had a smooth and fancy tongue, and I fell for it."

2. When Tom Mahon called Daniel Craig Deering four months after Sovereign went under, Deering, according to his answering machine, was doing business as A to Z Home Improvement.

3. Witnesses had told Mason that when Daniel moved out of his suburban home, they saw piles and piles of manuscripts stacked out on the curb waiting to be picked up by the garbage truck.

25. Pleading Not Guilty

1. The article, by Linton Weeks, with the subtitle "Shady Literary Agents Take Advantage of Growing Ranks of Would-Be Writers," was published on September 28, 1999.

26. Dorothy's Last Deal

1. Interview with Dorothy Deering, December 16, 2001.

Epilogue

1. The day after the sentencing, the class-action suit brought by Diane Goshgarian and the other Deering victims was withdrawn.

Sources and Acknowledgments

THE BULK OF MY INVESTIGATION into the genteel racket was conducted between September 1997 and January 1999. That phase of the research consisted of gathering promotional literature from several agencies, agency listings in publishing directories, magazine advertisements, data online, correspondence, author-agent contracts, and publishing agreements. I interviewed writers who had experienced problems with various fee agents, book doctors, and joint venture publishers; conducted a survey; and ran a manuscript sting—that is, the submission of a badly written or incomplete manuscript to determine whether a particular fee agent will accept it for the fee. I also interviewed several fee agents, book doctors, and a joint venture publisher.

The results of my general inquiry were published in a thirty-page booklet called *The Fisher Report,* distributed between January and May of 1999 by Bill Martin through his company, Agent Research and Evaluation, in New York City. Another by-product of my investigation, "The Fisher Scale," a weighted formula to help aspiring writers identify and avoid certain literary agents, appeared in several publications read by aspiring writers.

In July 2001, I decided to write a book about Dorothy Deering, her enterprises, and her associates and accomplices. This project required additional, more focused research that took six months and led to the interviews of, among others, Dorothy Deering and FBI special agent Clay Mason.

I thank the following people who contributed, in various ways, to this book: Professor E. Ernest Wood, Edinboro University of Pennsylvania;

Special Agent Clay Mason; Ann C. Crispin and Victoria Strauss of Science Fiction and Fantasy Writers of America; Kimberly Reese of The Write Connection; attorney Charles E. Petit; and Bill and Beverly Martin of Agent Research and Evaluation. I am extremely grateful to William Cox, a novelist and a friend, whose criticisms and editorial advice were immensely helpful.

Special thanks also to the following: Dan Ammerman, Craig Andrews, Ellen Brazer, Craig Etchison, Carole Fox-Breeding, Diane Goshgarian, Ronald J. Howell Sr., Glenda Ivey, Diana Kemp-Jones, John Kirk, Thomas E. Mahon, Jim Russo, and Carolyn Steinmetz. And last, but not least, thanks to my Edinboro colleague Linda Sayers, who typed the manuscript.

Interviews and Consultations

Dorothy L. Deering, federal prisoner 072-18032, Federal Prison Camp, Lexington, Kentucky—12/14/01, 12/15/01, 12/16/01.

Clay Mason, special agent, FBI, Frankfort Resident Agency, Louisville Field Division—2/16/00, 8/27/01, 8/31/01, 10/5/01, 12/11/01, 12/17/01, 1/16/02, 2/16/02, 2/26/02, 3/27/02, 4/11/02, 7/31/02, 8/12/02.

Deering Employees

Stephanie Baker, 8/14/98; Jim Russo, 9/18/01; Ron Spriggs, 2/19/02; Carolyn Thue, 12/21/01.

Other Deering Interviews

Shirley Allen Cunningham Jr., 3/26/02; Robert Helm, 2/24/02, 3/3/02; Pat Sullivan, 3/18/02, 3/19/02; Charlene Walls, 2/24/02, 3/10/02.

Deering Victims

Dan Ammerman, 1/18/02; Craig Andrews, 4/4/98; Ellen Brazer, 2/6/02, 3/10/02; Carole Fox-Breeding, 6/4/98; Mike A. Fuller, 5/24/98; Glyn J. Godwin, 6/5/98; Diane Goshgarian, 8/23/01; Ronald J. Howell Sr., 9/22/98, 8/21/01; Glenda Ivey, 4/21/98; Diana Kemp-Jones, 3/30/98; Carl Kirby, 4/1/99; John Kirk, 8/17/02; Diane Klein, 8/15/98; Thomas E. Mahon, 5/24/98, 8/20/01; Will D. Mitchell, 9/17/98; Ted Nottingham, 5/14/98; Laurie Pettit, 9/10/98; Patrick E. Robinson, 6/6/98; Paul D. Shackelford, 4/16/98, 5/27/98; Carolyn Steinmetz, 12/20/01; Lee Travis, 9/11/98; James P. Zimmerman, 6/2/98.

Victims of the Genteel Racket Generally

James D. Barnes, 10/16/98; Constance D. Casserly, 7/14/98; Linda Courtney, 4/27/98; Craig Etchison, 1/13/98; Mike A. Fuller, 5/24/98; Francis Gallagher, 1/5/98; Howard Goldsmith, 12/22/97; Harold E. Jervey Jr., 8/8/98; William B. Kerr, 2/7/02; Diane Klein, 8/5/98; Diane E. Lau, 12/22/97; Daniel Lynch, 1/7/98; Marsha Lytle, 4/8/98; Stephen Moxie, 8/31/98; Phil Petit, 8/21/98; Jack Powell, 9/12/98; Michael Schultz, 4/9/98; Doyle Schwab, 8/22/98; Judy Singer, 5/27/98; Lisa Stout, 4/2/98; Cindy Weigard, 4/21/98; John L. Young, 4/19/98.

Writers' Advocates

Ann C. Crispin, vice president, Science Fiction and Fantasy Writers of America, 7/7/98, 12/27/98, 12/31/98, 1/30/99, 5/1/99; Bill Martin, Agent Research and Evaluation, Inc., publisher of *Talking Agents,* a monthly newsletter, 25 Barrow St., New York, NY 10014, first consulted 12/12/97, dozens of contacts in 1998, 1999, and 2000; Charles E. Petit, consumer fraud and intellectual properties attorney, Urbana, Illinois, first consulted 10/17/99, dozens of contacts in 2000, 2001, and 2002; Kimberly Reese, founder, The Write Connection, first consulted 3/30/98, correspondence in 1998, 1999; Victoria Strauss, Science Fiction and Fantasy Writers of America, first consulted 5/1/99, last contacted 2/13/02, correspondence.

Law Enforcement

Leela Fireside, attorney general's office, Austin, Texas, 5/11/00; Jared Garlipp, attorney general's office, Buffalo, New York, 9/2/99; Sharon Hilborn, attorney general's office, Frankfort, Kentucky, 9/15/99; Judy A. Luther, U.S. postal inspector, Atlanta, Georgia, 1/31/01; Scott Sutherland, attorney general's office, Frankfort, Kentucky, 4/1/99, 9/21/99.

Literary Agents

Oscar Collier, author of (with Frances Spatz Leighton) *How to Write & Sell Your First Novel* and *How to Write & Sell Your First Nonfiction Book,* 11/7/97; Jeff Herman, The Jeff Herman Agency, LLC, New York, NY, publisher of *Writer's Guide to Book Editors, Publishers and Literary Agents,* correspondence on 12/17/98, 1/29/99; Donald Maass, Donald Maass Literary Agency, New York, NY, president, Association of Authors' Representatives, 10/11/00.

Writers' Organizations

Penny Dickens, executive director, The Writers' Union of Canada, Toronto, Canada, 8/5/98; Jack Handler, consumer rights attorney, National Writers Union, New York, NY, 7/14/99, 8/30/99, 9/12/99, 10/15/99, 1/12/00, 4/25/00; Alec McEachern, director, Canadian Authors Association, Toronto, Canada, 12/22/97; Ralph Sevush, associate director, Dramatists Guild of America, New York, NY, 9/22/99.

Journalists

John Cheves, *Lexington Herald-Leader,* 9/14/01; Jim Jordan, *Lexington Herald-Leader,* 8/24/01; Charles Mandel, freelance for *Edmonton Journal,* 6/3/98.

Writer's Digest Magazine

Annette Ferguson, classified manager, 1/11/02.

Documents

AGK	attorney general of Kentucky		HG	Howard Goldsmith
AJF	A. Jim Fisher		JDB	James D. Baines
BDB	Brian David Bruns		JP	Jack Petit
BR	Bill Richardson		JR	Jim Russo
CA	Craig Andrews		JVT	James Van Treese
CD	Charles Deering		JPZ	James P. Zimmerman
CE	Craig Etchison		KR	Katie Rearden
CFB	Carole Fox-Breeding		KRT	Kenneth R. Taylor
CR	Courtney Remekie		KV	Kallya Valanus
CT	Carolyn Thue		LCE	Lisa Coffman-Eitner
DCD	Daniel Craig Deering		MKK	Mary Kay Kindhauser
DA	Dan Ammerman		PD	police department
DD	Dorothy Deering		PS	Paul Shackelford
DG	Diane Goshgarian		SE	Steve Esrati
DKJ	Diana Kemp-Jones		TM	Thomas E. Mahon
DP	Donald Phelan		VR	Vicki Richardson
GG	Glyn Godwin		WM	Will D. Mitchell
GI	Glenda Ivey			

Deering Literary Agency

LETTERS

CA to DD, 7/5/91; VR to DKJ, 7/29/91; DKJ to VR, 10/8/91; DD to DKJ, 12/18/91; manuscript update for DKJ, 9/2/92; manuscript update for DKJ, 10/7/92; DD to TM, 4/4/94; CD to DKJ, 4/25/94; CD to DKJ, 5/3/94; CD to DKJ, 5/17/94; DD to DKJ, 6/15/94; DD to CA, 7/19/94; DD to CA, 10/6/94; DD to TM, 10/12/94; DD to CFB, 2/17/95; all-author memo, 8/17/95; manuscript update for CFB, 9/18/95; CD to GG, 12/30/95; GG to CD, 1/5/96; all-author memo, 4/2/96; manuscript update for TM, 5/96; CA to DD and CD, 5/17/96; all-author memo, 6/16/96; CD to CA, 1/3/97; CD to CFB, 5/16/97; CD to GI, 8/26/97; CD to GI, 8/26/97; DCD to CFB, 8/28/97; CFB to CD, 9/5/97; GI to DCD, 9/8/97; CA to DCD, 12/1/97; CA e-mail to CD and DD, 1/8/98; CD e-mail to CA, 1/14/98; To Whom It May Concern memo from TM, 3/24/98; TM to Lexington BBB, 3/31/98; CFB e-mail to DD, 7/19/98; CFB to DD and CD, 7/21/98; CD e-mail to CFB, 7/21/98; CFB e-mail to CD, 7/23/98; GG e-mail to CD, 7/24/98; CD e-mail to TM, 7/26/98; CD e-mail to TM, 7/27/98; To Whom It May Concern e-mail from CD, 7/27/98; all-author memo from KRT, 9/21/99.

CONTRACTS

Author-agent agreement between DD and DKJ, 1/13/92; author-agent agreement between DD and CA, 9/2/92; author-agent agreement between DD and CFB, 2/17/95; author-agent extension agreement (eight manuscripts) between DD and DKJ, 6/15/95; author-agent agreement between DD and CA, 7/14/95; author-agent agreement between DD and JPZ, 9/26/95; author-agent agreement between DD and GG, 12/30/95; author-agent agreement between DD and TM, 1/16/96; author-agent agreement between DD and CFB, 1/24/96.

NEWS & NOTES

May 1995; Summer 1995; August-September 1995; October-November 1995; December 1995; Spring-Summer 1996 (pink edition).

WHITE PAPER

Twenty-one-page paper entitled "The Problems and Scandals Surrounding the Deering Agency and the Publishing Companies with Whom They Have Dealt and Personally Owned" by Thomas E. Mahon. Published on the Internet.

VICTIMS' CORRESPONDENCE TO AUTHOR

TM e-mail, 4/1/98; PS e-mail, 4/3/98; GI letter, 4/6/98; JPZ e-mail, 4/11/98; WM e-mail, 4/13/98; GI e-mail, 4/14/98; GI letter, 4/25/98; GI letter, 5/6/98; GG e-mail, 5/11/98; GG e-mail, 5/12/98; TM e-mail, 5/13/98; DKJ e-mail, 5/18/98; WM e-mail, 5/23/98; JPZ letter, 6/3/98; CFB e-mail, 6/19/98; CFB letter, 6/25/98; CFB e-mail, 7/20/98; CFB e-mail, 5/6/99; KV e-mail, 7/28/99; TM e-mail, 8/30/01; TM fax, 8/31/01.

Atlantic Disk Publishers, Inc.

MISCELLANEOUS DOCUMENTS

Press release, 7/20/93; 1994 spring catalogue; all-author memo, summer 1994; royalty statement to TM, 1/18/95; all-author memo, summer 1995; all-author memo, 9/12/95; fall catalogue, 1995.

LETTERS

DD to TM, 8/11/92; DD to DKJ, 8/23/93; DD to TM, 12/8/93; DD to TM, 1/21/94; DD to CA, 8/29/94; DD to DKJ, 8/29/94; DD to DKJ, 12/20/94; DD to TM, 1/18/95.

CONTRACTS

Publishing agreement between DD and DKJ, 8/10/93; publishing agreement between DD and TM, 8/11/93; publishing agreement between DD and TM, 12/8/93.

Northwest Publishing, Inc.
MISCELLANEOUS DOCUMENTS

Spring 1994 catalogue; Notice of Hearing on Trustee's Motion for an Order Converting Case (BR96B-22890) to a Chapter 7 and Status Report, 7/17/96; Notice of Commencement of Case under Chapter 7 of the Bankruptcy Code, 8/7/96; Trustee's Second Status Report, 11/25/96; Trustee's Third and Final Status Report, 4/14/97; Utah attorney general's office notice re: filing of criminal charges against James Van Treese and others, 12/10/97; letter to author from attorney Duane H. Gillman, 1/20/98; bankruptcy court judgment making James Van Treese personally liable for NPI's debts, 10/9/98.

LETTERS

JVT to DKJ, 3/16/94; JVT to TM, 3/30/94; JVT to DKJ, 3/31/94; JVT to CA, 8/2/94; all-author memos from Coalition of Concerned Authors, 4/96, 6/96, 7/18/96.

CONTRACTS

Publishing agreement between JVT and DKJ, 3/24/94; publishing agreement between JVT and TM, 3/30/94; publishing agreement between JVT and CA, 7/22/94; publishing agreement between JVT and JPZ, 10/3/94.

VICTIMS' CORRESPONDENCE TO AUTHOR

TM e-mail, 4/1/98; JPZ e-mail, 4/11/98; TM e-mail, 5/23/98.

Canadian Literary Associates
LETTERS

DP to CE, 4/14/94; DP to CE, 6/1/94; DP to CE, 7/13/94.

Commonwealth Publications, Inc.
MISCELLANEOUS DOCUMENTS

"Warning: Commonwealth Publications," by Craig Etchison, 1/98 (two-page memo; transcript of CBC *Marketplace* segment aired 1/13/98; "Steve Esrati's Tale of Woe #22," O'Neal Web site, 5/7/98; class action filed and judgment obtained against Commonwealth Publications, Inc., 6/23/98.

LETTERS

DP to DKJ, 7/20/95; DP to CFB, 11/20/95; all-author memos, 10/1/96, 11/12/96, 11/21/96; DP to CFB, 3/1/97; all-author memos, 3/6/97, 12/15/97; AJF to CPI, 12/23/97; CFB to DP, 1/3/98; DP e-mail to CA, 1/6/98; CR to AJF, 1/15/98; CA to DP, 1/26/98; AJF to CR, 1/30/98; all-author memo, 2/1/98; CA to DP, 2/1/98; CR to AJF, 2/10/98; CA to crown attorney, 2/16/98; CA e-mail to DP, 2/26/98.

CONTRACTS

Publishing agreement between DP and DKJ, 7/8/95; publishing agreement between DP and CFB, 11/20/95; publishing agreement between DP and JPZ, 1/11/96; publishing agreement (three books) between DP and CA, 3/7/96; publishing agreement between DP and AJF (author declined), 2/10/98.

WRITERS' CORRESPONDENCE TO AUTHOR

CE letter, 1/17/98; HG letter, 2/1/98; CE letter, 2/27/98; Marilyn Meredith e-mail, 4/1/98; JPZ e-mail, 4/11/98; LCE letter, 4/16/98; CE letter, 4/25/98; Linda Courtney e-mail, 4/28/98; LCE e-mail, 4/28/98; HG letter, 4/30/98; Mike A. Fuller e-mail, 5/13/98; JPZ letter, 6/3/98; SE e-mail, 6/20/98; CFB e-mail, 6/19/98; CFB letter, 6/25/98; Constance D. Casserly e-mail, 6/30/98; HG letter, 9/19/98; CE letter, 10/20/98; SE e-mail, 11/12/98; CFB e-mail, 12/13/98; HG letter, 12/30/98; HG letter, 1/4/99; KV e-mail, 7/28/99; SE e-mail, 1/18/00.

O'NEAL WEB SITE

"CPI Legal Cases," 2/2/98; "Former CPI Employee Talks," 2/24/98; "Phelan's House Up for Sale," 4/21/98; "Phelan Wanted for Fraud by 8,000 Writers," 5/13/98; "31 CPI Authors Who Posted Their Contract Information"; "Another Ex-Employee Talks," 5/22/98; "Tales of Woe," 2/98–6/98.

Sovereign Publications, Inc.

MISCELLANEOUS DOCUMENTS

Sovereign Digest, Winter 1998 edition

LETTERS

JR to PS, 1/13/98; CT to DG, 2/13/98; DG to CT, 2/18/98; DD and CD to DG, 2/20/98; DG to DD, 3/6/98; all-author memo from BR, 3/9/98; BR to DG, 3/13/98; DG's attorney to DD, 4/1/98, 4/22/98; BR to DG's attorney, 4/25/98; DG's attorney to BR, 4/27/98; BR to DG's attorney, 4/28/98; DG's attorney to BR, 5/14/98; BR to DG, 5/7/98; DG to AGK, 5/9/98; AGK to DG, 5/28/98; BR to AGK, 6/2/98; DG to AGK, 6/24/98; TM e-mail to BR, 6/25/98; AGK to DG, 7/6/98; DG to AGK, 7/15/98; DG to FBI, 7/26/98; DG to AGK, 7/27/98; AGK to DG, 7/29/98; DG to AGK, 7/31/98; CD to AGK, 8/14/98; AGK to DG, 8/20/98; Lexington BBB to DG, 8/27/98; DG to AGK, 9/2/98; AGK to DG, 9/14/98; DG to FBI, 10/5/98; DG to AGK, 10/6/98; DG to FBI, 10/11/98; DG to Lexington PD, 10/19/98; DG to FBI, 10/24/98; DG to Lexington PD, 11/5/98; JR to Clay Mason, 3/9/99; all-victim memo from KRT, 9/21/99.

CONTRACTS

Publishing agreement between DD and DG, 6/19/96; publishing agreement between DD and JDB, 4/29/97 (author declined).

White Paper

Six-page report prepared by Mary Kay Kindhauser that includes Sovereign ISBN sequence for one hundred titles.

Sovereign Thousand-Dollar Gift Certificates

One for each of the following: JDB, 11/14/97; Jonathan Holman, 5/18/98; DKJ, 6/3/98; TM, 6/3/98; DG, 6/26/98; David Smith, 7/2/98.

Victims' Correspondence to Author

PS e-mail, 4/3/98; PS e-mail, 4/5/98; PS e-mail, 4/15/98; TM e-mail, 5/13/98; JP e-mail, 9/7/98; PS e-mail, 9/7/98; BDB e-mail, 9/11/98; JP and Laurie Pettit e-mails, 9/19/98; Helen Larson e-mail, 9/26/98; DG e-mail, 10/31/98; Kim Sullivan e-mail, 10/31/98; DG e-mail, 11/5/98; Ted Nottingham e-mail, 11/16/98; Mandy Kuchna e-mail, 5/6/99; Laura McClay e-mail, 5/11/99; MKK letter, 10/17/99; JR e-mail, 9/18/01.

Daniel Craig Deering

Miscellaneous Documents

Manuscript evaluation, December 1997; five-page statement by Dan Ammer-man that details his dealings with Daniel Craig Deering.

Letters

DCD to DA, 12/9/97; DCD to DA, 12/18/97; DCD to DA, 1/16/98; KR to DA, 7/10/98; DCD to DA, 7/16/98; all-client memo, 12/18/98; DA fax to DCD, 1/21/99.

Contracts

Agent-author agreement between DCD and DA, 12/9/97; Internet Web site agreement between DCD and DA, 12/18/97.

Victims' Correspondence to Author

BDB e-mail, 4/4/99; TM e-mail re: interview of KR, 7/14/99; KV e-mail, 7/28/99; MKK letter, 10/17/99; DA letter, 2/4/02; DA letter, 2/6/02.

Federal Court Documents

Indictments

Thirteen-page document re: the Deerings and William Paul Watson setting out counts, charges, and evidence, including a five-page attachment identifying potential witnesses and other incriminating evidence.

Plea Agreements

Agreements between assistant U.S. attorney Kenneth R. Taylor and Dorothy Deering, Charles Deering, William Paul Watson, and Daniel Craig Deering.

Docket

Criminal case docket for case #99-CR-76-ALL, United States District Court, Eastern District of Kentucky, Judge Karl S. Forester, Terminated Counts and Dispositions.

Indictment of David Brannon

Seven-page document setting out counts, charges, and evidence, including potential witnesses and incriminating evidence.

Plea Agreement

Agreement between assistant U.S. attorney Kenneth R. Taylor and David Brannon, criminal action no. 01-20.

Audiotapes

Telephone conversation taped by Ellen Brazer of Miami, Florida, between herself and Bill Richardson on January 14, 1998; telephone conversations taped by Dan Ammerman of Houston, Texas, between himself and Daniel Craig Deering, 6/4/98, 7/98, 8/98, 9/4/98. The audiotapes were made available on 3/26/02 by FBI agent Clay Mason of the Frankfort, Kentucky, resident agency. Ellen Brazer and Dan Ammerman granted this author written permission to publish the content of these conversations.

Videotape

CBC-TV *Marketplace* segment about Commonwealth Publications, Inc., aired 1/13/98, featuring interviews of its employees and victims. Fifteen minutes. Victims: Craig Etchison, Anita Guest, and Jacqueline Sevigny. Former employees: Yolanda Fast, Angela Balabash, and Jen Delward.

Published Sources (by date)

Kapos, Shia. "At Northwest Press, All Is Vanity." *Salt Lake Tribune,* April 4, 1996.

O'Connor, Clint. "Author's Dream Dashed: Publisher's Woes Stop Woman's Book." *Cleveland Plain Dealer,* June 4, 1996.

Hoover, Bob. "The Path to Enlightenment Leads One Author to Despair, Another to Hope." *Pittsburgh Post-Gazette,* July 7, 1996.

Oberbeck, Steven. "Trustee Seeks Fire Sale of Bankrupt Publishing House." *Salt Lake Tribune,* July 28, 1996.

Friedman, Rick, and Marcy Rein. "Commonwealth Publications and the Perils of Subsidy Presses: Joint Venture or Risky Venture?" *American Writer,* Summer 1997.

Carricaburu, Lisa. "Northwest Publishing Principals Charged." *Salt Lake Tribune,* December 10, 1997.

Gillis, Charlie. "Authors Want Story on Publishing Runaround." *Edmonton Journal,* January 31, 1998.

Loome, Jeremy. "Phone Disconnected, Doors Locked at Vanity Publishers." *Edmonton Sun,* March 27, 1998.

Loome, Jeremy. "Publisher Ordered to Cough Up Back Pay." *Edmonton Sun,* April 7, 1998.

Mandel, Charles. "Edmonton Publisher Wants Distance from Local Book Distributor." *Edmonton Journal,* May 1, 1998.

Mandel, Charles. "Commonwealth Disappears from View." *Quill & Quire,* May 1998.

Mandel, Charles. "Canadian Vanity Publisher Disappears after Author Threats." *Publishers Weekly,* May 18, 1998.

Mandel, Charles. "Writers Launch Suit Against Publisher." *Globe and Mail,* May 30, 1998.

Mandel, Charles. "Publisher Blames 'Conspiracy' for Firm's Collapse." *Edmonton Journal,* May 31, 1998.

Mandel, Charles. "Two Thousand Authors Lost up to $8M." *Edmonton Journal,* June 2, 1998.

Mandel, Charles. "Writers in Lawsuit." *Globe and Mail,* June 30, 1998.

Massing, Dana. "Agents Who Scam Would-Be Authors." *Erie Times News,* December 6, 1998.

Jordan, Jim. "Writer Sues, Alleges Local Publisher Took Money, Made Excuses." *Lexington Herald-Leader,* March 27, 1999.

Cheves, John. "Couple, Two Relatives Accused of Cheating Hundreds of Writers." *Lexington Herald-Leader,* September 4, 1999.

Weeks, Linton. "Publishing Schemes Prove to Be Pure Fiction." *Washington Post,* September 28, 1999.

Cheves, John. "One Pleads Guilty in Publisher Fraud." *Lexington Herald-Leader,* December 11, 1999.

Cheves, John. "Two Admit They Bilked Writers." *Lexington Herald-Leader,* December 23, 1999.

Lynch-Kimbro, Patricia. "Couple Sentenced in $1.5 Million Publishing Fraud." *Lexington Herald-Leader,* April 1, 2000.

Hunt, Stephen. "Judge Sentences Fake Publisher to 30 Years in Prison." *Salt Lake Tribune,* February 10, 2001.

Index

New York Times Book Review, 32

Northwest Publishing, Inc. (NPI), 17–18, 90, 156, 164; author concerns about, 30–31; bankruptcy proceedings, 61, 91; catalogue, 19; check-cashing fees, 48; closure, 58–61; contracts, 22–24; Deering's break with, 39, 40, 46; employees, 48–49, 57–58, 60; investigation of, 57–58, 62; Mahon and, 29–30; nonvanity books, 21, 66–67; revenues, 47, 57–58; takes manuscripts, 21–22

Nottingham, Ted, 26, 116, 141, 191n. 1 (chap. 14); as Deering's first client, 5, 13–14; Sovereign Publications and, 67, 75, 80, 98; visits Deering, 6–7

Oliver, Richard, 45

O'Neal, David, 91–94, 95

overseas representation, 55; Russia as market, 24–25, 40, 44, 72, 164–65, 169

parting fee, 51

Pentagon fraud, 144

Pettit, Laurie, 192n. 1 (chap. 19)

Phelan, Donald T., 32–34, 35–38, 40–42, 63, 91, 92–93; Deering's visit to, 54–55; investigation of, 185; lawsuit against, 55–56. *See also* Commonwealth Publishing, Inc.

Phelan, Lorraine (L. Faye Hillman), 33, 47, 185

Phelan, Michael, 47, 95

Phelan, Ryan, 47, 95

pitch book, 77–78, 79, 177

"Planned Death" (Steinmetz), 133

Presentation and Submission Package, 51

puffing, 5–7, 14, 160–61

Ray, Wayne, 46

reading fees, 5, 8–9, 16, 39, 119–20

Redmoor International, 96

Red Sky (Mullane), 19, 66–67

Reese, Kimberly (Kim), 126–28, 142

Richardson, Bill (William Paul Watson), 76–81, 82–85, 134, 139–40, 167; arrest of, 126, 139; employees and, 78, 82–83, 97, 155, 191n. 4 (chap. 12); feud between Deering and, 76, 79, 83, 86, 150; as fugitive, 76, 81, 147; interview of, by Mason, 170–72; John Kirk and, 116–17; memos to authors by, 106–7; personality problems of, 112–14; pleads guilty, 178–79; Russo and, 149–50; sales pitches of, 98–100; sentence of, 182, 184; summons of, 174; threatening letters by, 109–13

Richardson, Blake, 3–4, 6, 13, 29; Watson impersonates, 76, 85–86

Richardson, Vicki Watson, 1–2, 6, 7, 13, 22, 29, 40, 46, 71, 101, 152; writes short stories, 3–4

Rising Sun Literary Group, A, 13, 22, 46, 63–64, 71, 85, 101, 132, 152

royalties, 15, 17, 36–37

Russia, as market, 24–25, 40, 44, 72, 164–65, 169

Russo, Jim, 83–86, 88–89, 150, 179; letter to Shackelford, 148–49

Science Fiction and Fantasy Writers of America (SFWA), 127, 142, 192n. 2 (chap. 20)

Scott, Chris, 46, 71–72, 101, 132, 152, 193n. 1 (chap. 22)

Scott, Randolph, 46, 152

Scott, Vicki Richardson. *See* Richardson, Vicki Watson

"Sebastian Yard" (Mahon), 28–29

Shackelford, Paul D., 148, 175, 193n. 6 (chap. 21)

Jim Fisher, a graduate of Vanderbilt University School of Law, a former FBI agent, and a professor of criminal justice at Edinboro University of Pennsylvania, has published five books, two of which were nominated for the Mystery Writers of America's Edgar awards.